CONTENTIOUS ELECTIONS

From Afghanistan to Zimbabwe the world has witnessed a rising tide of contentious elections ending in heated partisan debates, court challenges, street protests, and legitimacy challenges. In some cases, disputes have been settled peacefully through legal appeals and electoral reforms. In the worst cases, however, disputes have triggered bloodshed or government downfalls and military coups. Contentious elections are characterized by major challenges, with different degrees of severity, to the legitimacy of electoral actors, procedures, or outcomes.

Despite growing concern, until recently, little research has studied this phenomenon. The theory unfolded in this volume suggests that problems of electoral malpractice erode confidence in electoral authorities, spur peaceful protests demonstrating against the outcome, and, in the most severe cases, lead to outbreaks of conflict and violence. Understanding this process is of vital concern for domestic reformers and the international community, as well as attracting a growing new research agenda.

The editors, from the Electoral Integrity Project, bring together scholars considering a range of fresh evidence—analyzing public opinion surveys of confidence in elections and voter turnout within specific countries, as well as expert perceptions of the existence of peaceful electoral demonstrations, and survey and aggregate data monitoring outbreaks of electoral violence. The book provides insights invaluable for studies in democracy and democratization, comparative politics, comparative elections, peace and conflict studies, comparative sociology, international development, comparative public opinion, political behavior, political institutions, and public policy.

Pippa Norris is the McGuire Lecturer in Comparative Politics, John F. Kennedy School of Government at Harvard University, Laureate Research Fellow and Professor of Government and International Relations at the University of Sydney, and Director of the Electoral Integrity Project.

Richard W. Frank is Lecturer in International Relations, School of Politics and International Relations at the Australian National University and Senior Research Fellow (non-resident) at the Electoral Integrity Project.

Ferran Martínez i Coma is a Research Associate in the Electoral Integrity Project at the University of Sydney.

CONTENTIOUS ELECTIONS

From Ballots to Barricades

Edited by
Pippa Norris, Richard W. Frank,
and Ferran Martínez i Coma

Part of the Electoral Integrity Project

Routledge
Taylor & Francis Group

NEW YORK AND LONDON

THE ELECTORAL INTEGRITY PROJECT
WHY ELECTIONS FAIL AND WHAT WE CAN DO ABOUT IT

First published 2015
by Routledge
711 Third Avenue, New York, NY 10017

and by Routledge
2 Park Square, Milton Park, Abingdon, Oxon, OX14 4RN

Routledge is an imprint of the Taylor & Francis Group, an informa business

© 2015 Taylor & Francis

Library of Congress Cataloging in Publication Data
Contentious elections : from ballots to barricades / edited by Pippa
    Norris, Richard W. Frank, and Ferran Martínez i Coma.
    pages cm
    Includes bibliographical references and index.
    1. Contested elections. 2. World politics—1989– I. Norris, Pippa.
    JF1001.C5735 2015
    324.6—dc23
    2014037264

ISBN: 978-1-138-85302-7 (hbk)
ISBN: 978-1-138-85303-4 (pbk)
ISBN: 978-1-315-72306-8 (ebk)

Typeset in Bembo and Stone Sans by
Florence Production Ltd, Stoodleigh, Devon, UK

Printed and bound in the United States of America by
Edwards Brothers Malloy on sustainably sourced paper

CONTENTS

FIGURES AND TABLES

Figures

Tables

CONTRIBUTORS

Katherine Collin is a Doctoral Researcher at American University, School of International Service. Previously, she earned her BA in UC Berkeley and her MA in International Policy Studies at the Monterey Institute of International Studies. She is currently researching and writing her dissertation on the use of referendums in peace processes. She is an electoral expert, having worked around post-conflict elections in Kosovo, Afghanistan, Iraq, Nepal, South Sudan, and Libya. She specializes in training, procedures, capacity building, and out-of-country registration and voting operations. She has published research reports on behalf of the United Nations High Commissioner for Refugees and the United Nations Development Programme on work in Romania and Afghanistan.

Richard W. Frank is a Lecturer in the School of Politics and International Relations at the Australian National University (ANU). Prior to joining ANU, Dr. Frank was the Electoral Integrity Project Manager and a Research Fellow in the Department of Government and International Relations at the University of Sydney and an Assistant Professor at the University of New Orleans. His research focuses on the causes of electoral violence, civil conflict, and human trafficking. His work has recently appeared in the *Journal of Democracy*, *Journal of Peace Research*, *Conflict Management and Peace Science,* and *International Interactions*, among other outlets. He co-edited *Advancing Electoral Integrity* (Oxford University Press 2014).

Masaaki Higashijima is a Doctoral Candidate of Political Science at Michigan State University. He earned his BA and MA at Waseda University, Japan. His primary interests lie in comparative and international political economy, post-communist countries, and political methodology (quantitative and qualitative methods). In his dissertation, he explores the causes and consequences of autocratic elections by combining cross-national statistical analysis with comparative case studies of developing countries, especially those in the post-Soviet region. More specifically, his dissertation deals with crucial questions concerning elections under dictatorships, such as when dictators decide to hold elections, what encourages autocrats to refrain from resorting to election violence and fraud, why and when dictators change electoral rules and institutions, and the impacts of autocratic elections on political and economic outcomes, including political business cycles and regime breakdown.

Patrick M. Kuhn is a Lecturer in Comparative Politics in the School of Government and International Affairs at Durham University, England. Before joining the faculty at Durham University, he served as Lecturer in the Woodrow Wilson School of Public and International Affairs and was a Postdoctoral Research Associate in the Empirical Studies of Conflict Project at Princeton University. He received his undergraduate degree in Political Science from the University of Zurich and an MA and PhD in Political Science from the University of Rochester. His doctoral studies focused on comparative political economy, with a special interest in development and conflict. His dissertation examined the causes and dynamics of electoral violence, including the micro-mechanism of pre-electoral violence, the link between ethnic voting and campaign violence in Sub-Saharan Africa, and the role of information and uncertainty with regard to post-electoral protests.

Ferran Martínez i Coma is a Research Associate at the Electoral Integrity Project in the Department of Government and International Relations at the University of Sydney. He has published in *Electoral Studies*, the *Journal of Democracy*, and *Party Politics*. Prior to arriving in Sydney he worked at the Ministry of Interior, in the General Direction of Interior Policy, in charge of organizing the elections, and in the Prime Minister's Office. He was also an Assistant Professor at Centro de Investigacion y Docencias Economicas (CIDE) in Mexico City. He co-edited *Advancing Electoral Integrity* (Oxford University Press 2014).

Olena Nikolayenko is Assistant Professor in the Department of Political Science at Fordham University, New York. She received a PhD in political science from the University of Toronto and was a SSHRC post-doctoral scholar at Stanford University's Center on Democracy, Development, and the Rule of Law. Her research interests include comparative democratization, social movements, public opinion, and youth, with the regional focus on Eastern Europe. She has published *Citizens in the Making in Post-Soviet States* (Routledge, 2011), and articles in the *Canadian Journal of Political Science*, *Comparative Politics*, *International Political Science Review*, *Youth and Society*, and other journals. Her current book project focuses on nonviolent youth movements in the post-communist region.

Pippa Norris is the McGuire Lecturer in Comparative Politics at the John F. Kennedy School of Government, Harvard University, Laureate Fellow and Professor of Government and International Relations at the University of Sydney, and Director of the Electoral Integrity Project. A political scientist and public speaker, her research compares election and public opinion, political communications, and gender politics. Recent books include *Why Electoral Integrity Matters* (Cambridge University Press 2014), *Advancing Electoral Integrity* (Oxford University Press 2014, co-edited) and *Comparing Democracy 4* (Sage 2014, co-edited). She also served as Director of the Democratic Governance Group in the United Nations Development Programme, NY, and as an expert consultant to many international organizations. Author or editor of more than 40 books, she has been awarded the Johan Skytte prize and the Karl Deutsch award.

Richard Rose was a founder Professor of the Politics Department at Strathclyde University and in 1976 established the Centre for the Study of Public Policy, the first public policy institute in a European university. He has pioneered the study of comparative politics and public policy in Europe. Rose has published more than 40 books, lectured in 45 countries, his writings have been translated into 17 languages, and his research has been funded by grants from various inter-governmental agencies such as the World Bank, the United Nations Development Programme and the European Commission. Rose was one of the founding members of the European Consortium for Political Research.

Alesia Sedziaka graduated from Stetson University and is a PhD candidate in the School of Government and Public Policy at the University of Arizona. Her dissertation focuses on the causes and consequences of perceived election unfairness in electoral authoritarian regimes. Her broad research interests include governance, social movements, and sustainability.

PREFACE AND ACKNOWLEDGMENTS

Elections that work well are essential for democracy. Alas, there are many contests around the world that end in heated disputes, generating mass protests, deadly violence, and even revolutionary upheavals. Sore losers commonly challenge the process and outcome, with cries of fraud, whether based on legitimate grievances or mistrustful suspicions. In fragile states, such as Kenya, Afghanistan, or Thailand, the result can be disastrous for stability, peace, and development. Even long-established democracies such as the United States and Canada are not immune from growing party polarization, increased public debate, and litigious appeals over the rules of the electoral game.

To address concern about these issues, this book brought together a wide range of scholars and practitioners. The volume is part of the Electoral Integrity Project (EIP), a six-year research project generously funded by the award of the Kathleen Fitzpatrick Australian Laureate from the Australian Research Council, and at Harvard by support from the Weatherhead Center for International Affairs, the Roy and Lila Ash Center for Democratic Governance and Innovation, and the Australian Studies Committee. The project focuses on the challenges of electoral integrity around the world, including why it matters, why electoral integrity fails, and what can be done to address these problems. Draft research papers, which formed the basis for these chapters, were originally presented at the pre–American Political Science Association (APSA) Workshop on Challenges of Electoral Integrity held in Chicago on August 28, 2013. As well as the contributors, we would also like to thank all the workshop participants, who provided such lively and stimulating comments, especially the panel discussants including Jan Teorell, André Blais, and Nikolay Marinov.

As always, this book also owes immense debts to many friends and colleagues. The EIP project is located in the Department of Government and International

Relations at the University of Sydney and the John F. Kennedy School of Government at Harvard University. We are deeply indebted to Michael Spence, Duncan Ivison, Simon Tormey, Allan McConnell, and Graeme Gill for facilitating the arrangement at the University of Sydney, as well as to all colleagues at Sydney and Harvard. The book would not have been possible without the research team and visiting fellows at Sydney who have played an essential role in stimulating ideas, providing critical feedback and advice, generating related publications, and organizing events, especially developing the Perception of Electoral Integrity (PEI) dataset. We would especially like to thank Elin Bjarnegard, Hilde Coffe, Ignacio Lago, Lawrence LeDuc, Carolien van Ham, and Par Zetterberg for stimulating ideas and feedback as fellows during the book's gestation, as well as invaluable contributions at research seminars and related events by Ian McAllister, Ben Reilly, Ben Goldsmith, Rodney Smith, Anika Gauja, Jorgen Elklit, and Andrew Reynolds. In particular, we greatly appreciate the contribution of Max Grömping and Minh Trinh, who helped with research on the project as they pursued their studies.

1

CONTENTIOUS ELECTIONS

From Votes to Violence

*Pippa Norris, Richard W. Frank,
and Ferran Martínez i Coma*

During the post-Cold War era, concern has risen about the proliferation of contentious elections and the number of polls held in a pervasive climate of fraud, mistrust, and intolerance that have ignited massive protests and violence.[1] Far from having beneficial consequences, contentious elections raise red flags by potentially undermining democratic transitions in countries emerging from dictatorship, furthering instability and social tensions in fragile states, increasing uncertainty and risks for investors, and jeopardizing growth and development in low-income economies (Paris 2004; Doyle and Sambanis 2006; Paris and Sisk 2009; Collier 2009).

The most violent and disruptive contests are exemplified by the 2007 Kenyan election, which attracted global headlines and international concern when rival community leaders organized tit-for-tat coercion. This led to thousands injured, widespread rape, an estimated 1,200 deaths, about 42,000 houses and many businesses looted or destroyed, and more than 300,000 people displaced, costing the country more than one billion dollars and deterring potential investors (UNHCR 2008; Kiai 2008; Chege 2008; Gutierrez-Romero 2013). The extent of the disruption was exceptional. But, alas, the 2007 Kenyan election was not an isolated occurrence. During the last decade, estimates from the Hyde and Marinov NELDA dataset suggest that around 12 percent of all elections worldwide saw opposition boycotts, 17 percent experienced post-election riots or protests, and 18 percent had electoral violence involving at least one civilian fatality.[2]

To address these concerns and to deepen our understanding of these phenomena, this book brings together research from a wide range of scholars of international relations, comparative politics, and political behavior. This introductory chapter advances a new conceptual and theoretical framework useful for understanding the risks of contentious elections. Building upon this foundation, we then outline the overall plan of the book and indicate how contributors build on this theory. Using both surveys within specific countries, as well as broader types of cross-national evidence, successive chapters focus on how contentious elections affect citizens' attitudes and behavior, as well influencing broader challenges to stability arising from leadership overthrow, electoral violence, and nationalist demands for secession. The conclusion presents a global perspective and cross-national evidence demonstrating that the risks of contentious elections are heightened under three conditions: in hybrid regimes (which are neither full-blown democracies nor dictatorships), in contests lacking fair procedures and impartial electoral authorities to serve as umpires, and in some of the world's poorer societies and most fragile states. The conclusion also summarizes the book's main findings and considers their broader implications for social science and for the public policy agenda.

The Concept of Contentious Elections

The subject of contentious politics has attracted a substantial literature, following the seminal work of Sidney Tarrow, Charles Tilly, and Doug McAdam (Tilly 1979; McAdam, Tarrow and Tilly 2001; Tilly and Tarrow 2006). This subfield has generated a wide range of research on diverse phenomenon such as social movements, collective actions, ethno-religious conflict, political strikes, civil wars, civil disobedience, resistance, terrorism, genocide, insurrection, and revolutions (e.g. Tarrow 1992; Kriesi et al. 1995; McAdam, McCarthy and Zald 1996; Kriesi, Della Porta, and Rucht 1998; Della Porta and Diani 1999; Aminzade et al. 2001) As McAdam and Tarrow (2010) note, however, the literatures on social movements and on electoral studies commonly travel along parallel tracks, with little cross-fertilization, despite the potential for fruitful interaction.

Drawing ideas loosely from this broad and rich research agenda, the concept of "contentious elections" is defined in this book as contests involving major challenges, with different degrees of severity, to the legitimacy of electoral actors, procedures, or outcomes. Using this conceptualization, contentious elections occur where deep disputes exist that challenge the legitimate authority of (i) electoral actors (such as concern about the lack of impartiality, authority, and independence of electoral management bodies, EMBs); (ii) the electoral procedures used throughout the electoral cycle (including disagreements about the rules of the game used to draw boundaries, register voters, candidates, and parties, allocate elected offices, regulate campaign finance and media, cast ballots, and translate votes into seats); and/or (iii) the electoral outcomes and thus challenges to the legitimacy of those winning office (including leaders, representatives, and political parties).

Contentious elections therefore reflect fundamental disagreements about the legitimacy of the contest. In general, the overarching concept of "legitimacy" represents broad acceptance of the underlying rules of the game, so that all actors willingly consent to the authority of the regime, without the need for force.

Legitimacy, in Seymour Martin Lipset's (1983: 64) words: "involves the capacity of a political system to engender and maintain the belief that existing political institutions are the most appropriate and proper ones for the society."

What are the sources of legitimate authority? In his seminal exposition, Max Weber posited several ideal types, including *traditional* authority (such as customary patrimonial arrangements for leaders and elites or the belief that the monarch is divinely sanctioned to rule in theocracies), *charismatic* authority (flowing from the personal popularity of the leader), and *rational-legal* authority (where authority is derived from the institutional office allocated by the rule of law and constitutional principles). Each of the first two classic Weberian ideal types of authority can still be observed in a handful of contemporary states. Nevertheless the global spread of elections for the national legislatures in nearly all countries worldwide, and the use of direct elections for many executives, means that in most countries today governing authority derives from holding offices determined by the formal constitutional principles and electoral laws (Gandhi and Lust-Okar 2009; Norris 2014). This is true not just in long-established democracies, but also in popularly elected autocracies. Elections for national office are held today in most independent nation states worldwide, with the exception of a handful of outliers where the executive rules through one-party regimes lacking the fig-leaf of any direct elections for the national legislature (such as in Communist China), through family connections in absolute monarchies (such as emirs governing Saudi Arabia and Oman), through military juntas (such as in Egypt, after the army seized power and the Muslim Brotherhood was imprisoned and outlawed), and in personal dictatorships lacking direct elections (such as Colonel Gaddafi's Libya). Legitimacy crises are triggered in states for diverse reasons. For instance, a major money-in-politics corruption scandal can bring down leaders. A government can be blamed for a severe failure of public policy, such as a financial disaster or currency crisis, which rocks the foundation of the state. Deadly violence can undermine the state's capacity to protect its peoples and borders due to inter-communal tensions, demands for secession, civil wars, or military invasions. Or a ruling leader may die in office or be deposed by a coup without an obvious successor. But a crisis of legitimacy through contentious elections represents another additional risk— one that is greatly heightened by the spread of popular contests around the globe; and the dangers are compounded in many divided societies holding elections as part of peace-building initiatives after decades of bloodshed.

Therefore consensual elections ideally provide a mechanism to settle disputes over legitimate authority in a peaceful, democratic, lawful, and orderly way. Such contests can channel and curb competition among rival visions of society, leaders and political parties by securing agreement over the underlying rules of the game. Legitimacy flowing from the ballot box is one of the most effective and efficient mechanisms to ensure that citizens comply with the authority of elected rulers, facilitating the process of governance by voluntarily respecting the rule of law, and providing the state with revenues through complying with the honest payment of taxes. In the absence of electoral legitimacy, ruling elites can seek to govern through multiple alternative non-democratic mechanisms, including through patronage and clientelism, through populist and ideological appeals to followers, and, in repressive states, through the threat or use of force and coercion (Svolik 2012). Contentious elections, however, are expected to prove deeply problematic for regime stability, because they raise fundamental doubts about the legitimate authority of electoral management bodies, actors, and the rules of the game. Such challenges, by their nature, cannot be resolved easily through the standard mechanisms of the ballot box or the regular policy-making process.

Measuring the Concept of Contentious Elections

What evidence would allow us to better understand this phenomenon? When it comes to defining and measuring examples of contentious elections, at one level, like art, "we all know it when we see it." During 2013 alone, for example, journalists reported large-scale demonstrations and riots challenging the legitimacy of elections in states as diverse as Malaysia, Venezuela, Mozambique, Cameroon, Uganda, Zambia, Cambodia, Thailand, Bangladesh, and Pakistan (Norris, Frank, and Martínez i Coma 2014). Few would dispute these are contentious elections. In some cases, however, post-election protests quickly faded away, and court cases were dismissed. In others, by contrast, mass discontent triggered security counter-reactions, partisan stalemate, social instability, inter-communal bloodshed, and deadly violence. Clearly such extremely diverse cases as the 2000 US election and Kenya in 2007 suggest a wide continuum of dissimilar disputes, making the relatively abstract concept of contentious elections difficult to measure with any degree of clarity and precision.

The phenomenon of a contested election can be detected most effectively, we argue, by examining empirical evidence for several symptoms, including:

1. low or declining trust and confidence in elections by citizens and elites;
2. contests generating peaceful mass demonstrations, opposition boycotts, or court challenges; and, in the most serious cases,
3. incidents of electoral violence occurring during or after polling day and nonpeaceful protests involving the deployment or threat of coercive tactics, the destruction of property, and/or physical harm to people.

Each of these elements underlying the overarching concept of contentious elections is expected to be related, generating a downward spiral deepening the severity of an electoral legitimacy crisis, as illustrated by the heuristic model presented in Figure 1.1. Several case studies presented subsequently in this book—focused on hybrid regimes such as Russia, Ukraine, and Azerbaijan—as well as cross-national comparative studies, demonstrate the connections theorized to exist among these elements.

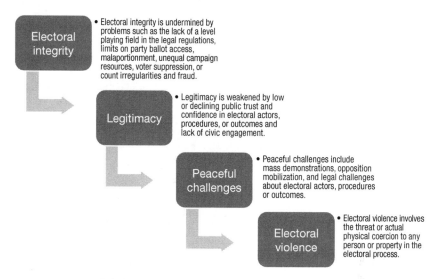

FIGURE 1.1 A model of contentious elections

Although evidence to examine this phenomenon remains less than ideal on several aspects, a growing range of empirical indicators, which are useful to diagnose both mild and virulent symptoms of contentious elections, are becoming available from several sources. These indicators include reports from international election observer organizations, representative mass surveys monitoring attitudes and reported behavior within and across countries, events-based datasets derived from news media content analysis, forensic analysis of outliers in polling results and turnout at local level, crowd-sourcing election watch initiatives, and official legal records of court disputes and prosecutions. Chapters in this book seek to analyze diverse sources of evidence, tracing the underlying relationship connecting each of these elements—utilizing public opinion surveys of confidence in elections and voter turnout within specific countries, as well as expert perceptions of the existence of peaceful electoral demonstrations, and survey and aggregate data monitoring outbreaks of electoral violence.

> Step 1: Electoral malpractices encourage low or declining public confidence in electoral actors, processes, and outcomes.

To clarify the reasoning, the first step in the model predicts that flawed and failed contests will usually damage public trust and confidence in electoral authorities, procedures, and outcomes. Malpractices that prevent elections from meeting international standards can occur for many reasons: as demonstrated elsewhere, some of the most overt malpractices used by rulers include imprisoning dissidents, harassing adversaries, coercing voters, vote-rigging counts, and finally, if losing, blatantly disregarding the people's choice (see Norris, Frank, and Martínez i Coma 2014). Serious violations of human rights, undermining electoral credibility, are widely condemned by domestic observers and the international community. Elsewhere, however, more minor administrative irregularities are common, arising from lack of technical capacity—exemplified by inaccurate voter registers, maladministration of polling facilities, lack of security in absentee ballots, pro-government media bias, ballot miscounts, and gerrymandering.

Where problems of electoral malpractices are widely perceived, so that ordinary people believe that the outcome was fraudulent, corrupt or stolen, this book's theory posits that this is likely to erode public trust and confidence in the electoral process and its authorities. A direct link connecting actual or perceived problems of electoral integrity with subsequent violence has long been suspected. Thus, a United Nations Development Programme (UNDP) report examining electoral conflict in South and South East Asia concluded:

> The mere suspicion or allegation of fraud is often enough, in democracies where there is a lack of confidence in authorities, for people to react violently ... Massive cheating or fraud such as conspiracies to bribe voters, tampering with ballots, dishonest counting or rigged voter lists can be the stimulus for a violent reaction by those, including the general public, who believe that they have been cheated.
>
> (Finley and Khan 2011: 6)

More systematic evidence derived from several social surveys covering different geographic regions, published in a series of studies conducted by several scholars, lends empirical support to the claim that perceptions of the honesty or fairness of elections are indeed commonly linked with social-psychological indicators of legitimacy, including low or declining feelings of trust in elected authorities, lack of confidence in the fairness of electoral procedures and authorities, and skepticism about the honesty of the outcome (Birch 2010; Carreras and Irepoglu 2013; Kerr 2014; Norris 2014).

Nevertheless, several mediating conditions are expected to affect this relationship, operating at both individual and macro-levels, before political attitudes (public perceptions of electoral malpractice) translate into contentious actions challenging electoral authorities, procedures, or the legitimate authority of the outcome. Empirical evidence establishing the underlying steps in this process are therefore explored in more detail in successive chapters.

In particular, even if electoral malpractices occur, many citizens may remain unaware of any problems, especially if they arise from highly technical issues (such as the malapportionment or gerrymandering of district boundaries), or from obscure legal regulations which are complex to grasp, not reported by the news media, and far removed from direct personal experience. Thus the specific type of malpractice, and the stage at which it occurs during the electoral cycle, may have important consequences for public perceptions of electoral integrity.

Moreover the type of media messages is another factor predicted to condition this relationship. Thus with "two-sided" messages, of the "he-said-she-said variety," supporters of the incumbent party may choose to believe the cues provided by government leaders, and officially appointed constitutional courts or electoral authorities, rather than the allegations made by opposition parties (with an incentive to cry wolf), domestic observer watchdogs, or international monitoring agencies.

Awareness of malpractices can also be expected to be strengthened at individual level by the usual social and demographic factors that commonly lead towards a more sophisticated grasp of political knowledge, including access to information from the independent media (where investigative reports are most likely to highlight any problems), by the cognitive skills and knowledge provided by formal education (which help citizens to process and make sense of technical information), and by government and opposition party leadership messages (where processes of framing and priming are expected to cue supporters in debates about electoral integrity). The type of actions that flow from any public dissatisfaction with the contest, and thus the links between attitudes and behaviors, also need to be determined. Critical citizens who doubt the integrity of the electoral process, with little trust in the authorities or faith in the outcome, may have little confidence in any parties or politicians, and thus decide to stay home, rather than cast a ballot for opposition parties. Therefore, building upon the existing comparative literature (Norris 2014), it is essential to establish further steps in the underlying mechanisms as many questions remain. Subsequent chapters use detailed national surveys to produce a fuller understanding of the first step in the theory.

Step 2: Lack of trust leads to peaceful electoral challenges.

In the second step, the core model in this book theorizes that widespread lack of public trust in electoral authorities, procedures, and outcomes in turn, is likely to provide a climate which opposition forces can exploit to mobilize peaceful mass protests, legal challenges to the process and results, and boycotts of the contest, all of which characterize contentious acts. In particular, a pervasive belief that the election outcome is fraudulent, rigged, or stolen, as well as a lack of confidence in the impartiality, honesty, or independence of electoral authorities (whether true or false), provides a climate of public opinion that facilitates direct political actions mobilized by anti-government forces, notably opposition boycotts, political strikes, and peaceful or violent mass demonstrations and rallies protesting against the process and outcome. In response, the regime may organize counter-demonstrations and public meetings to demonstrate support for the government.

This process is commonly observed. For example, large-scale Russian protests against Vladimir Putin's return to the Kremlin (as discussed in detail in Chapter 3), were mobilized following widely perceived problems during the 2011 State Duma and 2012 presidential contest, despite the crackdown by security forces and new laws restricting demonstrations (BBC News Europe 2012; Volkov 2012). Similar movements were evident in the so-called "colored revolutions" in Eastern Europe, where mass mobilization reportedly led to the reversal of the results of several elections that were widely regarded as fraudulent (Thompson and Kuntz 2004; Kalandadze and Orenstein 2009). Tucker argues that blatantly stolen or rigged presidential or parliamentary contests provide critical opportunities for mass protest and revolutionary action because the event serves as a single rallying point for opposition forces seeking to overthrow a regime, thereby overcoming collective action problems (Tucker 2007; Thompson and Kuntz 2009). Opposition parties and dissident movements may be deeply divided in their ideas and beliefs, as well as being drawn from dissimilar communities, regions, and ethnic identities, but anti-government forces can coalesce in mass street protests and legal challenges focused against a rigged election by the incumbent party.

Whether any public disaffection about the election is translated into sustained and widespread public protests, however, also deserves closer scrutiny. After all, some demonstrations can prove sporadic, quickly fading after polling day. Others, however, persist for weeks or months during and after the contest, like Thailand in 2013, generating a pervasive climate of political instability (Grömping 2014). Chapters therefore seek to establish the underlying conditions and individual characteristics that generate mass activism. These draw upon the extensive body of social-psychological research on public opinion, voting behavior, and political activism which has long examined the individual roots of contentious politics, including more recently how far trust in elections is associated with patterns of voting turnout or protest activism (Birch 2010; Carreras and Irepoglu 2013; Kerr 2014; Norris 2014).

Early studies of protest participation in post-industrial societies and Western democracies, during the 1960s and 1970s reported that direct activism disproportionately engaged students, the well-educated, and the professional middle classes, although in recent decades the traditional profile of protest demonstrators has gradually normalized to a broader cross-section of the electorate in affluent societies (Barnes and Kaase 1979; Topf 1995; van Aelst and Walgrave 2001; Norris 2002). Given this literature, among the individual predictors, several groups are expected to be disproportionately engaged in electoral protests, including supporters from the losing side in any multiparty contest (although counter-demonstration may also be mobilized among government forces), as well as the younger generation, those who are most attentive to traditional news reports and networks through social media, and urban populations. Elsewhere in developing societies, however, the social profile established from previous research is less clear, and several recent cases such as Bangladesh, Thailand, and Cambodia suggest that poorer sectors of the population, workers, and ethnic communities may also be mobilized in election demonstrations, depending upon the social characteristics of the supporters of opposition parties.

Step 3: Mass protests heighten the risks of electoral violence.

Finally, in states where normal political and legal channels fail to resolve disputes, and public disaffection with elections remains deeply rooted, the model predicts the highest risks of peaceful protests tipping into a tit-for-tat spiral of outright electoral violence. The failure of conventional channels for mobilizing dissent, in a state where there are also weak institutional mechanisms for the resolution of legal disputes through the authorities, are predicted to heighten the risks of outbreaks of electoral violence, reflecting the most severe manifestation of contentious elections. Electoral violence is understood in this book as acts of physical coercion, or threats of such acts, involving any person or property at any stage of the long electoral cycle, including before, during, or after polling day.[3] This problem may arise from coercion designed to suppress party rallies, threaten opponents, or intimidate citizens, as well as from riots and blockages by dissidents protesting the outcome, and reprisals by the policy and military force directed against opposition forces. Perpetrators and victims can include many actors, including governing elites, the security forces, opposition party leaders and supporters, terrorists and warlords, community leaders and groups, ordinary citizens, and international actors. As the use of elections has spread around the globe, however, so disputes have burgeoned over the legitimate authorities, processes, and results. Flawed contests are increasingly falling short of democratic ideals (Norris 2014: Ch.4).

Previous studies of this process have commonly focused upon specific case studies of particular contentious elections, using process tracing to understand outbreaks of electoral violence, especially in Sub-Saharan Africa (Basedau, Erdman, and Mehler 2007; Gilles 2011; Bekoe 2012). Scholars of international relations have sought to determine whether electoral violence can be blamed for the onset or recurrence of civil wars, especially where contests are held in fragile states, in multiethnic societies, and in some of the world's poorest countries lacking economic development and societal modernization (Collier, Hoeffler, and Sambanis 2005; Höglund 2009; Collier 2009; Collier and Vicente 2011). Rational choice perspectives have examined the strategic incentives for insurgents, warlords, and terrorist groups to deploy either violence or electoral strategies (Newman 2012; La Calle and Sanchez-Cuenca 2013). Others have analyzed the deterrents to repression constraining the deployment of electoral violence by ruling elites (Davenport 1997; Dunning 2011). Explanations for successful multiparty elections mitigating violence in post-conflict settings have commonly emphasized several positive factors, including the sustained engagement of the international community (Bermeo 2003), the level of state capacity (Reilly 2002, 2004), and repeated experience of elections (Lindberg 2006, 2009). Many scholars have also highlighted the risks of contentious elections for state-building and peace-building processes in countries where the international community has facilitated negotiated settlements in fragile states, low-income economies, and deeply divided plural societies with a recent history of conflict and minimal, if any, experience of democracy, exemplified by Afghanistan, DRC, and Iraq.[4]

Nevertheless there is no consensus about the causes of electoral violence and several alternative perspectives can be identified in the research literature. Do elections function as an institutional mechanism capable of channeling political differences and thereby resolving and overcoming conflict—a process termed here the *domestic democratic peace* thesis?[5] Or do elections potentially deepen the risks of violence (the *electoral conflict* thesis), where party competition generates strategic incentives for politicians to highlight ethnic hatreds and inter-communal tensions in the pursuit of popular support? Or alternatively, as we believe, is the problem poorly specified if the risks of contentious elections are conditional upon several macro-level factors, including the type of regime, the institutional arrangements, and prior structural conditions. Our argument suggests that the risks of contentious elections are highest in hybrid regimes, in states which lack impartial and effective electoral authorities capable of avoiding or resolving disputes, and in societies with underlying structural conditions which makes them particularly vulnerable to conflict.

Elections as Agencies of Democratic Peace

From the first perspective, democratic theories have long suggested that elections are the most legitimate and acceptable way to channel and resolve political tensions in any polity, encouraging a broad agreement among rival actors, parties and groups, and orderly mechanisms for leadership succession and elite turnover without the sanction of force. In consensual elections, all actors go along with the procedures for determining winning candidates and parties, including the losers who accept defeat (Anderson et al. 2005). Theories of liberal democracy suggest that when elections work well, they select representatives and governments, determine policy priorities, link citizens (as principals) with representatives (as agents), generate inclusive legislatures, confer legitimacy on elected authorities, hold leaders to account, and provide the main arena for most ordinary people to participate in politics.[6] Elections provide opportunities for the peaceful resolution of social conflict, the aggregation and expression of political demands, and the orderly transfer of government office. Where losers accept the rules of the game, in the belief that there are opportunities to gain votes, seats, and office in subsequent contests, elections maintain a stable equilibrium among contenders (Przeworski 2005). For all these reasons, contests meeting international standards of integrity are widely regarded as the main mechanism for the peaceful and orderly allocation of government office, linking citizens and the state through the ballot box. From this perspective, any violence around election day can be regarded as an unfortunate temporary by-product of the transition to democracy, or a residual problem likely to fade away once the rotation of parties in government and opposition consolidates through a series of regular elections (Lindberg 2006, 2009).

Elections as Causes of Deepening Violence?

Or, alternatively, however, do contests potentially magnify, exacerbate, and escalate any fault-line divisions, the *electoral conflict* thesis, by providing incentives for vote-seeking politicians to heighten inter-communal tensions as a way to mobilize support? This perspective is developed by several authors, notably by Mansfield and Snyder (2007), who argue that the international community's rush to implement elections as part of the early stages of the peace-building process is foolhardy and misguided if electoral competition in hybrid regimes produces strong incentives for new parties to play up nationalist fears and ethnic hatreds, in the pursuit of popular support, and if the state lacks other effective institutions to maintain order, including rule of law and control of security forces (Snyder 2000; Wilkinson 2006; Mansfield and Snyder 2007; Bracanti and Snyder 2011). Yet terrorist groups and radical insurgents may also have heightened incentives to use violent attacks to undermine the process in the weeks running up to polling day. A week before the 2014 Afghan elections to replace President Hamid Karsai, for example, the Taliban targeted the Independent Electoral Commission in Kabul by attacking the compound in an attempt to destabilize the contest and to deter citizens from casting a ballot.

A growing rational choice literature theorizes that electoral violence is a strategic tool in the competition for office in states with weak rule of law, with repressive techniques used mainly by unconstrained incumbents to deter opponents and to mobilize voting support (Chaturvedi 2005; Collier and Vicente 2011). For example, studies have asserted that ethnic nationalism was used instrumentally by elites to mobilize support following the break-up of the former Yugoslavia, generating outbreaks of armed conflict in the Balkans during the 1990s. In addition, Steve Wilkinson (2006) argues that Hindu–Muslim riots are fomented in India to help win elections, but whether state governments decide to stop them or not depends upon electoral calculations about whether doing so will win or lose them voters. If elections provide a public forum potentially heightening the incentives for deploying conflict and coercion then, in accordance with the "first-do-no-harm" rule of physicians, the well-meaning interventions by the international community to promote democratic elections in inhospitable climates may backfire and prove an expensive mistake. In bitterly divided and fragmented polities that have recently experienced deep-rooted violence, in states such as Afghanistan, the Democratic Republic of Congo, or Sri Lanka, this thesis suggests that elections will serve to perpetuate or even worsen conflict.

Institutional and Structural Conditions Leading to Contentious Elections

Alternatively, however, do the risks of contentious elections rise under certain institutional and structural conditions? At the macro-level, we argue that the type of regime is predicted to prove particularly important for heightening the odds of electoral disputes, with the dangers greatest in hybrid regimes, which are neither the most repressive autocracies nor established democracies. Figure 1.2 illustrates this relationship. We also predict that problems will worsen if states lack impartial and effective electoral authorities, capable of mediating and resolving any disputes in a timely fashion. Finally, we also predict that several structural conditions commonly associated with other forms of conflict, such as extreme poverty and lack of development, will be important, in making outbreaks of contentious elections more likely. Several reasons lead us to suggest this link, with the evidence examined in more detail later in this book.

Types of Regimes

Why do we believe that the risks of disputes escalating into violence are highest in hybrid regimes? In the most repressive regimes, any explicit public criticism or protests about electoral procedures are probably going to be censored and stifled, and states also have the capacity and lack of constraint to deploy force to coerce dissenters. Thus any public disaffection seems unlikely to be expressed by mass demonstrations in states where public protests are brutally suppressed by the security forces that are willing to deploy tactics of coercion in service of the ruling party.

By contrast, long-established democracies have multiple channels for the expression of dissent and for legal redress, allowing criticisms an outlet through peaceful mechanisms. In stable and peaceful societies and Western democracies, any minor problems of electoral malpractice that arise are likely to be resolved and disputes mediated through legal and constitutional channels. Long-established democracies are not immune from problems of electoral integrity. Challenges to the procedures and outcome are exemplified most notoriously by the 2000 US presidential elections. Since then, rival claims of voter fraud (by Republicans) and voter suppression (by Democrats) have become bitterly polarized, with legal battles fought in state legislatures and courtrooms across America (Minnite 2010; Hasen 2012; Wang 2012). These issues have even spilled over the borders to infect Canadian politics, exemplified by the Harper government's Fair Elections Bill, as well as occurring in other long-established democracies, such as Britain, Italy, and Japan (Wingrave and Hannay 2014). Such events periodically generate alarmist chatter about a 'crisis of democracy' (Crozier, Huntington, and Watanuki 1975). In fact, however, setting aside the hyperbole, from a global perspective, these problems reflect a non-lethal form of this disease. Long-established democracies can be regarded as similar to healthy patients, where institutions have

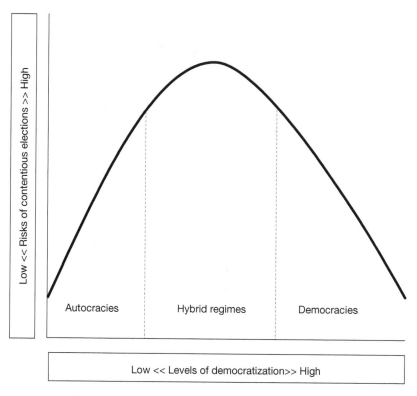

FIGURE 1.2 The predicted risks of contentious elections in hybrid regimes

accumulated cultural reservoirs of acceptance over successive elections that make them largely immune from a severe legitimacy crisis.

For these reasons, it is hybrid regimes, which are neither absolute autocracies nor yet consolidated democracies, which seem most at risk from the dangers of contentious elections likely to generate a full-blown legitimacy crisis. In hybrid regimes, which have started to liberalize from absolute autocracies, however, authorities may have less capacity or willingness to deploy force against public dissent, providing conditions under which opposition forces can mobilize more easily and protests can flourish. We theorize that hybrid regimes are common in states that have recently emerged from absolute autocracy, that have experienced a history of civil conflict and inter-communal violence, or that are only newly democratized. As such, hybrid regimes have had little time or opportunity to accumulate the deep reservoirs of legitimacy that facilitates acceptance of governance authority in good times and bad. Thus the risks that contentious elections will spark a crisis should not be underestimated in this context. Evidence examining this argument is presented later in the concluding chapter of this book.

The Role of Electoral Authorities

Whether or not elections are linked with conflict may also be conditional upon a state's particular institutional arrangements. In particular, theories of consociational democracy proposed by Arend Lijphart have long argued that in divided societies, power-sharing arrangements reduce the grievances underlying conflict. In particular, proportional representation electoral systems (along with parliamentary executives, and decentralized levels of governance) provide opportunities for the representation of members of minority groups and political parties in elected office. By contrast majoritarian "winner-take-all" arrangements, concentrating power in the hands of the largest party, are predicted to prove conflictual in divided societies (Lijphart 1999; Norris 2008).

Among institutional arrangements, we predict that the role of electoral management bodies and the courts, which have received growing attention, are also likely to prove important, as the key umpires adjudicating any electoral disputes (Opitz, Fjelde, and Höglund 2013). A major report published by International IDEA suggested that the de facto independence of electoral authorities from the ruling party is important for their performance; those under direct control of the government, such as electoral authorities employed as civil servants located within a ministry, are thought more vulnerable to suspicions of partisan manipulation and favoritism (Wall et al. 2006). More autonomous bodies, by contrast, are freer to act (and to be seen to act) in an impartial and fair manner as an "ombudsman" or "umpire" above the partisan fray. This seems likely to prove particularly important when adjudicating between governing and opposition parties in any electoral disputes, especially resolving disputes in a timely and transparent fashion. Although the role of EMBs is likely to be important, empirical evidence classifying the independence and impartiality of these bodies has been limited in previous research, so the final chapter presents some new evidence for this claim.

Finally, the structural conditions that are most commonly associated with civil wars and internal conflict are also mediating factors that seem likely to prove important. The litany of "usual suspects" commonly highlights the existence of deep-rooted poverty, under-development, and socioeconomic inequality, high levels of ethnic heterogeneity, the "curse" of natural resources, levels of corruption, and a recent history of prior armed conflict. Structural social conditions are often believed to heighten the general risks of societal struggles, functioning as the "deep-drivers" of electoral violence.[7] Therefore the book's theoretical argument suggests that holding elections per se is not a problem for violence, but neither is it an automatic panacea generating peace. Rather the risks of contentious elections are affected at macro-level by the type of regime, the institutional arrangements, and the structural conditions in each society, and at micro-level by many factors which link together perceptions of electoral malpractice, the propensity to engage in peaceful demonstrations, and the willingness to become involved in violent conflict.

Plan of the Book

Chapters in this book examine several key questions concerning different aspects of the underlying theory, using diverse forms of national and cross-national evidence to assess the risks, and to understand the causes, of contentious elections. The research examines a series of related questions. What are the individual-level determinants of how citizens perceive the legitimacy of the electoral process and outcomes? When do perceptions of stolen or fraudulent elections trigger peaceful or violent protests? Who participates in such actions and what underlying social conditions are associated with mass activism? When do contentious elections lead to leadership overthrow, deadly violence, and demands for succession? And what types of regimes and electoral institutions are most vulnerable to electoral disputes?

The emerging research agenda studying the causes and consequences of electoral integrity throws some light on these issues through analyzing why contests succeed, or fail to meet international standards and global norms, also provides insights into these issues (Norris 2013). This body of work provides invaluable insights, despite the importance of this phenomenon for democratic legitimacy, peace-building, and regime stability, comprehensive theories and systematic evidence determining the underlying conditions and proximate triggers of contentious elections remain unduly fragmented and compartmentalized among a mélange of disparate sub-disciplinary fields.

Whether elections either mitigate or exacerbate social tensions, political conflict and deadly violence ideally requires analysis of both macro-level conditions—including understanding the broader environment set by the type of regime and levels of democratization and development, the design of electoral institutions and procedures, the historical legacy of civil wars, the distribution of predominant cultural values, patterns of party competition and communal cleavages within the electorate – as well as the more fine-grained micro-level of the underlying drivers operating among citizens living within specific societies and contests, including how political actors respond to their electoral environments, how citizens and parties form perceptions about the legitimacy of elections, and how the behavior of political actors reflects their electoral environment, these perceptions, and specific short-term events occurring within the electoral arena.

Part I: Corroding Public Trust and Triggering Protest

Chapters in the first section of the book build upon these ideas and present empirical evidence for several of the mechanisms that we predict in the first step in the model, establishing the links between perceptions of electoral integrity and citizen trust in the electoral authorities and processes.

In Chapter 2, Olena Nikolayenko turns to issues of how far contentious elections dampen turnout. Recent empirical research shows that mass perceptions of electoral integrity are positively associated with electoral participation.

This chapter argues that party identification affects this relationship in non-democracies. Specifically, this chapter suggests that the turnout decision by supporters of opposition political parties is more likely to be influenced by their perceptions of electoral integrity, given a higher level of concern about political rights and civil liberties violations among regime opponents. Using the case of the 2005 parliamentary elections in Azerbaijan, this chapter demonstrates that supporters of opposition political parties were much more likely to report the intent to vote if they anticipated even a modicum of electoral fairness. In contrast, mass perceptions of electoral integrity exert a weaker effect on turnout by supporters of the ruling party. These findings provide an explanation for low levels of electoral participation among supporters of opposition political parties in non-democracies.

What about unconventional forms of political activism? In Chapter 3, Alesia Sedziaka and Richard Rose look at how far contentious elections trigger electoral protest. Recent research focuses on electoral authoritarian regimes, which use limited political competition and manipulated elections to enhance legitimacy and maintain incumbent rule. But to what extent and under what conditions do elections lacking in integrity enhance or erode support for regime? More specifically, when do unfair elections increase support for electoral protest? To address these questions in the context of Russia, this chapter uses evidence from the New Russia Barometer nationwide survey, conducted shortly after the 2011 State Duma election that triggered electoral protests. This evidence is complemented by surveys of Muscovites and Moscow protesters. The study tests the effects of several conditions on support for electoral protest: direct experience of procedural unfairness, perceived decisiveness of procedural violations for election outcomes (substantive unfairness), knowledge of the election observers' critical assessments, and voting for winners or losers. The chapter concludes by discussing the implications of election unfairness for protest attitudes in electoral authoritarian regimes.

In Chapter 4, Masaaki Higashijima explores the conditions under which contentious elections generate leadership overthrow. When dictators call elections, the chapter suggests that they need to solve two problems to take advantage of the informational benefits that elections bring. First, they need to secure an overwhelming majority to show regime invincibility. Second, in addition to winning big, they need to do so in credible ways, namely, a landslide victory via less-fraudulent elections. The chapter suggests that, if dictators fail to satisfy either of these two conditions, elections can backfire on dictators in two different ways. If they do not demonstrate overwhelming popular support, the results can reveal the weakness of dictators, thereby strengthening the likelihood of potential leadership change due to post-electoral bargaining within ruling coalitions or simply via electoral victory for the opposition. On the other hand, if contentious elections are clearly fraudulent, this can encourage post-electoral protest movements. Cross-national statistical analysis of 72 authoritarian countries (from 1975 to 2004) supports the two hypotheses: when dictators underuse electoral fraud, they are more likely to face political turnover after elections. When dictators overuse fraud, on the other hand, elections are more likely to be followed by popular protests.

Part II: Catalyzing and Preventing Electoral Violence

In Chapter 5, Patrick Kuhn focuses upon how far contentious contests trigger electoral violence in a comparison of states in Sub-Saharan Africa. Election campaigns are violent in many developing countries, costing hundreds of lives and displacing thousands of people each year. This chapter contributes to the growing academic literature on the causes and consequences of electoral violence by providing a systematic empirical evaluation of the main assumptions and predictions of three frequently cited theoretical models of pre-electoral violence. It does so by using both cross-national and individual-level data on multiparty elections in Sub-Saharan Africa. The empirical analysis provides four main results. First, the study finds that violence and intimidation reduce electoral turnout. Second, there is a robust positive association between a country's degree of ethnic voting and pre-electoral violence. Third, the chapter finds no evidence of any single group of voters being the predominant target of campaign violence. Instead, the results suggest that the identity of the victims varies across countries. Finally, the chapter suggests that the incumbent party is the primary perpetrator of pre-electoral violence. Overall, neither of the three models is fully supported by the empirical evidence, pointing towards the need for more empirical research on the micro-mechanisms of campaign violence to refine existing theoretical models.

In Chapter 6, Katherine Collin examines the growing use of referendums to either build peace or else to perpetuate conflict by changing state structures: territory, citizenship, center–periphery relations. The universe of cases is established, using the history of sovereignty referendums held in the context of conflict since World War I. The risks and contributions of peacemaking referendums are explored, with reference to their similarities and differences to post-conflict elections. A typology of such referendums is presented, demonstrating the changing nature of risks and mitigation strategies depending on the context of the conflict and the peace process. Generally, the chapter argues that the risks of peacemaking referendums have been exaggerated. Most effectively incorporate mitigation strategies into their design. In cases when this is not possible, the real risks of the referendum are weighed against the risks of returning to conflict. The fact that there are a number of outstanding mandates for peacemaking referendums, and that they are increasingly incorporated into peace processes, indicate that for scholars and practitioners it is important to improve our knowledge and understanding of these referendums.

Conclusions

Finally in Chapter 7, the editors summarize the key findings from the book and then consider new evidence for several macro-level conditions which are also regarded as important for this phenomenon, namely the type of regime that is in power, the role of the electoral authorities, and the underlying social structural conditions closely associated with contentious elections. The evidence suggests that the risks of contentious outcomes are gravest in hybrid regimes that are neither full-blown democracies nor dictatorships. The dangers are also highest in contests lacking fair procedures and impartial electoral authorities, as well as in some of the world's poorer societies. The conclusion reflects upon the general implications of the book's findings for theories of elections, democracy, and contentious politics, as well as the lessons for public policy initiatives seeking to strengthen electoral integrity around the globe.

Notes

1   See, for example, Global Commission (2012).
2   Estimates are derived from Hyde and Marinov (2011). See also estimates by Straus and Taylor (2012).
3   For a similar conceptualization, see Straus and Taylor (2012).
4   See the summary literature review in Höglund (2009).
5   See also Davenport (2007).
6   See, for example, Powell (2000).
7   See the summary literature review in Höglund (2009).

References

Aelst, Peter van, and Stefaan Walgrave. 2001. "Who is That (Wo)man in the Street? From the Normalization of Protest to the Normalization of the Protester." *European Journal of Political Research* 39: 461–486.

Aminzade, Ronald, Jack A. Goldstone, Doug McAdam, Elizabeth J. Perry, William H. Sewell, Sidney Tarrow, and Charles Tilly. 2001. *Silence and Voice in the Study of Contentious Politics.* New York: Cambridge University Press.

Anderson, Christopher J., Andre Blais, Shaun Bowler, Todd Donovan, and Ola Listhaug. 2005. *Losers' Consent: Elections and Democratic Legitimacy.* New York: Oxford University Press.

Barnes, Samuel, and Max Kaase. 1979. *Political Action: Mass Participation in Five Western Democracies.* Woodland Hills, CA: Sage.

Basedau, Matthais, Gero Erdman, and Andreas Mehler. 2007. *Votes, Money and Violence: Political Parties in Sub-Saharan Africa.* Sweden: Nordiska Afrikainstitutet.

BBC News Europe. 2012. "Russia Protests: Putin Opponents March in Moscow." June 12. Available from www.bbc.co.uk/news/world-europe-18405306 (accessed December 1, 2014).

Bekoe, Dorina, Ed. 2012. *Voting in Fear: Electoral Violence in Sub-Saharan Africa.* Washington, DC: United States Institute of Peace.

Bermeo, Nancy. 2003. "What the Democratization Literature Says or Doesn't Say About Postwar Democratization." *Global Governance* 9: 159–177.

Birch, Sarah. 2010. "Perceptions of Electoral Fairness and Voter Turnout." *Comparative Political Studies* 43(12): 1601–1622.

Bracanti, Dawn, and Jack L. Snyder. 2011. "Rushing to the Polls: The Causes of Premature Post-conflict Elections." *Journal of Conflict Resolution* 55(3): 469–492.

Carreras, Miguel, and Yasmin Irepoglu. 2013. "Trust in Elections, Vote Buying, and Turnout in Latin America." *Electoral Studies* 32(4): 609–619.

Chaturvedi, Ashish. 2005. "Rigged Elections with Violence." *Public Choice* 125(1/2): 189–202.

Chege, Michael. 2008. "Kenya: Back from the Brink." *Journal of Democracy* 19(4): 125–139.

Collier, Paul. 2009. *Wars, Guns and Votes: Democracy in Dangerous Places.* New York: HarperCollins.

Collier, Paul, Anke Hoeffler, and Nicholas Sambanis. 2005. "The Collier-Hoeffler Model of Civil War Onset and the Case Study Project Research Design." In *Understanding Civil War*, edited by Paul Collier and Nicolas Sambanis. Washington, DC: The World Bank, pp. 1–33.

Collier, Paul, and Pedro Vicente. 2011. "Violence, Bribery and Fraud: The Political Economy of Elections in Sub-Saharan Africa." *Public Choice* 153(1): 1–31.

Crozier, Michel, Samuel P. Huntington, and Joji Watanuki. 1975. *The Crisis of Democracy: Report on the Governability of Democracies to the Trilateral Commission.* New York: New York University Press.

Davenport, Christian. 1997. "From Ballots to Bullets: An Empirical Assessment of how National Elections Influence State Uses of Political Repression." *Electoral Studies* 6(4): 517–540.

Davenport, Christian. 2007. *State Repression and the Domestic Democratic Peace.* New York: Cambridge University Press

Della Porta, Donatella, and Mario Diani. 1999. *Social Movements.* Oxford: Blackwell.

Doyle, Michael W., and Nicholas Sambanis. 2006. *Making War and Building Peace.* Princeton, NJ: Princeton University Press.

Dunning, Thad. 2011. "Fighting and Voting: Violent Conflict and Electoral Politics." *Journal of Conflict Resolution* 55(3): 327–339.

Finley, Simon Alexis, and Sophie Khan. 2011. *Elections, Violence and Conflict Prevention.* Bangkok: UNDP Asia-Pacific.

Gandhi, Jennifer, and Ellen Lust-Okar. 2009. "Elections under Authoritarianism." *Annual Review of Political Science* 12: 403–422.

Gillies, David, Ed. 2011. *Elections in Dangerous Places: Democracy and the Paradoxes of Peacebuilding.* Montreal: McGill Queens University Press.

Global Commission on Elections, Democracy and Security. 2012. *Deepening Democracy: A Strategy for Improving the Integrity of Elections Worldwide.* Stockholm: International IDEA.

Grömping, Max. 2014. "Echo Chambers: Partisan Facebook Groups During the 2014 Thai Election." *Asia Pacific Media Educator* 24(1): 39–59.

Gutierrez-Romero, Roxana. 2013. "To What Extent Did Ethnicity and Economic Issues Matter in the 2007 Disputed Kenyan Elections?" *Development Policy Review* 31(3): 291–320.

Hasen, Richard L. 2012. *The Voting Wars: From Florida 2000 to the Next Election Meltdown.* New Haven: Yale University Press.

Höglund, Kristine. 2009. "Electoral Violence in Conflict-ridden Societies: Concepts, Causes, and Consequences." *Terrorism and Political Violence* 21(3): 412–427.

Hyde, Susan D., and Nikolay Marinov. 2011. *Codebook for National Elections across Democracy and Autocracy (NELDA)* 3rd release.

Kalandadze, Katya, and Mitchell A. Orenstein. 2009. "Electoral Protests and Democratization Beyond the Color Revolutions." *Comparative Political Studies* 42(11): 1403–1425.

Kerr, Nicholas. 2014. "Public Perceptions of Election Quality in Africa: A Cross-national Analysis." In *Advancing Electoral Integrity*, edited by Pippa Norris, Richard W. Frank, and Ferran Martínez i Coma. New York: Oxford University Press, pp. 189–210.

Kiai, Maina. 2008. "The Crisis in Kenya." *Journal of Democracy* 19(3): 162–168.

Kriesi, Hanspeter, Ruud Koopmans, Jan Willem Dyvendak, and Marco G. Guigni. 1995. *New Social Movements in Western Europe: A Comparative Analysis*. Minneapolis, MN: University of Minnesota Press.

Kriesi, Hanspeter, Donatella Della Porta, and Dieter Rucht, Eds. 1998. *Social Movements in a Globalizing World*. London: Macmillan.

La Calle, Luis de, and Ignacio Sanchez-Cuenca. 2013. "Killing and Voting in the Basque Country: An Exploration of the Electoral Link Between ETA and its Political Branch." *Terrorism and Political Violence* 25(1): 94–112.

Lijphart, Arend. 1999. *Patterns of Democracy*. New Haven: Yale University Press.

Lindberg, Staffan. 2006. *Democracy and Elections in Africa*. Baltimore, MD: The Johns Hopkins University Press.

Lindberg, Staffan, Ed. 2009. *Democratization by Elections: A New Mode of Transition*. Baltimore, MD: The Johns Hopkins University Press.

Lipset, Seymour Martin. 1983. *Political Man: The Social Bases of Politics* (2nd ed.) London: Heinemann.

Mansfield, Edward D., and Jack Snyder. 2007. *Electing to Fight: Why Emerging Democracies go to War*. Cambridge, MA: MIT Press.

McAdam, Doug, and Sidney Tarrow. 2010. "Ballots and Barricades: On the Reciprocal Relationship Between Elections and Social Movements." *Perspectives on Politics* 8(2): 529–542.

McAdam, Doug, Sidney Tarrow, and Charles Tilly. 2001. *Dynamics of Contention*. New York: Cambridge University Press.

McAdam, Doug, John D, McCarthy and Mayer N. Zald, Eds. 1996. *Comparative Perspectives on Social Movements*. New York: Cambridge University Press.

Minnite, Lorraine Carol. 2010. *The Myth of Voter Fraud*. Ithaca: Cornell University Press.

Newman, Lindsay Shorr. 2012. "Do Terrorist Attacks Increase Closer to Elections?" *Terrorism and Political Violence* 25(1): 8–28.

Norris, Pippa. 2002. *Democratic Phoenix: Reinventing Political Activism*. New York: Cambridge University Press.

Norris, Pippa. 2008. *Driving Democracy: Do Power-Sharing Institutions Work?* New York: Cambridge University Press.

Norris, Pippa. 2013. "The New Research Agenda Studying Electoral Integrity." *Electoral Studies* 32(4): 563–575.

Norris, Pippa. 2014. *Why Electoral Integrity Matters*. New York: Cambridge University Press.

Norris, Pippa, Richard W. Frank, and Ferran Martínez i Coma. 2014. *The Year in Elections, 2013*. Sydney: Electoral Integrity Project, University of Sydney.

Opitz, Christian, Hanne Fjelde, and Kristine Höglund. 2013. "Including Peace: The Influence of Electoral Management Bodies on Electoral Violence." *Journal of Eastern African Studies* 7(4): 713–731.

Paris, Roland. 2004. *At War's End: Building Peace after Civil Conflict.* Cambridge: Cambridge University Press.

Paris, Roland, and Timothy D. Sisk, Eds. 2009. *The Dilemmas of Statebuilding.* Oxford: Routledge.

Powell, G. Bingham. 2000. *Elections as Instruments of Democracy.* New Haven, CT: Yale University Press.

Przeworski, Adam. 2005. "Democracy as an Equilibrium." *Public Choice* 123: 253–273.

Reilly, Benjamin. 2002. "Elections in Post-conflict Scenarios: Constraints and Dangers." *International Peacekeeping* 9(2): 118–139.

Reilly, Benjamin. 2004. "Elections in Post-conflict Societies." In *The UN Role in Promoting Democracy: Between Ideals and Reality,* edited by Edward Newman and Roland Rich. Tokyo: United Nations University Press, pp. 113–134.

Snyder, Jack. 2000. *From Voting to Violence: Democratization and Nationalist Conflict.* New York: Norton.

Straus, Scott, and Charles Taylor. 2012. "Democratization and Electoral Violence in Sub-Saharan Africa, 1990–2008." In *Voting in Fear: Electoral Violence in Sub-Saharan Africa,* edited by Dorina Bekoe. Washington, DC: United States Institute of Peace, pp. 15–38.

Svolik, Milan W. 2012. *The Politics of Authoritarian Rule.* New York: Cambridge University Press.

Tarrow, Sidney. 1992. *Power in Movement.* Cambridge: Cambridge University Press.

Thompson, Mark R., and Philipp Kuntz. 2004. "Stolen Elections: The Case of the Serbian October." *Journal of Democracy* 15(4): 159–172.

Thompson, Mark R., and Philipp Kuntz. 2009. "More Than Just the Final Straw: Stolen Elections as Revolutionary Triggers." *Comparative Politics* 41(3): 253–272.

Tilly, Charles. 1979. *From Mobilization to Revolution.* Reading: Addison-Wesley.

Tilly, Charles, and Sidney Tarrow. 2006. *Contentious Politics.* New York: Oxford University Press.

Topf, Richard. 1995. 'Beyond Electoral Participation.' In *Citizens and the State,* edited by Hans-Dieter Klingemann and Dieter Fuchs. Oxford: Oxford University Press, pp. 52–91.

Tucker, Joshua. 2007. "Enough! Electoral Fraud, Collective Action Problems, and Post-Communist Colored Revolutions." *Perspectives on Politics* 5(3): 535–551.

United Nations High Commissioner for Human Rights (UNHCR). 2008. *Report from OHCHR Fact-Finding Mission to Kenya, 6–28 February 2008.* Geneva: UN/OHCHR.

Volkov, Denis. 2012. "The Protesters and the Public." *Journal of Democracy* 23(3): 55–62.

Wall, Alan, Andrew Ellis, Ayman Ayoub, Carl W. Dundas, Joram Rukambe, and Sara Staino. 2006. *Electoral Management Design: The International IDEA Handbook.* Sweden: International IDEA.

Wang, Tova Andrea. 2012. *The Politics of Voter Suppression: Defending and Expanding Americans' Right to Vote.* Ithaca: Cornell University Press.

Wilkinson, Steve. 2006. *Votes and Violence: Electoral Competition and Ethnic Riots in India:* New York: Cambridge University Press.

Wingrave, Josh, and Chris Hannay. 2014. "Everything You Need to Know About the Fair Elections Act." *Globe and Mail.* March 25. Available from: www.theglobeandmail.com/news/politics/what-is-the-fair-elections-act/article17648947/ (accessed December 1, 2014).

PART I

Corroding Public Trust and Triggering Protest

2

DO CONTENTIOUS ELECTIONS DEPRESS TURNOUT?

Olena Nikolayenko

The introductory chapter predicts that electoral autocracies are likely to have widespread discontent with elections (especially among opposition supporters); however, compared with hybrid regimes, this disaffection is more likely to be implicit, passive, and largely dormant, without major public outbreaks of contentious politics. Nevertheless, if citizens decide to stay at home on polling day in autocratic states this can also be seen as a clear statement of public disaffection.

To explore this issue, this chapter examines the linkage between perceived electoral integrity and the decision to turn out in the context of Azerbaijan's 2005 election, a case study of public attitudes and behaviors within one of the world's most repressive electoral autocracies. In particular, this chapter argues that opposition supporters are more likely to stay at home on polling day because they believe that the electoral process lacks legitimacy. Party identification usually refers to "an enduring affective attachment a voter feels towards a particular political party, which disposes him or her to vote for that party in elections" (Sanders 2003: 241). Furthermore, partisanship influences citizens' decisions to participate in an election. This chapter contends that the turnout decision of citizens identifying with opposition political parties (compared with those loyal to the ruling party) is more strongly affected by their perceptions of electoral integrity. The underlying assumption is that party identification in non-democracies has an additional layer of meaning. Identification with opposition political parties denotes not just attachment to a specific political force but also rejection of the legitimacy of the current political regime. By definition, regime opponents, compared with political conformists, are more likely to be concerned with violations of procedures during an election campaign, which in turn might weigh heavily upon their decision to turn out. It is unclear, however, whether supporters of opposition political parties with low levels of confidence in electoral processes are more likely to pursue the exit strategy—vote abstention—or the voice strategy—voting in large numbers—to defy authoritarian practices in the country.

This chapter's analysis differs from many previous studies and expands the scope of empirical research by focusing on electoral participation in the case of Azerbaijan. This country exemplifies a repressive electoral authoritarian regime; multicandidate, multiparty elections are regularly held, but electoral procedures systematically favor the incumbent ruler. Like most Central Asian states, Belarus, and Russia, Azerbaijan in 2005 was classified as "unfree" by Freedom House, signifying the widespread lack of civil liberties and political rights in the former Soviet republics.[1] Given the prevalence of authoritarian practices in these countries, citizens are likely to employ a similar line of reasoning to weigh costs and benefits of participation in contested elections. So the results derived from this study can be generalized to a large subset of contemporary electoral authoritarian regimes.

The remainder of this chapter is organized as follows. The next section situates this chapter within extant scholarship on voter turnout and electoral integrity. It then discusses electoral malpractices during the 2005 parliamentary election in Azerbaijan. Data sources and the measurement of key variables are then described. The results are explored, and the concluding section summarizes the main findings.

Review of the Literature and Theoretical Framework

Since the end of the Cold war, there has been an increased interest in the study of elections in hybrid regimes and electoral autocracies. A dominant assumption in the literature is that an authoritarian incumbent uses elections as a mechanism for the distribution of state resources among the ruling elite to bolster his political longevity (Boix and Svolik 2013; Lust-Okar 2006; Magaloni 2008). Yet, incentives for citizens' participation in these flawed elections are less clear. A growing volume of empirical research analyzes voting behavior in such societies by using arguments and hypotheses developed in established democracies (Colton 2000; Fornos, Power and Garand 2004; Seligson et al. 1995; Tucker 2002, 2006).

The concept of electoral integrity needs to be integrated in the study of voting behavior in non-democracies. Norris (2013: 564) defines electoral integrity as "international conventions and global norms, applying universally to all countries worldwide throughout the electoral cycle, including during the pre-electoral period, the campaign, on polling day, and its aftermath." According to the International Institute for Democracy and Electoral Assistance (IDEA), internationally recognized electoral standards include the right to universal and equal suffrage, the right to contest elections without discrimination, the right to freedom of expression and freedom of association, independence and impartiality of electoral management bodies, secrecy of the ballot, fair, honest and transparent vote count, presence of election observers during various stages of election processes, and effective mechanisms and remedies for the enforcement of electoral rights.[2] Most elections in non-democracies are dubbed as "not free and fair" or "flawed" because they fail to meet international standards for democratic elections, albeit the type and the magnitude of electoral malpractices might vary from one country to another or from one election to another.[3] The burgeoning comparative authoritarianism literature documents a wide array of electoral malpractices in non-democracies around the globe (Alvarez, Hall and Hyde 2008; Birch 2010; Magaloni 2006; Myagkov, Ordershook and Shakin 2009; Schedler 2006). It is plausible to assume that a high rate of international electoral standards violations dampens public confidence in electoral processes, which in turn negatively affects the rate of electoral participation. Most empirical work, however, has overlooked behavioral consequences of public confidence in electoral fairness.

To date, a handful of studies have analyzed the impact of perceived electoral integrity on voting behavior (Birch 2010; Carreras and Irepoglu 2013; McAllister and White 2013; Norris 2014; Simpser 2012). In a path-breaking study, McCann and Dominguez (1998) find that popular perceptions of electoral fraud negatively affect voter turnout in Mexico, but such perceptions have little direct effect on the likelihood of voting for the political opposition. Similarly, Carreras and Irepoglu (2013) demonstrate that low levels of confidence in electoral processes depress the likelihood of voting in Latin America, while vote buying has the opposite effect. Using data from 31 countries around the globe, Birch (2010) reaffirms the positive relationship between perceptions of electoral fairness and the propensity to vote. Another finding in this literature is that mass perceptions of electoral fairness exert indirect effects on electoral participation. Citizens' evaluations of electoral integrity may affect their level of external political efficacy, the belief in one's capacity to influence political processes, which in turn influences voter turnout (McAllister and White 2013; Norris 2014).

This study contributes to this literature by investigating the effect of party identification on the relationship between perceived electoral integrity and turnout in an authoritarian regime. This chapter contends that perceptions of electoral integrity are more likely to affect the turnout decision made by opposition political party supporters, compared to political conformists. This argument derives from previous research on political legitimacy. Public confidence in political institutions and support for regime norms are positively associated with political participation (Gronlund and Setala 2007; Mishler and Rose 2005). Chen and Zhong (2002), for example, find that citizens with a high level of support for the communist regime are more likely to vote than citizens with democratic orientations in the People's Republic of China. The main hypothesis to be tested in this study is as follows:

Hypothesis 1: Perceptions of electoral integrity are more likely to depress turnout among supporters of opposition political parties, compared to supporters of the ruling party.

The Azerbaijan Context and the 2005 Parliamentary Election

Bordering Iran and Russia, Azerbaijan is an oil-rich state with a population of approximately 8.8 million people and is the only former Soviet republic where executive power was transferred from an incumbent president to his son. Since the collapse of communism and independence in 1991, most elections in Azerbaijan have fallen far short of international standards for democratic elections, and the Aliyev dynasty has steadily consolidated its grip on power.[4] Heydar Aliyev, a former KGB chief (1967–1969) and leader of the Communist Party of Soviet Azerbaijan (1969–1982), was elected as the third president of Azerbaijan in 1993 and re-elected for another five-year term in 1998. At the age of 80, the ailing Aliyev dropped out of the 2003 presidential race in favor of his 42-year old son, Ilham. Aliyev's push for hereditary succession was fraught with a high level of electoral malpractices, including inaccurate voter lists, the intimidation of both precinct election commission members and voters, restrictions on domestic and international election observation, onerous restrictions on political rallies, an absence of an effective mechanism for the resolution of election disputes, and the post-election detention of opposition political party activists (OSCE 2004). According to official election results, Ilham Aliyev won 76.8 percent of the vote, while Isa Gambar, a prominent opposition leader and chair of the Musavat Party, came in second with 13.9 percent (OSCE 2004: 25). Despite pervasive electoral irregularities, political parties still nominated candidates for the 2005 parliamentary election. Voters, in turn, had to decide whether or not to vote.

The parliamentary election scheduled for November 6, 2005 appeared to be quite competitive. The Central Election Commission (CEC) registered 2,063 of 2,148 applicants as candidates representing 48 political parties and blocs (OSCE 2006a: 9). However, nearly one quarter of registered candidates withdrew their candidacies before election day, citing threats of criminal prosecution, business closure, or concerns about family security (Franklin 2006: 2). Of the remaining 1,539 candidates, at least 431 represented the ruling party Yeni Azerbaijan Party (YAP), 116 represented the electoral bloc *Azadlyq* (Freedom) which was composed of three main opposition political parties (Azerbaijan Democratic Party, Azerbaijan Popular Front Party, and Musavat Party), 69 represented the electoral bloc *Yeni Siyaset* (New Policy) formed by smaller political parties critical of the incumbent government, and 68 represented the Liberal Party of Azerbaijan.[5] In accordance with new electoral rules, all candidates vied for seats in the 125-member national parliament in single-member districts based upon the first-past-the-post principle.

The parliamentary election was marred with a litany of electoral malpractices, including the manipulation of electoral rules, vote choice, and electoral administration.[6] After 2003, the Azerbaijani legal framework had slightly improved with the adoption of amendments to the Election Code and two presidential decrees on elections. For example, the presidential decree *On Urgent Measures for the Preparation and Conduct of Elections* lifted the ban on the registration of local nongovernmental organizations (NGOs) with more than 30 percent of foreign funding as domestic electoral observers. Yet, this decree had a negligible substantive impact because it was signed after the deadline for registration of domestic election observers. By mid-October, the Azerbaijani NGO Election Monitoring Center (EMC) completed the cumbersome process of individually registering 2,300 election observers (EMC 2006: 5). One of the main electoral malpractices during the campaign period was interference of local authorities and the police in electoral processes and in particular the obstruction of campaign activities by opposition political parties. Since the adoption of a new mass media law in 2002, the National Council on TV and Radio (which was staffed with presidential appointees) did not approve any new broadcasting licenses, thereby securing the ruling party's dominance of national TV coverage. Moreover, the May 2005 murder of investigative journalist Elmar Huseynov had a chilling effect on independent media, further limiting the opposition's media access.

Two allegedly prevented coup d'états added to the climate of fear during the election year. Ruslan Bashirli, the 27-year old leader of the youth movement *Yeni Fikir* (New Thinking), was arrested in August 2005 for allegedly plotting a coup at the behest of Armenian secret service agents (Human Rights Watch 2005: 17–22). State-controlled media also insinuated a homosexual relationship between Bashirli and Ali Karimli, leader of the Azerbaijan Popular Front Party, so Bashirli's arrest was an indirect blow to the public image of the opposition political party (Radio Free Europe/Radio Liberty 2005). Another coup was allegedly plotted by the former speaker of the national parliament and exiled leader of the Azerbaijan Democratic Party, Rasul Guliyev. Having received political asylum in the United States, Guliyev had announced his intent to return to Azerbaijan in October 2005, but he was threatened with embezzlement charges if he returned. Furthermore, the police arrested more than a dozen of Guliyev's political allies for their alleged involvement in plotting a coup on the eve of the parliamentary election (Ismayilov 2005).

Furthermore, vote buying and family voting were among the common electoral malpractices in this election. The EMC (2006: 3) reported cases of vote buying in 107 out of 125 electoral districts. In addition, international election observers witnessed cases of family voting at nearly one-fifth of the polling stations they visited on election day (OSCE 2006a: 19). Family voting in Azerbaijan usually means men voting on behalf of female family members. This social practice reflects the dominant social norms regarding the status of women in Azerbaijani society. Opinion polls suggest that politics is seen predominantly as a male domain. When prompted to assess whether women have greater, fewer, or the same opportunities in several areas of life, 65 percent of Azerbaijanis reported that women had fewer opportunities than men in politics, while 48 percent stated that women had more opportunities in education and healthcare sectors (Sharma 2006: 27–28). By the same token, only 54 percent of Azerbaijani men believe that women's participation in the labor market is good for Azerbaijani society (Sharma 2006: 28).

The post-election stage was also fraught with electoral irregularities. The OSCE reported cases of tampering with election results and the non-transparent handling of election complaints. According to official figures, voter turnout was 42.2 percent (OSCE 2006a: 20), down from 68 percent in the previous parliamentary election (OSCE 2001: 12). Upon the end of voting, state authorities also encroached upon citizens' freedom of expression and assembly by interfering with the organization of public rallies against vote rigging and violently dispersing a sit-in action in downtown Baku (BBC 2005; Peuch 2005). Overall, the OSCE observation mission concluded that the parliamentary election failed to meet a number of international standards for democratic elections (OSCE 2006a: 3).

Research Design

Data

This study uses data from a public opinion poll conducted by the International Foundation for Election Systems (IFES) on June 4–26, 2005.[7] An advantage of using this survey is that it was conducted before election day (November 6, 2005), which enables us to exclude the possibility that mass perceptions of electoral integrity were affected by the act of voting. Had the pre-election IFES survey been administered a few weeks, rather than months, prior to election day, partisanship differences in the evaluation of electoral processes would have been even more pronounced. The government's alleged exposure of two attempted coups and the state harassment of opposition political parties since the administration of the pre-election survey would have likely lowered even further opposition party supporters' confidence in the election's integrity.

Variable Measurement

The dependent variable, *the decision to vote*, was measured with the help of the following survey item, "How likely are you to vote in the parliamentary election that will take place later this year?" In a follow-up open-ended question, potential nonvoters were asked to disclose their motives for nonvoting. The independent variable, *mass perceptions of electoral integrity*, was measured with the help of the following question, "Please rank on a scale from 0, least fair, to 6, most fair, how free and fair, in your opinion, the parliamentary election will be?" The index was recoded into a dichotomous variable, with 0 equals unfair and 1 equals fair. Party identification was measured with the help of a survey item, which prompted respondents to name a political party that best represented the aspirations of people like them. The analysis below distinguishes between supporters of the ruling party YAP and supporters of the opposition electoral bloc *Azadlyq*.

In addition, the multivariate analysis includes several control variables commonly associated with electoral participation: socio-demographic character-istics (age, gender, educational attainment, and urban residence), measures of psychological involvement in politics (interest in politics, external political efficacy, and internal political efficacy), and correlates of economic voting (assessment of the national economy and satisfaction with the family financial situation).[8]

Scholars identified multiple individual-level determinants of voting.[9] A major argument in the literature is that socioeconomic status affects the likelihood of voting (Brady, Verba, and Schlozman 1995; Milbrath and Goel 1977; Wolfinger and Rosenstone 1980). Socioeconomic status is considered as one of the strongest predictors of voter turnout. Ample empirical evidence shows that better-educated individuals are more prone to vote (Blais, Gidengil and Nevitte 2004; Brady, Verba, and Schlozman 1995; Nie, Junn, and Stehlik-Barry 1996). Education reduces cognitive costs of voting because it enables citizens to comprehend complex election-related issues, compare party platforms, and make informed decisions regarding vote choice. In addition, education might foster a sense of civic duty, providing an incentive for electoral participation. A related finding in the literature is that citizens with high levels of income tend to vote at higher rates than those from disadvantaged socioeconomic backgrounds (Leighley and Nagler 1992; Rosenstone and Hansen 1993).

Additional socio-demographic characteristics associated with electoral participation are age, gender, and rural residence. Empirically, there is a curvilinear relationship between age and turnout (Bhatti, Hansen, and Wass 2012; Niemi and Barkan 1987; Strate et al. 1989). The middle-aged tend to turn out at higher rates than both younger and older voters. This trend can be attributed to lifecycle effects on political participation. The level of electoral participation tends to peak when citizens develop a higher stake in the political system and assume more responsibility at home and at work. Historically, men turned out at higher rates than women (Glaser 1959). In recent years, however, the gender gap in turnout has dramatically narrowed in established democracies (Childs 2004; Inglehart and Norris 2003; Norris 2002). Another finding in the literature is that voters in rural areas are more likely to cast a ballot than urbanites (Mo, Brady, and Ru 1991; Monroe 1977; Wright 1976). For example, Darr and Hesli (2010) find that traditional rural networks, rather than formal associations, play a central role in mobilizing voters in the Kyrgyz Republic. A possible explanation for higher voter turnout in rural areas is the development of more closely knit communities and a stronger reinforcement of certain social norms among farmers.

As measures of socioeconomic status, this chapter uses the level of educational attainment and employment status. Only 8.5 percent of Azerbaijanis have not finished high school, and three-quarters of respondents completed secondary education. Given this school completion rate, university education is treated as a measure of the above-average socioeconomic status. Another common measure of socioeconomic status, income level, is not included in the survey due to the sensitive nature of the question in a transition economy.

Another strand of research focuses on such psychological factors as interest in politics, party identification, and political efficacy (Finkel 1985; Soderlund, Wass, and Blais 2011). Higher levels of interest in politics are associated with higher likelihoods of political participation. Empirical evidence also suggests that both internal political efficacy—one's belief in the capacity to understand and participate in politics—and external political efficacy—one's belief in the responsiveness of the political system to citizens' demands—affect turnout intentions. In addition, identification with a political party increases the likelihood of voting. Scholars, for example, attribute a decline in US voter turnout to the weakening of partisan attachments (Abramson and Aldrich 1982; Gray and Caul 2000). Therefore this study controls for several psychological factors commonly linked with turnout.

Results

Sixty-eight percent of the Azerbaijani electorate reported their intent to vote in the 2005 parliamentary election. Consistent with previous research (Abramson and Aldrich 1982; Gray and Caul 2000), the level of anticipated electoral participation was higher among citizens with partisan attachment. Specifically, 84.9 percent of YAP sympathizers and 72.1 percent of *Azadlyq* supporters were intent on voting, while only 55.2 percent of respondents without any political party identification intended to vote. It must also be noted that self-reported voter intent needs to be considered with some caution. Turnout over-reporting is a common problem in public opinion research due to a social desirability bias. Traugott and Katosh (1979), for example, find that 78 percent of participants in the American National Election Study reported voting in the 1976 presidential election, while only 61 percent of the surveyed individuals voted, according to the official records. Likewise, the level of anticipated voter turnout (based upon citizens' self-reported voting intentions) was much higher than the official turnout figure reported by the government-run Central Election Commission of Azerbaijan after the election. According to the official results, 44 percent of voting-age citizens ended up voting on election day (CEC 2005). The OSCE observation mission, however, noted "serious violations during the count" and inconsistencies in the tabulation of election results (OSCE 2006a: 22–23), which makes it difficult to estimate the actual rate of electoral participation in Azerbaijan.

On the list of factors that survey respondents mentioned to explain their intent not to vote in the upcoming election, remarkably, more than one-third of potential non-voters (38.7 percent) cited a high incidence of electoral malpractices as a factor. Additional reasons for nonvoting included a lack of external political efficacy and a lack of trust in the national parliament. A handful of respondents mentioned a lack of resources (e.g. time or money) to vote. In sum, these survey responses provide prima facie evidence that mass perceptions of electoral integrity decrease the likelihood of one's participation in elections.

Table 2.1 displays the distribution of mass perceptions of electoral integrity by party identification. Overall, party identification had a strong impact on mass perceptions of electoral integrity. Consistent with previous research on winners and losers in an electoral contest (Anderson and Tverdova 2003; Anderson et al. 2005), the ruling party's voters reported a higher level of confidence in electoral processes than voters for the political opposition. Specifically, almost two-thirds of the ruling party's sympathizers reported confidence in the electoral process while only one-fourth of *Azadlyq* supporters did so. In contrast, 69 percent of *Azadlyq* supporters anticipated a high level of electoral irregularities during the parliamentary election. Clearly, most voters with a partisan attachment were inclined to espouse diametrically divergent opinions of the electoral process depending on their party affiliation. Another noteworthy finding is that almost one-fifth of respondents without party identification (over double those with a party affiliation) reported difficulty in assessing the degree of electoral fairness in the country. Statistical analysis (not reported here) shows that young female respondents with a low level of education were those more likely to choose the "don't know" option.

Further analysis confirms that the relationship between mass perceptions of electoral integrity and the turnout decision is affected by party identification. Although not reported here, non-partisans' intent to vote increased by 33.2 percent if they placed a great deal of confidence in the electoral process. Similarly, the intent to vote was over 30 percent higher among those *Azadlyq* supporters who

TABLE 2.1 Mass perceptions of electoral integrity by party identification

Mass perceptions of electoral integrity	Party identification		
	The ruling party	Opposition parties	None
Fair	63	22	39
Unfair	28	69	40
	100	100	100
	(834)	(165)	(1,061)

Note: Each column reports percentages, with the total number of respondents in parenthesis.

Source: 2005 IFES Survey

anticipated a high level of electoral integrity. This bivariate analysis indicates that the impact of mass perceptions of electoral integrity on the intent to vote was smallest among supporters of the ruling party. Still, YAP supporters are 16 percent more likely to report their intent to vote if they placed a high level of confidence in electoral processes.

Table 2.2 presents logistic regression results of models with the turnout decision as the dependent variable. Model 1 includes a common set of socio-economic and psychological variables associated with the turnout decision, while Model 2 adds a measure of electoral integrity. A likelihood ratio test indicates that there is a statistically significant difference between the two models with Model 2 as the preferred one. Model 3 includes two interaction terms, estimating the interaction effect of perceived electoral integrity and party identification. The results clearly demonstrate that perceptions of electoral integrity are strongly associated with the turnout decision. As seen in Model 2, the coefficient for electoral integrity is positive and statistically significant, indicating that public confidence in electoral fairness increases the likelihood of one's intent to vote. In fact, perceived electoral integrity is found to be the strongest determinant of one's intent to vote in the specified models.

As expected, regression coefficients for most attitudinal and socio-demographic variables are statistically significant and in the expected direction. Interest in politics and political efficacy are positively associated with the turnout decision. Those interested in politics are more likely to report the intent to vote. The results also indicate that satisfaction with the personal financial situation increases one's intent to vote, while a subjective assessment of the performance of national economy is weakly related to the turnout decision. Among socio-demographic variables, gender is the strongest determinant of electoral participation. Given predominant cultural norms in Azerbaijan, it is not surprising that male voters are more likely to report their intent to vote than female voters.

Furthermore, this study finds that party identification has a significant impact on the turnout decision. The coefficient for opposition party identification is negative and statistically significant, indicating that supporters of the opposition political parties are less likely to vote than supporters of the ruling party. Likewise, the odds of electoral participation are significantly lower among non-partisans. The coefficients for interaction terms appear to be statistically insignificant in the nonlinear model, but it should not be inferred from the output presented in Table 2.2 that the impact of mass perceptions on the turnout decision is not conditional upon party identification. Berry, DeMeritt, and Esarey (2010: 265), for example, point out that "one can glean no definitive information about the nature of interaction among independent variables in influencing $Pr(Y)$ from the sign and magnitude of a product term coefficient in a binary logit or probit model." Unlike the interaction effect in linear models, the interaction effect in nonlinear models is conditional on independent variables (on this point, see Ai and Norton 2003; Norton, Wang, and Ai 2004).

TABLE 2.2 The propensity to vote

Variable	Model 1		Model 2		Model 3	
	B	Exp(B)	B	Exp(B)	B	Exp(B)
Perceived electoral integrity			1.627***	5.090	1.487***	4.425
			(.147)		(.250)	
Party ID: opposition[a]	−.967***	.380	−.614*	.541	−.822**	.439
	(.224)		(.248)		(.284)	
Party ID: none[a]	−1.325***	.266	−1.213***	.297	−1.276***	.279
	(.132)		(.154)		(.209)	
Electoral integrity * party ID: opposition					1.459	4.300
					(.892)	
Electoral integrity * party ID: none					.133	1.142
					(.300)	
Interest in politics	.579***	1.785	.798***	2.221	.812***	2.254
	(.128)		(.152)		(.153)	
Internal political efficacy	.427***	1.533	.418**	1.519	.423**	1.526
	(.127)		(.148)		(.148)	
External political efficacy	.399**	1.490	.457**	1.579	.466**	1.594
	(.137)		(.160)		(.161)	
Satisfaction with financial family situation	.456**	1.578	.351*	1.420	.336*	1.399
	(.147)		(.167)		(.168)	
Assessment of national economy	.116	1.123	−.027	.974	−.025	.975
	(.141)		(.163)		(.163)	
Gender (male = 1)	.407***	1.502	.227†	1.255	.234†	1.264
	(.118)		(.138)		(.138)	
University education	.159	1.173	.231	1.260	.246	1.278
	(.170)		(.192)		(.192)	
Employment status	.128	1.136	.101	1.106	.101	1.106
	(.126)		(.145)		(.146)	
Young[b]	−.005	.995	.023	1.023	.023	1.024
	(.132)		(.153)		(.154)	
Old[b]	−.021	.979	−.001	.999	.005	1.005
	(.157)		(.184)		(.184)	
Urban	−.174	.840	.165	1.179	.165	1.179
	(.118)		(.144)		(.144)	
Constant	.615	1.849	−.303	.738	−.253	.777
	(.187)		(.240)		(.260)	
Log-likelihood	1896.995		1437.523		1433.925	
Pseudo R-square	.228		.330		.332	
N	1,801		1,564		1,564	

Note: Cell entries are regression coefficients b with standard errors in parenthesis and the odds ratio exp(b) in italics and the propensity to vote in Azerbaijan in 2005. The models use binary logistic regression. Significance levels: ***p < .001; ** p <.01; *p < .05; † < .10.

a   Identification with the ruling party is the reference category.
b   The middle-aged is the reference category.

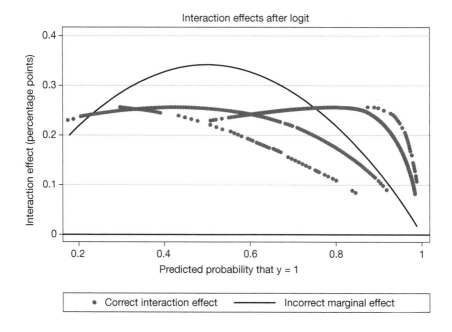

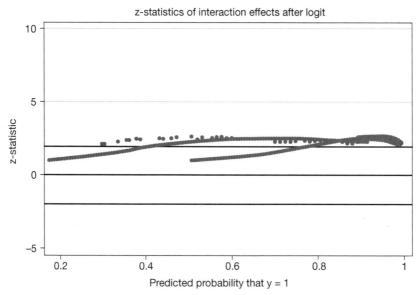

FIGURE 2.1 Interaction effect for electoral integrity ⋆ party identification (*Azadlyq*)

Note: The graphs are generated using the Stata command inteff; mean for z score = 2.17, min = .99, max = 2.66.

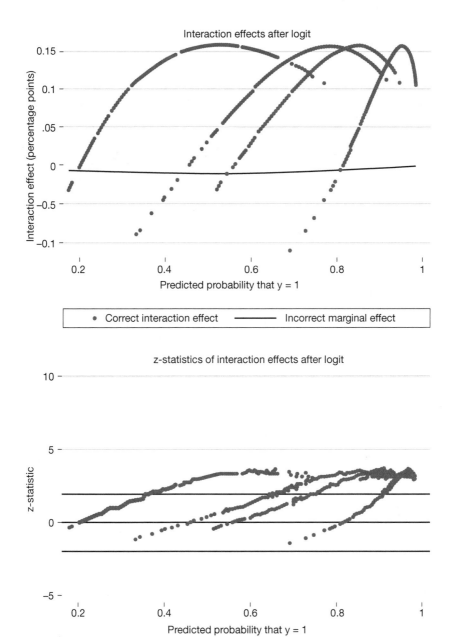

FIGURE 2.2 Interaction effect for electoral integrity ★ party identification (none)

Note: The graphs are generated using the Stata command inteff; mean for z score = 2.39, min = −1.39, max = 3.62.

The next step is to test the statistical significance of the interaction effect in the binary logistic regression model.[10] As shown in Figure 2.1a, the predicted probability of voting is 20 percent for those observations toward the left end of the figure, and the predicted probability of voting increases to 90 percent for some observations toward the right end of the figure, implying that the magnitude of the interaction effect varies. Overall, it is also safe to conclude that the interaction effect is statistically significant.

Furthermore, this study investigates how mass perceptions of electoral integrity affect the turnout decision by running the same model separately for three subsets of the population: (1) supporters of the ruling party; (2) supporters of *Azadlyq*; and (3) non-partisans. Table 2.3 summarizes the results of logistic regression models with the intent to vote as the dependent variable, controlling for party identification. The results confirm that mass perceptions of electoral integrity produce the strongest impact on one's intent to vote among regime opponents. As shown in Model 2 (Table 2.3), the intent of vote increases by 27 times if supporters of the opposition political parties anticipate a modicum of electoral integrity. The impact of perceived electoral integrity is also positive and statistically significant among supporters of the ruling party and non-partisans, albeit to a lesser extent. Another interesting finding is that youthful supporters of both the ruling party and the opposition political parties are significantly less likely to vote than the middle-aged, while young nonpartisans are more likely to vote than the middle-aged without any party attachment. These results suggest that most political parties were unable to mobilize young voters in Azerbaijan.

Conclusion

Using the case of the 2005 parliamentary election in Azerbaijan, this chapter demonstrates that the impact of mass perceptions of electoral integrity on the likelihood of voting depends, in part, on party identification. In particular, supporters of opposition political parties are much more likely to report their intent to vote if they anticipate a low level of electoral malpractices. The results also show that mass perceptions have a significant, albeit smaller, impact on the likelihood of electoral participation among supporters of the ruling party and non-partisans. Overall, these findings confirm the importance of incorporating a measure of perceived electoral integrity in empirical analysis of voting behavior in non-democracies.

The findings presented here can be generalized to non-democracies in the post-Soviet region and beyond. By the nature of the regime, elections in a repressive political regime are fraught with violations of democratic procedures. For example, the 2004 presidential election in Ukraine, the 2006 presidential election in Belarus, and the 2011 parliamentary election in Russia were marred with a high incidence of electoral malpractices (OSCE 2004, 2006b, 2012). Under such circumstances, voters need to decide whether to participate in flawed

TABLE 2.3 Propensity to vote, controlling for party identification

Variables	Model 4 Identification with the ruling party		Model 5 Identification with the political opposition		Model 6 Lack of identification with a political party	
	B	Exp(B)	B	Exp(B)	B	Exp(B)
Perceived electoral integrity	1.347***	3.846	3.322***	27.726	1.686***	5.397
	(.273)		(.980)		(.190)	
Interest in politics	1.039***	2.827	.868	2.383	.790***	2.203
	(.309)		(.617)		(.193)	
Internal political efficacy	.059	1.060	.620	1.859	.481**	1.617
	(.305)		(.594)		(.187)	
External political efficacy	.569†	1.767	.750	2.118	.304	1.355
	(.304)		(.487)		(.217)	
Satisfaction with financial family situation	.121	1.129	−.462	.630	.594**	1.810
	(.308)		(.601)		(.227)	
Assessment of national economy	.498	1.645	.648	1.912	−.426*	.653
	(.304)		(.744)		(.215)	
Gender (male = 1)	.456†	1.578	−.237	.789	.268	1.308
	(.270)		(.172)		(.179)	
University education	−.212	.809	.541	1.717	.304	1.355
	(.330)		(.569)		(.272)	
Employment status	−.219	.803	.475	1.607	.181	1.199
	(.282)		(.483)		(.192)	
Young[a]	−.485†	.616	−1.149*	.317	.431*	1.539
	(.287)		(.522)		(.202)	
Old[a]	−.192	.825	−.366	.694	.180	1.197
	(.378)		(.606)		(.237)	
Urban	.272	1.312	.057	1.059	.145	1.156
	(.295)		(.540)		(.185)	
Constant	−.026	.974	−.733	.481	−1.648	.192
	(.426)		(.856)		(.250)	
Log-likelihood	423.651		125.844		831.563	
Pseudo R-square	18.3%		33.8%		28.1%	
N	663		132		736	

Note: Cell entries are regression coefficients b with standard errors in parenthesis and the odds ratio exp(b) in italics and the propensity to vote in Azerbaijan in 2005. The models use binary logistic regression. Significance levels: ***p < .001; **p < .01; *p < .05; † < .10.

a The middle-aged is the reference category.

elections. It is reasonable to assume that mass perceptions of electoral integrity in interaction with partisan orientations affect voting behavior.

These results have implications for the organization of get-out-the vote (GOTV) campaigns in non-democracies. Opposition political parties tend to invest a lot of resources into raising public awareness of electoral malpractices, but opposition politicians are less adept at generating public outrage and converting mass dissatisfaction with the current regime into a high voter turnout. Political parties in non-democracies need to mobilize voters to turn out in spite of their low levels of confidence in the election's fairness. Otherwise, low voter turnout gives the ruling party an additional advantage by securing their electoral victory through the mobilization of a relatively small share of its supporters and the gross manipulation of electoral results in low turnout districts. Had all the voters identifying with the *Azadlyq* bloc (7.9 percent) participated in the 2005 election, the opposition political parties might have received more seats in the national parliament. According to official records (OSCE 2006a: 29), the *Azadlyq* bloc secured 6 out of 115 seats in the national parliament (5.2 percent). Nonetheless, a higher voter turnout of opposition political party supporters would not have drastically changed the outcome of the 2005 parliamentary election due to low levels of public trust in opposition political parties. Opposition politicians in Azerbaijan still face the challenge of how to establish rapport with the majority of voters.

Notes

1 For details, see country report for Azerbaijan in *Freedom in the World 2006*, available at: www.freedomhouse.org/report/freedom-world/2006/azerbaijan#.UuAOS7Qo 7IU.
2 For a full list, see IDEA (2002).
3 See Lehoucq (2003).
4 On the country's history and politics, see Cornell (2011).
5 For details, see Inter-Parliamentary Union (2005).
6 On the conceptualization of these terms, see Birch (2010).
7 A total of 2,120 respondents participated in the survey, including a base nationally representative sample (N = 1,500) and an oversampling of urban residents in five cities: Barda, Ganja, Guba-Khachmaz, Lenkoran, and Zaqatala (N = 620). A weight variable was used to approximate the distribution of responses in the general population. Since 2002, IFES contracted the Sorgu Social Studies Center, a local polling company, to implement data collection. This company was selected through a competitive bidding process, and it has a large portfolio of international clients, including BBC and the World Bank. Sorgu staff administered the face-to face survey using the Kish selection method. The first sampling stage was drawing a random sample of households. The second sampling stage was the random selection of an adult per household. If the selected respondent declined to participate in the survey, an adult from another household was recruited as a substitute. All interviews were conducted in respondents' homes and in their language of choice (89 percent in Azeri and 11 percent in Russian).
8 Though some scholars consider religious institutions as agents of electoral mobilization, a measure of religiosity—attendance of religious services—is not included in the statistical models. Nearly 95 percent of respondents in the IFES survey self-identified with Islam,

but 86 percent of them reported that they never attended a Friday prayer. These findings provide some grounds to conclude that religious institutions play a negligible role in mobilizing voters in Azerbaijan.

9 For a recent review of this literature, see Smets, Kaat, and van Ham (2013).

10 For this purpose, it is necessary to estimate the cross-derivative of the expected value of the dependent variable using the Stata command *inteff* (Norton, Wang and Ai 2004). This command also enables the researcher to plot interaction effects. The first graph plots interaction effects against predicted probabilities, and the second graph plots z-statistics of the interaction effect against predicted probabilities.

References

Abramson, Paul and John Aldrich. 1982. "The Decline of Electoral Participation in America." *American Political Science Review* 76(3): 502–521.

Ai, Chunrong and Edward Norton. 2003. "Interaction Terms in Logit and Probit Models." *Economics Letters* 80: 123–129.

Alvarez, Michael, Thad Hall, and Susan Hyde, Eds. 2008. *Election Fraud: Detecting and Deterring Electoral Manipulation*. Washington, DC: Brookings Institution Press.

Anderson, Christopher and Yuliya Tverdova. 2003. "Corruption, Political Allegiances, and Attitudes Toward Government in Contemporary Democracies." *American Journal of Political Science* 47(1): 91–109.

Anderson, Christopher, André Blais, Shaun Bowler, Todd Donovan, and Ola Listhaug. 2005. *Losers' Consent: Elections and Democratic Legitimacy*. New York: Oxford University Press.

BBC. 2005. "Thousands in Fresh Azeri Protest." November 19. Retrieved from www. news.bbc.co.uk/2/hi/europe/4452174.stm (accessed November 15, 2013).

Berry, William, Jacqueline DeMeritt, and Justin Esarey. 2010. "Testing for Interaction in Binary Logit and Probit Models: Is a Product Term Essential?" *American Journal of Political Science* 54(1): 248–266.

Bhatti, Yosef, Kasper Hansen, and Hanna Wass. 2012. "The Relationship between Age and Turnout: A Roller-Coaster Ride." *Electoral Studies* 31(3): 588–593.

Birch, Sarah. 2010. "Perceptions of Electoral Fairness and Voter Turnout." *Comparative Political Studies* 43(12): 1601–1622.

Blais, Andre, Elisabeth Gidengil, and Neil Nevitte. 2004. "Where Does Turnout Decline Come From?" *European Journal of Political Research* 43(2): 221–236.

Boix, Carles and Milan Svolik. 2013. "The Foundations of Limited Authoritarian Government: Institutions and Power-sharing in Dictatorships." *Journal of Politics* 75(2): 300–316.

Brady, Henry, Sidney Verba, and Kay Lehman Schlozman. 1995. *Voice and Equality: Civic Voluntarism in American Politics*. Cambridge, MA: Harvard University Press.

Carreras, Miguel and Yasemin Irepoglu. 2013. "Trust in Elections, Vote Buying, and Turnout in Latin America." *Electoral Studies* 32(4): 609–619.

CEC (Central Election Commission of the Republic of Azerbaijan). 2005. *Elections to the Milli Majlis of the Republic of Azerbaijan November 6, 2005: Protocol on General Voting Results by CEC of the Republic of Azerbaijan*. Retrieved from www.cec.gov.az/en/4millimajlis 2005/report/report.htm (accessed November 15, 2013).

Chen, Jie and Yang Zhong. 2002. "Why Do People Vote in Semicompetitive Elections in China?" *Journal of Politics* 64(10): 178–197.

Childs, Sarah. 2004. "A British Gender Gap? Gender and Political Participation." *Political Quarterly* 75(4): 422–424.

Colton, Timothy. 2000. *Transitional Citizens: Voters and What Influences Them in the New Russia.* Cambridge, MA: Harvard University Press.

Cornell, Svante. 2011. *Azerbaijan Since Independence.* Armonk, NY: M.A. Sharpe.

Darr, Benjamin and Vicki Hesli. 2010. "Differential Voter Turnout in a Post-Communist Muslim Society: The Case of the Kyrgyz Republic." *Communist and Post-Communist Studies* 43(3): 309–324.

EMC (Election Monitoring Center). 2006. *Final Report on the Results of the Monitoring of the Elections to the Milli Majilis of the Republic of Azerbaijan Held on November 6, 2005.* Baku, Azerbaijan: EMC. Retrieved from www.smdt.az/files/file/Parlament%20 seckileri/Final_Report_Parlament_2005. pdf.

Finkel, Steven. 1985. "Reciprocal Effects of Participation and Political Efficacy: A Panel Analysis." *American Political Science Review* 29(4): 891–913.

Fornos, Carolina, Timothy Power and James Garand. 2004. "Explaining Voter Turnout in Latin America, 1980 to 2000." *Comparative Political Studies* 37(8): 909–940.

Franklin, Jeremy. 2006. *Azerbaijan: Parliamentary Elections 2005.* Oslo, Norway: The Norwegian Center for Human Rights/The Norwegian Resource Bank for Democracy and Human Rights.

Glaser, William. 1959. "The Family and Voting Turnout." *Public Opinion Quarterly* 23(4): 563–570.

Gray, Mark and Miki Caul. 2000. "Declining Voter Turnout in Advanced Industrial Democracies, 1950 to 1997." *Comparative Political Studies* 33(9): 1091–1122.

Gronlund, Kimmo and Maija Setala. 2007. "Political Trust, Satisfaction and Voter Turnout." *Comparative European Politics* 5: 400–422.

Human Rights Watch. 2005. "Azerbaijan Parliamentary Elections 2005: Lessons Not Learned." Human Rights Watch Briefing Paper. October 31.

Inglehart, Ronald and Pippa Norris. 2003. *Rising Tide: Gender Equality and Cultural Change Around the World.* New York: Cambridge University Press.

IDEA (International Institute for Democracy and Electoral Assistance). 2002. *International Electoral Standards: Guidelines for Reviewing the Legal Framework of Elections.* Stockholm, Sweden: IDEA.

Inter-Parliamentary Union. 2005. "Azerbaijan Elections in 2005." *Historical Archive of Parliamentary Election Results.* Retrieved from www.ipu.org/parline-e/reports/arc/ 2019_05.htm (accessed November 15, 2013).

Ismayilov, Rovshan. 2005. "Recent Arrests Fuel Controversy, but Bets Are Off on Outcome." *EurasiaNet.* November 1. Retrieved from www.eurasianet.org/azerbaijan/ news/coup_20051101.html (accessed November 23, 2013).

Lehoucq, Fabrice. 2003. "Electoral Fraud: Causes, Types, and Consequences." *Annual Review of Political Science* 6: 233–256.

Leighley, Jan and Jonathan Nagler. 1992. "Socioeconomic Class Bias in Turnout, 1964— 1988: The Voters Remain the Same." *American Political Science Review* 86(3): 725–736.

Lust-Okar, Ellen. 2006. "Elections under Authoritarianism: Preliminary Lessons from Jordan." *Democratization* 13(3): 456–471.

Magaloni, Beatriz. 2006. *Voting for Autocracy: Hegemonic Party Survival and Its Demise in Mexico.* New York: Cambridge University Press.

Magaloni, Beatriz. 2008. "Credible Power-Sharing and the Longevity of Authoritarian Rule." *Comparative Political Studies* 41(4–5): 715–741.

McAllister, Ian and Stephen White. 2013. "Electoral Integrity and Support for Democracy in Post-Communist Europe." *The Electoral Integrity Project Working Paper Series*. Cambridge, MA: Harvard University.

McCann, James and Jorge Dominguez. 1998. "Mexicans React to Electoral Fraud and Political Corruption: An Assessment of Public Opinion and Voting Behavior." *Electoral Studies* 17(4): 483–503.

Milbrath, Lester and Madan Lal Goel. 1977. *Political Participation: How and Why Do People Get Involved in Politics?* Chicago: Rand McNally College Publishing.

Mishler, William and Richard Rose. 2005. "What Are the Political Consequences of Trust: A Test of Cultural and Institutional Theories in Russia." *Comparative Political Studies* 38(9): 1050–1078.

Mo, Jongryn, David Brady, and Jaehun Ru. 1991. "Urbanization and Voter Turnout in Korea: An Update." *Political Behavior* 13(1): 21–32.

Monroe, Alan. 1977. "Urbanism and Voter Turnout: A Note on Some Unexpected Findings." *American Journal of Political Science* 21(1): 71–78.

Myagkov, Mikhail, Peter Ordershook, and Dimitri Shakin. 2009. *The Forensics of Electoral Fraud*. New York: Cambridge University Press.

Nie, Norman H., Jane Junn, and Kenneth Stehlik-Barry. 1996. *Education and Democratic Citizenship in America*. Chicago: University of Chicago Press.

Niemi, Richard and Joel Barkan. 1987. "Age and Turnout in New Electorates and Peasant Societies." *American Political Science Review* 81(2): 583–588.

Norris, Pippa. 2002. *Democratic Phoenix: Reinventing Political Activism*. New York: Cambridge University Press.

Norris, Pippa. 2013. "The New Research Agenda Studying Electoral Integrity." *Electoral Studies* 32(4): 563–575.

Norris, Pippa. 2014. *Why Electoral Integrity Matters*. New York: Cambridge University Press.

Norton, Edward, Hua Wang, and Chunrong Ai. 2004. "Computing Interaction Effects and Standard Errors in Logit and Probit Models." *Stata Journal* 4(2): 154–167.

OSCE (Organization for Security and Cooperation in Europe). 2001. *The Republic of Azerbaijan Parliamentary Election 5 November 2000 and 7 January 2001*. Warsaw, Poland: Office for Democratic Institutions and Human Rights.

OSCE (Organization for Security and Cooperation in Europe). 2004. *Presidential Election (Second Round) Ukraine, 21 November 2004: Statement of Preliminary Findings and Conclusions*. Warsaw, Poland: Office for Democratic Institutions and Human Rights.

OSCE (Organization for Security and Cooperation in Europe). 2006a. *The Republic of Azerbaijan Parliamentary Election 6 November 2005*. Warsaw, Poland: Office for Democratic Institutions and Human Rights.

OSCE (Organization for Security and Cooperation in Europe). 2006b. *The Republic of Belarus Presidential Election 19 March 2006: OSCE/ODIHR Election Observation Mission Report*. Warsaw, Poland: Office for Democratic Institutions and Human Rights.

OSCE (Organization for Security and Cooperation in Europe). 2012. *The Russian Federation Elections to the State Duma 4 December 2011: OSCE/ODIHR Election Observation Mission Report*. Warsaw, Poland: Office for Democratic Institutions and Human Rights. Warsaw, Poland: Office for Democratic Institutions and Human Rights.

Peuch, Jean-Christophe. 2005. "Baku Police Disperse Opposition Rally." *Radio Free Europe/Radio Liberty* November 26. Retrieved from www.rferl.org/content/article/1063263.html (accessed August 1, 2013).

Radio Free Europe/Radio Liberty. 2005. "Arrested Activist's Father Alleges Harassment by Azerbaijani Authorities." *Newsline* August 8. Retrieved from www.rferl.org/content/article/1143455.html (accessed August 1, 2013).

Rosenstone, Steven and John Mark Hansen. 1993. *Mobilization, Participation, and Democracy in America.* New York: Macmillan.

Sanders, David. 2003. "Party Identification, Economic Perceptions, and Voting in British General Elections, 1974–97." *Electoral Studies* 22(2): 239–263.

Seligson, Mitchell A. and John A. Booth. 1995. "Who Votes in Central America? A Comparative Analysis." In Mitchell Seligson and John A. Booth, Eds. *Elections and Democracy in Central America, Revisited.* Chapel Hill, NC: University of North Carolina Press, pp. 128–151.

Schedler, Andreas, Ed. 2006. *Electoral Authoritarianism: The Dynamics of Unfree Competition.* Boulder, CO: Lynne Rienner.

Sharma, Rakesh. 2006. *Public Opinion in Azerbaijan 2005: Findings from a Public Opinion Survey.* Washington, DC: International Foundation for Election Systems.

Simpser, Alberto. 2012. "Does Electoral Manipulation Discourage Voter Turnout? Evidence from Mexico." *Journal of Politics* 74(3): 782–795.

Smets, Kaat and Carolien van Ham. 2013. "The Embarrassment of Riches? A Meta-Analysis of Individual-level Research on Voter Turnout." *Electoral Studies* 32(2): 344–359.

Soderlund, Peter, Wass, Hanna, and Andre Blais. 2011. "The Impact of Motivational and Contextual Factors on Turnout in First- and Second-Order Elections." *Electoral Studies* 30(4): 689–699.

Strate, John, Charles Parrish, Charles Elder, and Coit Ford. 1989. "Life Span Civic Development and Voting Participation." *American Political Science Review* 83(2): 443–464.

Traugott, Michael and John Katosh. 1979. "Response Validity in Surveys of Voting Behavior." *Public Opinion Quarterly* 43(3): 359–377.

Tucker, Joshua. 2002. "The First Decade of Post-Communist Elections and Voting: What Have We Studied and How Have We Studied It?" *Annual Review of Political Science* 5: 271–304.

Tucker, Joshua. 2006. *Regional Economic Voting: Russia, Poland, Hungary, Slovakia, and the Czech Republic, 1990–1999.* New York: Cambridge University Press.

Wolfinger, Raymond and Steven Rosenstone. 1980. *Who Votes?* New Haven, CT: Yale University Press.

Wright, Gerald. 1976. "Community Structure and Voting in the South." *Public Opinion Quarterly* 40(2): 201–215.

3

DO CONTENTIOUS ELECTIONS CATALYZE MASS PROTESTS?

Alesia Sedziaka and Richard Rose

Recent research focuses on "electoral authoritarian" regimes, those regimes that use elections to enhance legitimacy, yet manipulate them to maintain incumbent rule (Levitsky and Way 2010; Schedler 2006a). Scholars have significantly advanced the conceptualization and measurement of electoral manipulation (Birch 2011; Kelley and Kolev 2010; Norris 2014); yet the extent to which contested elections contribute to the maintenance or breakdown of electoral authoritarian regimes remains disputed (Schedler 2013, 143). On the one hand, formally competitive elections should serve to legitimate rulers and to strengthen the show of support for regime (Gandhi and Lust-Okar 2009). On the other hand, critical opposition campaigns and allegations of election fraud in contentious elections introduce the risk of popular discontent and instability (Howard and Roessler 2006; Lindberg 2009).

The question persists: to what extent and under what conditions do contentious elections erode support for regime? More specifically, when do evaluations of election unfairness lead people to protest? Recent studies using evidence from Russia and other post-communist states show that perceived election unfairness has negative effects on support for the regime (Rose and Mishler 2009), feelings of political efficacy (McAllister and White 2011), and voter turnout (Birch 2010), but positive effects on support for protest (Chaisty and Whitefield 2013). Moreover, some scholars have theorized that rigged elections provide a critical opportunity for mass protests and can serve as rallying points for opposition forces (Kuntz and Thompson 2009; Tucker 2007), and there is some cross-national evidence supporting this claim (Norris 2014).

Nevertheless, we have yet to fully comprehend the conditions under which contentious elections are more or less likely to motivate protest. Drawing on psychological theories of procedural justice (Tyler and Lind 2001) and motivated political reasoning (Lodge and Taber 2000), as well as recent research focusing on winner–loser gap in elections (Anderson et al. 2005), we examine a series of competing hypotheses regarding the conditions that may affect the likelihood of popular support for election protest. More specifically, theories of procedural justice suggest that perceptions of an election's unfairness should contribute to protest support independent of the election's outcomes (Tyler 2006). In contrast, theories of substantive fairness hold that citizens' reactions to unfair elections will depend on the decisiveness of the violations for the election's outcomes (Hartlyn and McCoy 2006). Finally, theories of motivated political reasoning suggest that voter's political preferences should affect protest support by biasing the interpretation of election unfairness (Lodge and Taber 2000).

To evaluate these propositions, we use the nationwide XIX New Russia Barometer survey (Rose 2012), conducted by the Levada Center shortly after the December 2011 Russian State Duma election.[1] These data are compared to a unique survey of Moscow protesters at the December Sakharov Avenue rally against election fraud, in addition to a representative survey of all Muscovites (Levada Center 2012).

The 2011 State Duma election triggered unprecedented mass protests against election fraud (Volkov 2012). International observers concluded that this election did not meet "the necessary conditions for fair electoral competition" (OSCE/ODIHR 2012, 1). Unlike Western commentators and observers, Russian society was deeply divided in its attitudes towards the election and immediate post-election protests (Rose 2012). While 46 percent of Russians viewed the election as unfair, many thought it was fair (35 percent) or were undecided about its fairness (19 percent). Furthermore, while 43 percent of Russians said they supported the post-election protests, a comparable number of citizens opposed them (42 percent). More citizens perceived the election as unfair than in previous elections (see McAllister and White 2011; Rose and Mishler 2009), yet many citizens remained convinced that the elections were fair and opposed the election protests. The wide variation in reactions to election unfairness and protest make Russia an excellent setting for testing the delegitimizing effects of electoral manipulation. Next, we elaborate on the theoretical underpinnings of the conditions that may explain Russians' diverging attitudes.

The Consequences of Election Unfairness for Electoral Protest Support

The idea of diffuse support suggests that citizens will consent to unfavorable political outcomes if they have sufficient attachment to the regime or to the procedures that produced the unfavorable outcomes (Easton 1965, 272). Beliefs that regime norms and structures are "right and proper" are thought to promote citizens' voluntary compliance with authorities (Easton 1965; Tyler 2006).

If procedures matter, fair elections should increase support for regimes, and fraudulent elections should increase support for election protest (Norris 2014).

However, electoral manipulation is often hidden from ordinary citizens and is difficult to observe even for trained experts and election monitors (Hartlyn and McCoy 2006; Kelley 2012; Schedler 2009a). Assessments of election quality are complicated by uncertainties about the extent of manipulation and genuine popular preferences (Schedler 2006b). Kelley (2010, 2012) shows that election observers produce diverging assessments of elections which are subject to multiple biases and limitations of resources and time. Moreover, electoral manipulation is not limited to blatant types of cheating such as ballot box stuffing or miscounting of votes. It includes more subtle tools such as restricting opposing parties' and candidates' access to media and resources; selective application of law; and restrictive legal frameworks (Birch 2011; Ledeneva 2006; Levitsky and Way 2010). Manipulation is often ambiguous and potentially justifiable on legal grounds (Schedler 2009a; Simpser and Donno 2012). The complexity and ambiguity of electoral manipulation leave ample room for disagreement on its extent and significance, both among experts and ordinary citizens (Sedziaka 2014). Thus, the delegitimizing effects of electoral manipulation should not be taken for granted. The critical question is, to what extent and under what conditions does electoral manipulation affect support for election protest?

Procedural Unfairness: Direct Experience of Electoral Violations

Theories of procedural justice suggest that people's reactions to authorities depend on the perceived fairness of procedures used to make decisions and policies (Tyler and Lind 2001). There is evidence that procedural fairness affects attitudes to and compliance with authorities and the law (Tyler 1990, 2006). Furthermore, the fairness heuristic theory posits that people may use assessments of procedural fairness as a cognitive shortcut to guide them to acceptance or rejection of authorities' decisions (Lind et al. 1993; Tyler and Lind 2001; Tyler et al. 1997, 100). However, as Doherty and Wolak (2012) argue, the fairness of political processes is often ambiguous, and when it is, people rely on prior preferences to evaluate procedures. This means that election winners may discount information about election unfairness, while losers may exaggerate the extent and significance of election fraud.

Since people tend to attribute disproportional weight to salient information based on personal experience (Kaufmann 1994), procedural concerns will likely matter more when people experience procedural violations directly. In the context of elections, pressure to vote for the governing party exerted by local authorities or employers imparts direct knowledge of violations. This evidence should be more difficult to discount than allegations or second-hand reports of violations, and easier to interpret than structural bias such as limited access to media and resources. Therefore, we hypothesize that when citizens experience undue pressure from employers or authorities, the likelihood of protest support will increase.

> Hypothesis 1: Citizens who experienced direct pressure to vote for a particular party will be more likely to support electoral protest.

Knowledge of International Election Monitor Assessments

Due to the concealed nature of electoral manipulation, citizens may have little direct experience of procedural violations. Previous research shows that relatively few Russians report direct electoral pressure (McAllister and White 2011; Rose 2012). However, knowledge of international observers' critical assessments may increase indirect perceptions of procedural unfairness, thereby increasing protest support. The literature on election monitoring assumes that international observers' assessments of violations affect government legitimacy (Kelley 2012; Beaulieu and Hyde 2009). At the same time, some scholars argue that people may not understand the criteria that experts use to assess electoral violations (Birch 2011, 53). We test the proposition that knowledge of critical judgments by international election monitors increases protest support.

> Hypothesis 2: Citizens who know about international observers' critical assessments of elections will be more likely to support electoral protest.

Substantive Unfairness: Decisiveness of Violations for Election Outcomes

Instead of viewing procedural violations in absolute terms, citizens may consider their significance in relation to election outcomes. The focus on substantive outcome fairness means that the party that enjoys the most popular support ought to win (Rose, Mishler, and Munro 2011, 131).[2] Hartlyn and McCoy (2006, 50) argue that "even where significant irregularities have occurred, if they do not appear to have had an impact on the outcome, most of the actors are much more willing to accept the results, even if begrudgingly." Perceived support for the winner may affect attitudes towards both the election process and protest by suggesting that the result would have been the same even in a fairer contest (Silitski 2005). Structural bias against the opposition (manifested in biased laws, media coverage, and access to resources) may help the public's acquiescence to election results because the effects of such bias on the election outcome are difficult to measure; in addition, unlike blatant vote-rigging, structural bias is also difficult to observe (Hartlyn and McCoy 2006). However, when citizens believe that electoral manipulation had a significant impact on an election's outcome, they should be more supportive of electoral protest.

> Hypothesis 3: Citizens who think that procedural violations decisively affected election outcomes will be more likely to support electoral protest.

Finally, the experience of electoral pressure, knowledge of critical international monitor assessments, and substantive unfairness should all increase the likelihood of overall judgments of election unfairness. In turn, summary perceptions of election unfairness should increase the likelihood of protest support.

> Hypothesis 4: Citizens who perceive elections as generally unfair will be more likely to support electoral protest.

Motivated Reasoning and Winner–Loser Gap

The influence of election unfairness on protest support may depend on the significance that citizens attribute to unfairness. Theories of motivated political reasoning predict that people will devalue and rationalize information that contradicts their prior preferences (Lodge and Taber 2000; Taber and Lodge 2006; Taber, Lodge, and Glathar 2001). Furthermore, Gaines and colleagues (2007) show that even when people acknowledge the same facts, they interpret them differently in order to maintain partisan attitudes. Previous research found a winner–loser gap in attitudes towards both election fairness and protest (Anderson and Mendes 2006; Anderson et al. 2005). It follows that winners and losers should interpret election unfairness differently, which should result in a different likelihood of protest support.

More specifically, winners should devalue the importance of information about election fraud to make it consistent with their vote choice, while losers should attribute heightened significance to such information. This means that the same levels of perceived unfairness should result in a lower probability of protest support among winners, compared to losers. To test the idea that winners and losers attribute different significance to election unfairness, we use interactions between various measures of unfairness and winning. Prior research suggests that nonvoters are more likely to perceive elections as unfair (Anderson et al. 2005; Rose and Mishler 2009). In addition, the XIX New Russia Barometer survey shows that almost 30 percent of Russian nonvoters don't trust any of the current politicians (Rose 2012). We expect that nonvoters' attitudes towards protest will be similar to those of losers.

> Hypothesis 5a: Winners will be less likely to support electoral protest, compared to losers and nonvoters.

Hypothesis 5b: Assessments of electoral unfairness will be less likely to motivate protest support among winners, compared to losers and nonvoters.

Control Variables

We control for factors that previous research identified as important for election fairness assessments and political support (Chaisty and Whitefield 2013; Norris 2011; Rose, Mishler, and Munro 2011). Our control variables include democratic ideals and deficit, assessments of political and economic performance, and measures of socioeconomic status such as education, wealth, and age. For example, citizens' commitment to democratic values may determine both their attitudes towards elections and electoral protest. Alternatively, citizens' support for elections and protest may be driven by dissatisfaction with corruption or government economic performance (Rose, Mishler, and Munro 2011). Socioeconomic resources may also enable citizens to be more critical of elections and more supportive of protest (Magaloni 2006). Since the largest protest rallies took place in Moscow, we control for Moscow residence and its interaction with election unfairness. Last, we include interactions between measures of election unfairness and democratic values, to check if election quality may matter more among "strong" democrats.

Measures and Descriptive Statistics

To examine the impact of election unfairness assessments on support for electoral protest, we use data from the nationwide XIX New Russia Barometer survey (Rose 2012), complemented with surveys of Muscovites and Moscow protesters (Levada Center 2012). The nationwide survey was organized by the Centre for the Study of Public Policy at University of Strathclyde and conducted by the Levada Center soon after the December 4, 2011 State Duma election. A random sample of 1,600 Russians aged 18 and older was interviewed between December 16 and 20. The Levada Center organized separate surveys of Muscovites and Moscow protesters. A random sample of 998 Muscovites was interviewed between December 8 and 16. Finally, a sample of 791 Moscow protesters was interviewed at the Sakharov Avenue rally against election fraud on December 24, 2011. Using these data, we can trace some differences between the protesters, Muscovites, and Russians at large. The survey of Muscovites serves to check if any differences between the protesters and the general public are due to unique characteristics of the protesters, as opposed to all Muscovites.

The following survey question measures electoral protest support: "Generally speaking, do you support street protests against violations in the conduct of the [State Duma] election and falsification of the results?" The answers range from "entirely oppose" to "definitely support" on a five-point scale. The advantage of this measure is that it is specific to the context of unfair elections, allowing us to examine their immediate mobilizing effect. The nationwide survey shows that while 43 percent of Russians supported protest against election fraud, 42 percent opposed it, and 15 percent were neutral. In Moscow, a narrow majority (56 percent) supported protest (see Figure 3.1 for details).

According to the OSCE/ODIHR (2012) final report:

> Observers received numerous credible allegations of attempts to unduly influence voters' choices. These included allegations of civil servants being requested to sign letters in support of ER [United Russia], owners of big companies putting pressure on employees to vote for the governing party, and school directors being instructed by local authorities to ensure that their employees vote for ER.

The nationwide survey measures pressure to vote for one party by asking, "During the election campaign this year, did you notice any attempt to pressure or push you to take part in the election and support a particular party or candidate? And if so, by whom?" (Levada-Tsentr 2011a). We code a binary variable that indicates the presence or absence of pressure from "local authorities" or "bosses at work." Around 12 percent of Russians reported such pressure in the nationwide survey.[3]

The following survey question reflects the perceived decisiveness of procedural violations for election results: "In your opinion, were there violations in the

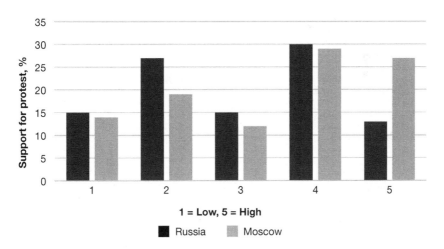

FIGURE 3.1 Support for protest against election fraud in Russia, December 2011

Source: New Russia Barometer XIX, Centre for the Study of Public Policy, University of Strathclyde (Rose 2012); Survey of Muscovites (Levada Center 2012)

counting of votes in the Duma election and if so, how significant were they?" Two- fifths of Russians thought that there were minor (29 percent) or no violations (12 percent); 20 percent thought that violations, although significant, hardly affected the results; and only 15 percent thought that the results were significantly altered, or substantively unfair. To separate substantive and procedural assessments, we code a set of dummy variables, omitting "no violations" as a reference category.

To gauge the knowledge of Russians about election monitoring, the survey asked, "Are you aware of critical Western assessments such as by observers, the resolution of the OSCE, the statement of US Secretary of State Hillary Clinton about the Duma election?" A small minority of 14 percent said they knew about such assessments; another 35 percent claimed that they had heard about them. These data show that the majority of Russians have little knowledge about election monitoring. Finally, the question on whether the State Duma election was conducted fairly measures the summary unfairness perceptions.

While relatively few Russians thought that violations in the vote count substantially altered the results, many said they had voted for the losing parties. We measure winning in elections by voting for the government-backed United Russia that officially received 49 percent of the vote.[4] In the nationwide survey, 46 percent of the voters reported voting for United Russia. The rest of the votes were distributed among the systemic opposition parties: Communist Party of the Russian Federation (17 percent), Fair Russia (12 percent), and Liberal Democratic Party of Russia (12 percent). Only a meager 3 percent of respondents said they had voted for the long-established opposition liberal-democratic party, *Yabloko*. United Russia had less support in Moscow: around one-third of Muscovites recalled voting for United Russia, and 12 percent for *Yabloko*.

Moscow Protesters at the Sakharov Avenue, December 24, 2011

The survey of Moscow protesters was conducted at a major rally against election fraud that took place around three weeks after the State Duma election on December 24, 2011. When asked about reasons for joining the protest, the largest number of protesters cited a "desire to express indignation with election fraud" (72 percent) and "accumulated dissatisfaction with the state of affairs in the country and with government policies" (73 percent).[5] Consistent with the expressed dissatisfaction, the protesters were overwhelmingly opposed to the dominant party and the presidential candidacy of Vladimir Putin, and had voted accordingly. Out of 791 interviewed protesters, only three voted for United Russia in the 2011 State Duma election. The top two contenders among the protesters were the liberal-democratic *Yabloko* (48 percent) and the Communist Party (24 percent). Furthermore, only four out of 791 respondents said they would vote for Vladimir Putin in the presidential election in March 2012. The protesters self-identified most frequently as democrats (38 percent) and liberals (31 percent), followed by communists (13 percent). Only 6 percent self-identified as nationalists.

The protesters' political preferences are highly unrepresentative of Russia at large as well as Moscow. It is telling that support for the liberal-democratic *Yabloko* is 16 times higher among the protesters than among Russians at large, and four times higher than among Muscovites. Moreover, the protesters are unrepresentative in terms of socioeconomic status. They are highly educated and well off by Russian and even by Moscow standards (see Figure 3.2).

Empirical Analysis

Given the disparities between the protesters and Russians at large, it is important to determine to what extent and when electoral unfairness contributes to protest support. We use ordered logit regression to test the effects of specific measures of procedural and substantive unfairness, summary unfairness perceptions, and motivated reasoning among winners and losers on the likelihood of electoral protest support. This is an appropriate strategy, given that the dependent variable is measured on a five-point scale (from "entirely oppose" to "definitely support" protest). The statistical analysis is based on the data from the nationwide XIX New Russia Barometer survey conducted shortly after the 2011 State Duma election. To facilitate the interpretation of individual variable effects, we first present the models that omit interaction terms; we then conduct a separate analysis of the interaction effects (see Table 3.1 for results).[6]

The results provide considerable support for our hypotheses. Model 1 shows the effects of specific indicators of unfairness and winning, while omitting summary unfairness perceptions as a potential mediator between these variables and protest support. Model 2 includes summary unfairness perceptions along with

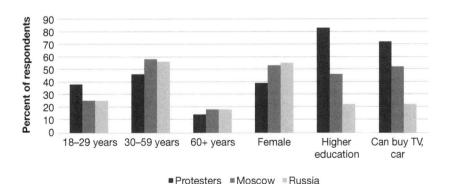

FIGURE 3.2 The socioeconomic background of protesters

Sources: New Russia Barometer XIX, Centre for the Study of Public Policy, University of Strathclyde (Rose 2012); Surveys of Muscovites and Moscow Protesters (Levada Center 2012)

TABLE 3.1 Support for electoral protest

Variables	Model 1 Specific Unfairness		Model 2 Overall unfairness		Model 3 Unfairness x winning		Model 4 All interactions	
Election unfair			0.73***	(0.12)	0.89***	(0.14)	1.75***	(0.35)
Pressure	0.89***	(0.22)	0.87***	(0.23)	0.93***	(0.23)	0.92***	(0.23)
Observer assessments	0.34***	(0.10)	0.29**	(0.10)	0.28**	(0.10)	0.32**	(0.10)
Decisive violations	1.99***	(0.31)	1.16***	(0.33)	1.16***	(0.33)	0.97**	(0.34)
Significant violations	1.12***	(0.26)	0.54*	(0.27)	0.62*	(0.28)	0.47	(0.28)
Undecided	0.46	(0.25)	0.15	(0.25)	0.26	(0.26)	0.10	(0.26)
Insignificant violations	0.58*	(0.23)	0.34	(0.23)	0.45	(0.23)	0.34	(0.24)
Winner	−1.03***	(0.16)	−0.85***	(0.16)	0.36	(0.57)	0.12	(0.58)
Democracy as ideal	0.04	(0.05)	0.06	(0.05)	0.07	(0.05)	0.43***	(0.12)
Democratic deficit	0.02	(0.04)	−0.00	(0.04)	−0.01	(0.04)	−0.01	(0.04)
Household economy	−0.17	(0.11)	−0.12	(0.11)	−0.11	(0.11)	−0.12	(0.11)
National economy	−0.01***	(0.00)	−0.01**	(0.00)	−0.01**	(0.00)	−0.01**	(0.00)
Corruption	0.03	(0.09)	−0.05	(0.09)	−0.04	(0.09)	−0.02	(0.09)
Education	−0.01	(0.04)	−0.01	(0.04)	−0.01	(0.04)	−0.00	(0.04)
Wealth	0.06	(0.09)	0.04	(0.09)	0.04	(0.09)	0.03	(0.09)
Age	0.00	(0.00)	0.00	(0.00)	0.00	(0.00)	0.00	(0.00)
Moscow	0.44	(0.27)	0.50	(0.27)	0.49	(0.27)	−3.72***	(1.00)
Interactions								
Election unfair ⋆ winner					−0.51*	(0.23)	−0.43	(0.23)
Election unfair ⋆ dem. ideal							−0.13**	(0.04)
Election unfair ⋆ Moscow							1.58***	(0.37)
Pseudo R^2	0.11		0.13		0.13		0.14	

Note: N = 800. Ordered logit estimates. Standard errors in parentheses. ⋆ p < 0.05, ⋆⋆ p < 0.01, ⋆⋆⋆ p < 0.001. "No violations" omitted as a reference category. Cutpoints omitted due to space considerations.

Source: New Russia Barometer XIX (Rose 2012)

all the other variables. In Model 1, pressure, knowledge of critical international monitor assessments, decisive violations, and winning are statistically significant and in the predicted direction. These variables remain statistically significant, even after taking into account summary unfairness perceptions. Since the effects of specific measures of unfairness were not subsumed by the summary judgments, the substantive interpretation of the results will focus on Model 2.

Hypothesis 1 concerning the impact of the experience of pressure to vote for a particular party is confirmed: electoral pressure does increase the likelihood of protest support. Table 3.2 summarizes the substantive meaning of our findings

TABLE 3.2 Change in protest support

	Mostly support		Definitely support	
Pressure	0.13	[0.08, 0.18]	0.08	[0.03, 0.14]
Decisive violations	0.18	[0.09, 0.27]	0.10	[0.04, 0.17]
Winner	−0.14	[−0.20, −0.09]	−0.06	[−0.08, −0.03]
Election unfair	0.09	[0.06, 0.13]	0.04	[0.03, 0.06]
National economy	−0.04	[−0.07, −0.02]	−0.02	[−0.03, −0.01]
Observer assessments	0.10	[0.03, 0.16]	0.05	[0.01, 0.08]

Note: Change in predicted probability, given change from 0 to 1 for pressure, decisive violations, winner; a standard deviation change for election unfair and national economy; moving from 1 to 3 for observer assessments. For each variable, all other variables are held at the mean. 95 percent confidence intervals in brackets. Differences in predicted probability are based on Model 2.

Source: New Russia Barometer XIX (Rose 2012)

by reporting the change in predicted probability of mostly or definitely supporting protest corresponding to the change in independent variables of interest. For example, when all the other variables are set at their mean, reported pressure increases the likelihood of mostly supporting protest by .13 (the 95 percent confidence interval is [.08, .18]). This implies that personal experience of pressure to vote for the dominant party may increase the delegitimizing potential of electoral manipulation.

Hypothesis 2 addressing the influence of the knowledge of critical international election monitor assessments receives support as well. Substantively, the probability of mostly supporting protest increases by .10 [.03, .16] when moving from "don't know" to "know" about observer assessments. This means that along with the direct experience of procedural unfairness, indirect knowledge of observer judgments may also provide motivation for protest support. This knowledge is not a function of higher levels of education or wealth, since neither of these variables achieves statistical significance in our models. Nonetheless, this finding should be treated with caution, because the effect of such knowledge may be endogenous to protest attitudes. In particular, citizens who are favorably oriented towards electoral protest may be especially likely to look for and learn about critical foreign observer judgments. In addition, international monitor assessments are not the only potential source of information about procedural unfairness.[7] Further research is needed to determine to what extent this and other sources of knowledge of electoral violations contribute to protest support.

Our results confirm Hypothesis 3 regarding the influence of substantive unfairness, or perceived decisiveness of violations for election outcomes, on the likelihood of protest support. In particular, compared to thinking that there were no violations, perceived decisiveness of vote count violations leads to an 18 percent increase in the likelihood of supporting protest. This finding implies that the significance people attribute to procedural violations in relation to substantive election outcomes is an important condition for electoral protest support. Furthermore, this means that we need to take into account not only how citizens assess procedural violations, but also how they judge the extent of popular support for the incumbents. Hypothesis 4, addressing the impact of summary unfairness perceptions, is supported as well. Model 2 in Table 3.1 shows that summary perceptions increase the likelihood of protest support, when controlling for specific indicators of unfairness. In particular, a standard deviation increase in perceptions that the election was unfair increases the predicted probability of mostly supporting protest by .09.

In contrast, winning reduces the likelihood of protest support (Hypothesis 5a), which confirms prior findings on the winner-loser gap in protest attitudes (Anderson and Mendes 2006). Substantively, the predicted probability of mostly supporting protest is −.14 lower for winners than for losers and nonvoters. The logic of motivated reasoning may partially explain this difference. As discussed earlier, theories of motivated political reasoning suggest that winners and losers may attribute different significance to information about election fraud in order to maintain prior preferences. Hypothesis 5b addresses the influence of motivated reasoning on protest support by examining the interactions between different indicators of election unfairness and winning. More specifically, if winners interpret election unfairness differently, the effect of the same levels of unfairness on protest support should be smaller among winners, compared to losers and nonvoters.

Hypothesis 5b on motivated political reasoning receives mixed support. Interactions between winning and specific indicators of unfairness (pressure, knowledge of international observer assessments, and decisive violations) do not achieve statistical significance when controlling for all other variables. Thus, our presentation focuses on the interaction between summary unfairness perceptions and winning. Model 3 in Table 3.1 shows that this interaction is statistically significant (p < .027). Model 4 controls for other statistically significant interactions. Here, the interaction between summary unfairness perceptions and winning no longer achieves conventional levels of statistical significance (p < .065). However, when generating predicted probabilities of protest support based on this model, we see statistically significant and consistent differences between winners and losers/nonvoters at various levels of perceived election unfairness.

Figure 3.3 illustrates the difference between winners and losers/nonvoters in predicted probabilities of definitely supporting protest over the range of summary perceptions of unfairness. The figure shows that this difference increases with higher values of perceived unfairness. For example, when citizens view the election as absolutely fair, there is no statistically discernable difference between winners and losers/nonvoters. However, when perceiving the election as "not very fair," winners are less likely than losers/nonvoters to definitely support protest by −.08 [−.11, −.06]. When perceiving the election as "not at all fair," this difference increases to −.19 [−.28, −.11]. These findings suggest that winners attribute less

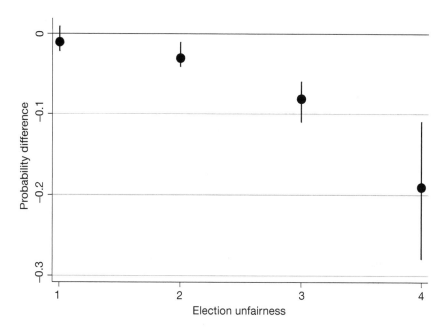

FIGURE 3.3 Probability of definitely supporting protest over electoral unfairness

Note: Differences between winners and losers/nonvoters in predicted probabilites. The vertical lines represent 95 percent confidence intervals. All other variables set at the mean. Differences in predicted probability based on Model 4 in Table 3.1. Along the x axis: 1 = absolutely fair; 2 = mostly fair; 3 = not very fair; 4 = not at all fair.

significance, compared to losers and nonvoters, to the same assessments of overall unfairness, which results in lower protest support. It follows that the strength of partisan bias in interpreting the information about electoral manipulation affects its mobilizing potential.

Among the control variables, only the effect of national economy assessments is statistically significant (see Model 2 in Table 3.1). For a standard deviation increase in positive assessments, the likelihood of mostly supporting protest declines by −.04 [−.07, −.02]. Thus, perceptions of positive macro-economic performance reduce the delegitimizing power of unfair elections. Other variables, including perceived corruption, household economy, democratic ideals and deficit, and measures of socioeconomic status (age, wealth, and Moscow residence) are not statistically significant. As Model 4 in Table 3.1 shows, however, democratic ideals and Moscow residence condition the effect of overall unfairness perceptions on protest support.

In particular, based on a standard deviation change, citizens with stronger preference for democracy are more likely to mostly support protest when they think the election is absolutely fair (the difference in predicted probability is .07

[.03, .12]). When citizens view the election as unfair, however, this difference is not statistically discernable. Thus, when elections are perceived as fair, higher preference for democracy may increase the likelihood of electoral protest support. In addition, living in Moscow strongly enhances the effect of perceived unfairness: when viewing the election as "not at all fair," the difference between Muscovites and other Russians in predicted probability of definitely supporting protest is .56 [.32, .79]. A higher proportion of educated and well-off citizens in the capital may at least partly explain this finding. However, the explanation may also lie in greater knowledge of and solidarity with the capital-centered protests.

Conclusions and Implications

Leaders in electoral authoritarian regimes use multiple strategies of manipulation to disadvantage opponents and ensure reelection (Levitsky and Way 2010; Schedler 2002, 2006a). Yet, we do not fully understand when electoral manipulation works to mobilize public support for regime, and when it leads citizens to support electoral protest. Theories of legitimacy suggest that institutions perceived as "right and proper" increase regime acceptance and compliance with authority (Easton 1965; Tyler 2006). Furthermore, recent research assumes that electoral manipulation carries significant costs of regime delegitimation (Birch 2011). Yet, this assumption cannot be taken for granted. Survey evidence collected soon after the 2011 Russian State Duma election that triggered protests against election fraud demonstrates that many citizens viewed the election as fair and opposed protest.

Drawing on psychological theories of procedural justice (Tyler and Lind 2001), motivated reasoning (Lodge and Taber 2000) and winner–loser gap (Anderson et al. 2005), we examined the following conditions that may explain how people react to unfair elections: the experience and knowledge of procedural unfairness; perceived substantive unfairness; and biased reasoning regarding unfairness among winners and losers. Overall, the results are consistent with the theoretical expectations and with the research on the consequences of perceived election unfairness (Norris 2014; McAllister and White 2011; Rose and Mishler 2009). The procedural considerations receive support in our analysis: both pressure to vote for one party and knowledge of critical international monitor assessments increase the likelihood of electoral protest support. However, the latter finding is inconclusive due to concerns about endogeneity, as citizens supportive of protest may purposefully pursue the validation of foreign observers. On the other hand, our findings underscore the importance of substantive unfairness (Hartlyn and McCoy 2006; Rose, Mishler, and Munro 2011), suggesting that when people perceive procedural violations as decisive for election results, they are more willing to support protest.

Nevertheless, as our findings show, the influence of unfairness assessments on protest support may be counteracted by motivated reasoning among winners and losers, which extends prior findings about winner–loser gap (Anderson et al. 2005).

While we do not find that specific measures of unfairness interact with winning, the same overall unfairness perceptions are less likely to motivate protest support among winners than among losers and nonvoters, as predicted by theories of motivated political reasoning (Lodge and Taber 2000). This finding implies that winners rationalize and attribute less significance to information about election fraud. In addition to election-related variables, assessments of national economy perform well in our models, suggesting that positive views of the economy reduce the delegitimizing potential of unfair elections.

Our analysis of electoral protest support in Russia has important implications for the broader debate on legitimation of electoral authoritarian regimes. First, while we find that experiencing pressure to vote during the election campaign increases support for electoral protest, only 12 percent of Russians reported encountering such pressure (Rose 2012). This means that the effects of direct experience of procedural unfairness may be limited insofar as electoral corruption remains concealed and takes on more sophisticated forms. The influence of international observer assessments on protest support has similar implications. According to the nationwide XIX New Russia Barometer survey, only 14 percent of citizens knew about international monitor judgments. Insofar as citizens in electoral authoritarian regimes have limited access to and interest in such information, it cannot contribute to widespread protest support.

Importantly, we find that protest support depends on whether citizens perceive election outcomes as unfair. When citizens perceive winners as popular, and vote rigging as not very significant for election results, protest appears less appealing. While experts recognize that electoral manipulation distorts vote choice well before the election day, the impact of structural bias on election outcomes is difficult to assess (Hartlyn and McCoy 2006). As a result, citizens in electoral authoritarian regimes may react to protest according to their perceptions of popular support for winners and losers rather than procedural violations. Insofar as such regimes succeed in reducing viable political alternatives, such perceptions may not favor the opposition (Schedler 2006b; Silitski 2009; Wilson 2005).

The results also suggest that attitudes towards electoral protest are at least partly driven by mechanisms of motivated political reasoning. Given potentially low exposure of citizens to procedural violations and obstacles to knowledge of election monitor assessments, substantive judgments about winners' popularity and partisan biases may be instrumental in shaping public opinion about protest. Future research should further explore when and to what extent electoral manipulation achieves its purpose of mobilizing public support, and when it leads to support for protest against the very foundation of electoral authoritarian regimes.

Acknowledgments

The authors acknowledge the Centre for the Study of Public Policy, University of Strathclyde, and the Levada Center, Moscow, as generous sources of data for this study. Earlier versions of this chapter were presented at the Midwest Political Science Association Annual Convention, April 11–14, 2013, Chicago, IL, and at the pre-APSA Workshop on Electoral Integrity, August 28, 2013, Chicago, IL. We thank William Mishler, Eugene Huskey, and Gary Goertz for their comments on earlier drafts. We also thank the editors of this volume for their constructive criticism.

Notes

1 Full details of the survey are available in Rose (2012). The English-language questionnaire is also available at www.cspp.strath.ac.uk.
2 Substantive fairness may also be conceptualized as the belief that the candidate or party who is "right" for the country ought to win, regardless of electoral violations. However, given the difficulty of disentangling this conceptualization from winning and losing, we do not explore it separately.
3 A representative survey of 1,600 Russians, conducted by the Levada Center shortly *before* the election (November 25–28, 2011) contains two questions on pressure during the campaign that specify the parties meant to benefit from it (Levada-Tsentr 2011b). Nine percent of the respondents said that they were urged to vote for United Russia by direct superiors or management of their company or educational institution. Answering a separate question, 12 percent claimed that representatives of regional or city authorities urged them to vote for United Russia. The percentage of citizens naming other parties was negligible.
4 See www.RussiaVotes.org for the official election results.
5 Other frequently cited answers included "the government does not care about what people like me think" (52 percent) and "disappointment with the promises of modernization politics, with Medvedev" (42 percent). See Volkov (2012) for a detailed discussion of the protesters and the general public.
6 The exclusion of interaction terms from the models allows for a more meaningful interpretation of the direct effects of their constituent variables.
7 As robustness checks, we controlled for media exposure. These variables are not statistically significant and are not included in our models.

References

Anderson, Christopher, André Blais, Shaun Bowler, Todd Donovan, and Ola Listhaug. 2005. *Losers' Consent: Elections and Democratic Legitimacy*. New York: Oxford University Press.

Anderson, Christopher, and Silvia Mendes. 2006. "Learning to Lose: Election Outcomes, Democratic Experience and Political Protest Potential." *British Journal of Political Science* 36(1): 91–111.

Beaulieu, Emily, and Susan D. Hyde. 2009. "In the Shadow of Democracy Promotion: Strategic Manipulation, International Observers, and Election Boycotts." *Comparative Political Studies* 42(3): 392–415.

Birch, Sarah. 2010. "Perceptions of Electoral Fairness and Voter Turnout." *Comparative Political Studies* 43(12): 1601–1622.

———. 2011. *Electoral Malpractice*. Oxford; New York: Oxford University Press.

Chaisty, Paul, and Stephen Whitefield. 2013. "Forward to Democracy or Back to Authoritarianism? The Attitudinal Bases of Mass Support for the Russian Election Protests of 2011–2012." *Post-Soviet Affairs* 29(5): 387–403.

Doherty, David, and Jennifer Wolak. 2012. "When Do the Ends Justify the Means? Evaluating Procedural Fairness." *Political Behavior* 34(2): 301–323.

Easton, David. 1965. *A Systems Analysis of Political Life*. New York: Wiley.

Gaines, Brian J., James H. Kuklinski, Paul J. Quirk, Buddy Peyton, and Jay Verkuilen. 2007. "Same Facts, Different Interpretations: Partisan Motivation and Opinion on Iraq." *The Journal of Politics* 69(4): 957–974.

Gandhi, Jennifer, and Ellen Lust-Okar. 2009. "Elections under Authoritarianism." *Annual Review of Political Science* 12(1): 403–422.

Hartlyn, Jonathan, and Jennifer McCoy. 2006. "Observer Paradoxes: How to Assess Electoral Manipulation." In *Electoral Authoritarianism: The Dynamics of Unfree Competition*, Ed. Andreas Schedler. Boulder, CO: L. Rienner Publishers, pp. 41–54.

Howard, Marc Morjé, and Philip G. Roessler. 2006. "Liberalizing Electoral Outcomes in Competitive Authoritarian Regimes." *American Journal of Political Science* 50(2): 365–381.

Kaufmann, Chaim D. 1994. "Out of the Lab and into the Archives: A Method for Testing Psychological Explanations of Political Decision Making." *International Studies Quarterly* 38: 557–586.

Kelley, Judith. 2010. "Election Observers and Their Biases." *Journal of Democracy* 21(3): 158–172.

———. 2012. *Monitoring Democracy: When International Election Observation Works, and Why It Often Fails*. Princeton, NJ: Princeton University Press.

Kelley, Judith, and Kiril Kolev. 2010. "Election Quality and International Observation 1975–2004: Two New Datasets." *SSRN eLibrary*. Available at: www.papers.ssrn.com/sol3/papers.cfm?abstract_id=1694654 (accessed March 3, 2012).

Kuntz, Philipp, and Mark R. Thompson. 2009. "More than Just the Final Straw: Stolen Elections as Revolutionary Triggers." *Comparative Politics* 41(3): 253–272.

Ledeneva, Alena V. 2006. *How Russia Really Works: The Informal Practices That Shaped Post-Soviet Politics and Bussiness*. 1st ed. Cornell University Press.

Levada Center. 2012. *Levada Center, Moscow: Profiling Russian Protesters*. Centre for the Study of Public Policy. CSPP Publications. University of Strathclyde, Glasgow, UK.

Levada-Tsentr. 2011a. "Rossiyane ob aktsiyakh protesta i proshedshikh vyborakh [Russians on protest events and recent elections]." *Levada-Tsentr*. Available at: www.levada.ru/28–12–2011/rossiyane-ob-aktsiyakh-protesta-i-proshedshikh-vyborakh (accessed August 9, 2013).

———. 2011b. "Za kogo pobuzhdali golosovat' rossiyan i kakim partiyam okazyvali sodeystviye mestnyye vlasti i izberkomy [Whom Russians were pushed to vote for and which parties received help from the local authorities and election commissions]." *Levada-Tsentr*. Available at: www.levada.ru/12–12–2011/za-kogo-pobuzhdali-golosovat-rossiyan-i-kakim-partiyamokazyvali-sodeistvie-mestnye-vlast (accessed July 22, 2013).

Levitsky, Steven, and Lucan Way. 2010. *Competitive Authoritarianism: Hybrid Regimes After the Cold War*. 1st ed. New York: Cambridge University Press.

Lindberg, Staffan I, Ed. 2009. *Democratization by Elections: A New Mode of Transition*. Baltimore, MD: Johns Hopkins University Press.

Lodge, Milton, and Charles S. Taber. 2000. "Three Steps toward a Theory of Motivated Political Reasoning." In *Elements of Reason: Cognition, Choice, and the Bounds of Rationality*, Eds. Arthur Lupia, Mathew D. McCubbins, and Samuel L. Popkin. Cambridge; New York: Cambridge University Press, pp. 183–213.

Magaloni, Beatriz. 2006. *Voting for Autocracy Hegemonic Party Survival and Its Demise in Mexico.* Cambridge; New York: Cambridge University Press. Available at: www.site.ebrary. com/id/10257508 (accessed May 3, 2013).

McAllister, Ian, and Stephen White. 2011. "Public Perceptions of Electoral Fairness in Russia." *Europe-Asia Studies* 63(4): 663–683.

Norris, Pippa. 2011. *Democratic Deficit: Critical Citizens Revisited.* New York: Cambridge University Press. Available at: www.site.ebrary.com/id/10460542 (October 24, 2012).

———. 2014. *Why Electoral Integrity Matters.* New York: Cambridge University Press.

OSCE/ODIHR (Organization for Security and Cooperation in Europe/Office for Democratic Institutions and Human Rights). 2011. *International Election Observation Statement of Preliminary Findings and Conclusions, Russian Federation: State Duma Elections, 4 December 2011.* Moscow: OSCE/ODIHR. Available at: www.osce.org/odihr/ elections (accessed August 9, 2013).

———. 2012. *Election Observation Mission Final Report, Russian Federation: Elections to the State Duma, 4 December 2011.* Warsaw: OSCE/ODIHR. www.osce.org/odihr/elections (August 9, 2013).

Rose, Richard. 2012. *New Russia Barometer XIX. The 2011 Duma Election.* Centre for the Study of Public Policy. CSPP Publications. University of Strathclyde, Glasgow, UK.

Rose, Richard, and William Mishler. 2009. "How Do Electors Respond to an 'Unfair' Election? The Experience of Russians." *Post-Soviet Affairs* 25(2): 118–136.

Rose, Richard, William Mishler, and Neil Munro. 2011. *Popular Support for an Undemocratic Regime. The Changing Views of Russians.* Cambridge; New York: Cambridge University Press.

Schedler, Andreas. 2002. "The Menu of Manipulation." *Journal of Democracy* 13(2): 36–50.

———, Ed. 2006a. *Electoral Authoritarianism: The Dynamics of Unfree Competition.* Boulder, CO: L. Rienner Publishers.

———. 2006b. "The Logic of Electoral Authoritarianism." In *Electoral Authoritarianism: The Dynamics of Unfree Competition*, Ed. Andreas Schedler. Boulder, CO: L. Rienner Publishers, pp. 1–23.

———. 2009a. "Electoral Authoritarianism." In *The SAGE Handbook of Comparative Politics*, Eds. Todd Landman and Neil Robinson. Los Angeles: SAGE, pp. 381–393.

———. 2013. *Politics of Uncertainty: Sustaining and Subverting Electoral Authoritarianism.* Oxford Scholarship Online. Available at: www.myilibrary.com?id=505882 (accessed November 11, 2013).

Sedziaka, Alesia. 2014. "The Causes and Consequences of Perceptions of Election Unfairness." Dissertation. The University of Arizona.

Silitski, Vitali. 2005. "Preempting Democracy: The Case of Belarus." *Journal of Democracy* 16(4): 83–97.

———. 2009. "Tools of Autocracy." *Journal of Democracy* 20(2): 42–46.

Simpser, Alberto, and Daniela Donno. 2012. "Can International Election Monitoring Harm Governance?" *The Journal of Politics* 74(2): 501–13.

Taber, Charles S., and Milton Lodge. 2006. "Motivated Skepticism in the Evaluation of Political Beliefs." *American Journal of Political Science* 50(3): 755–769.

Taber, Charles S., Milton Lodge, and Jill Glathar. 2001. "The Motivated Construction of Political Judgments." In *Citizens and Politics: Perspectives from Political Psychology*, Ed. James H. Kuklinski. Cambridge; New York: Cambridge University Press, pp. 198–226.

Tucker, Joshua A. 2007. "Enough! Electoral Fraud, Collective Action Problems, and Post-Communist Colored Revolutions." *Perspectives on Politics* 5(3): 535–551.

Tyler, Tom R. 1990. *Why People Obey the Law.* New Haven, CT: Yale University Press.
——. 2006. "Psychological Perspectives on Legitimacy and Legitimation." 57: 375–400.
Tyler, Tom R., Robert J. Boeckmann, Heather J. Smith, and Yuen J. Huo. 1997. *Social Justice in a Diverse Society.* Boulder, CO and Oxford, UK: Westview Press.
Tyler, Tom R., and E. Allan Lind. 2001. "Procedural Justice." In *Handbook of Justice Research in Law,* New York: Kluwer Academic/Plenum Publishers, pp. 65–92.
Volkov, Denis. 2012. "The Protesters and the Public." *Journal of Democracy* 23(3): 55–62.
Wilson, Andrew. 2005. *Virtual Politics: Faking Democracy in the Post-Soviet World.* New Haven: Yale University Press.

4

DO CONTENTIOUS ELECTIONS OVERTHROW LEADERS?

Masaaki Higashijima

Since the end of the Cold War, growing pressure from the international community has made it difficult for authoritarian leaders to avoid holding periodical elections. Coinciding with the proliferation of electoral autocracies (Diamond 2002; Schedler 2006; Levitsky and Way 2010),[1] scholars have asserted that authoritarian leaders may use elections as a tool to consolidate their rule (e.g. Magaloni 2006; Gandhi and Lust-Okar 2009; Blaydes 2011). Yet elections do not always benefit autocrats. Contentious elections often induce political conflicts like popular protests that may undermine authoritarian stability. For example, the color revolutions in post-Soviet countries (Georgia, Ukraine, and Kyrgyzstan) during the mid-2000s all occurred immediately after elections (Tucker 2007; Kuntz and Thompson 2009; Bunce and Wolchik 2010). Likewise after the Côte d'Ivoire 2000 elections, massive protests erupted in favor of opposition parties, which subsequently ousted the incumbent president Robert Guéï. Protests allow the opposition to send a clear signal of public dissent to the international community. Thus, even if subdued by dictatorial governments, the eruption of serious protests in contentious elections may threaten authoritarian stability in the long run, with international actors tightening economic sanctions and adopting coercive diplomacy.

Elections may also oust the incumbent leader. For instance, unpopular incumbent Prime Minister Bandaranaike lost the Sri Lankan 1977 elections by the largest margin in the country's history to increasingly popular opposition parties. This also strengthened the Tamil opposition move toward separatism (Samaraweera 1977, 1201), which contributed to the Sri Lankan civil war. Similarly, in December 1991, President Chadli Bendjedid called the first multiparty election in Algeria's history. This election also unexpectedly brought a sweeping victory to the radical Islamic Salvation Front opposition party, triggering a military coup and a civil war (Bouandel 1993). Separately, in the 1989 Polish elections, the opposition Solidarity Movement obtained an overwhelming majority both in the lower and upper houses, paving the way for a democratic transition. "No one in the political elite anticipated the replacement of a Communist government by a Solidarity government . . . The purpose of . . . election procedures was to permit Solidarity to enter Parliament but to preserve the continuation of Communist rule" (Olson 1993, 417).

Cross-national data[2] on 72 authoritarian countries (1977–2004) shows that a small but significant minority of authoritarian leaders face either political turnover or popular protests after elections: 14 percent of authoritarian elections experienced leadership turnover, whereas popular protests occurred in 19 percent of them. Political leaders in dictatorships like Indonesia (1997), Cameroon (1993), Azerbaijan (2000, 2003), and Mexico (1988, 1994) experienced post-election popular protests, while Uruguay (1984), Bolivia (1980), Chile (1988), Haiti (1995, 2000), Sri Lanka (1977) and Liberia (1997) saw their elections lead to political turnover. These contentious elections in authoritarian states leave us with several puzzles: why do authoritarian elections often backfire? Specifically, why do autocrats face threats of popular protests and political turnover after elections and how can we understand the sources of these distinct political conflicts?

In untangling the puzzling relationships among protests, turnover and authoritarian elections, this chapter suggests an answer: authoritarian leaders are likely to face either protests or overthrow when they fail to manipulate elections successfully in light of their mobilization power. To do so, I first describe the dilemma that political leaders face at the ballot box. Recent literature suggests that autocrats try to take advantage of elections to show their invincibility, as well as obtaining information about key actors' strengths (Magaloni 2006; Geddes 2006; Cox 2009; Blaydes 2011; Simpser 2013). To achieve these ends, elections need to be believable. On the one hand, if election results are seen to be completely predetermined, then authoritarian leaders cannot enjoy their informational benefits. On the other hand, if elections meet international standards of electoral integrity, it is more likely that autocrats will fail to win overwhelmingly. In other words, autocrats face a serious trade-off (which this chapter calls "the electoral dilemma" in authoritarian regimes) between the credibility of election results and the certainty of winning big. Under the constraint of this dilemma, authoritarian leaders need to make a careful decision about how much they should manipulate elections.

To what extent authoritarian leaders open up the electoral field will be determined by their ability to mobilize voluntary popular support (Higashijima 2013). When the political leader is able to buy a large portion of popular support through extensive pre-electoral economic distributions, he or she will be able to win big without relying much on election violence, electoral cheating and manipulation of electoral law. Thus, if the autocrat is financially strong, the more credibly she is able to signal her strength by producing an overwhelming majority at the polls without making the electoral field extremely favorable to herself. By contrast, when the authoritarian leader lacks such financial resources, she is unable to organize large-scale mobilization of popular support. In this case, fair elections are more likely to produce surprising results, so that the authoritarian leader has a strong interest in biasing election results by engaging in electoral manipulation.

If authoritarian leaders are able to overcome this electoral dilemma by optimally setting the level of electoral fraud according to their mobilization power, then elections contribute to authoritarian stability via the signaling and information-gathering functions. The more complicated fact, however, is that autocrats may have difficulties in setting the appropriate level of electoral fraud in light of their power. When this is the case, autocrats fail to solve the electoral dilemma, and they are more likely to face political conflict after contentious elections—popular protests or political turnover. More specifically, I argue that there are two distinct pathways through which authoritarian elections induce political conflict. First, when autocrats underuse electoral fraud relative to their power, election results are more likely to credibly reveal the weakness. This brings about leadership change as a result of post-electoral coups within ruling coalitions or via opposition parties' electoral victory. Second, when autocrats overuse electoral fraud relative to their power of mobilization, elections deteriorate the quality of electoral information and hence cannot work as a credible tool to show regime strength. This encourages post-electoral protest movements.

To test these empirical implications, this chapter uses a cross-national statistical analysis to compare 72 authoritarian countries from 1977 to 2004. A two-stage estimation is employed. A model predicting the level of electoral fraud is run to measure the mobilization power of authoritarian leaders and other controls. Then, using predicted values, the gap between the predicted level of electoral fraud that the autocrat is expected to employ and the real level of electoral fraud in the election is measured. In doing so, it is possible to observe how well the autocrat dealt with the electoral dilemma. The second-stage model estimates the likelihoods of leadership turnover and popular protests using this fraud gap variable. The analysis shows that underuse of electoral fraud by autocrats is more likely to lead to leadership change. By contrast, when the autocrat overuses electoral fraud, elections are more likely to be followed by popular protests.

Literature Review

Previous research contends that formal institutions play crucial roles in consolidating authoritarian rule. Since dominant parties institutionalize their patronage system and enable the autocrat to make credible commitment to the internal elite, dominant party regimes are more likely to survive than military and personalist regimes (Geddes 1999; Magaloni 2008). Multiparty legislatures also increase autocrats' survival rate, because it provides a forum through which autocrats can make policy concession to a large portion of society (Gandhi and Przeworski 2007;

Gandhi 2008), credibly share patronage with the elite (Malesky and Schuler 2010; Blaydes 2011; Boix and Svolik 2011), and divide and rule opposition parties (Lust-Okar 2004). For similar reasons, multiparty legislatures also make political order stable by preventing civil war and labor protests (Gandhi and Vreeland 2004; Kim and Gandhi 2010).

Among these institutions, elections have been seen as one of the most important political tools that autocrats can use to stay in power (Gandhi and Lust-Okar 2009; Blaydes 2011). First, elections are viewed as an institution for authoritarian leaders to *acquire* information about the competence of ruling and opposition elites. Semi-competitive elections provide information on the popularity of local officials and candidates in their electoral districts (Ames 1970; Shi 1999; Magaloni 2006). The total number of votes that candidates gain in their districts works as an opportunity for autocrats to judge who among the elites is powerful as well as who is loyal to the dictator (Blaydes 2011). Election results also render information on the geographical distribution of popular support for opposition parties (Magaloni 2006; Cox 2009; Miller 2012). Second, elections work as an efficient method to communicate with the elites by *conveying information* on regime strengths. By holding elections and winning them with a large margin, autocrats can credibly demonstrate to potential opponents that the regime is so unshakable that any rebellious attempt against the current ruler will fail (Simpser 2013; Magaloni 2006; Geddes 2006).

The current literature of authoritarian politics focuses on how elections help autocrats stay in power. Other strands of research, however, have suggested that elections in hybrid regimes and authoritarian regimes often contribute to democratization. Lindberg (2006, 2009) argues that repetitive elections in multiparty contexts contribute to further democratization and improve the quality of democracy in Africa. Employing a comprehensive cross-national dataset covering 193 countries between 1919 and 2004, Teorrel and Hadenius (2009) find both current and cumulative effects of holding elections on democratization, which resonates with Lindberg's finding in the context of Africa. In a similar vein, Roessler and Howard (2009) and Brownlee (2009) assert that competitive authoritarian regimes are more likely to democratize than both hegemonic and closed authoritarian regimes. In this context, Huntington (1991: 174), notes that "the lessons of the third wave [of democratization] is that elections are not only the life of democracy; they are also the death of dictatorship."

In a similar vein, researchers also maintain that contentious elections provide an opportunity for opposition parties and anti-regime supporters to protest (see previous chapters; Tucker 2007; Kalandadze and Orenstein 2009). Although most protests are repressively subdued, some involve large-scale, anti-government demonstrations. In some cases, these demonstrations lead to the breakdown of authoritarian regimes, which has occurred in the Philippines (1986), and the post-Soviet countries (the color revolutions, Tucker 2007; Kuntz and Thompson 2009).

In reconciling these different findings about authoritarian elections, scholars have begun to illuminate the background conditions determining the effect of elections on democratization, leadership change and protest movements. Conducting both a cross-national quantitative analysis of 31 competitive authoritarian countries and a Kenyan case study, Howard and Roessler (2006) find that election results tend to become more open when opposition parties succeed in forming coalitions and launching pre-election anti-government protests. Donno (2013) also asserts that competitive authoritarian states are more likely to democratize either when domestic oppositions form coalitions or when pre-electoral political and economic conditionality is imposed from international actors. In a study on electoral violence in developing countries, Hafner-Burton et al. (2013) provide cross-national evidence that serious pre-electoral violence is positively associated with the probability of post-electoral protests. Similarly, Kuhn (2012) shows that electoral fraud increases the propensity of popular protests after elections (only in fairly close elections however). And Bunce and Wolchik (2010) emphasize the importance of the opposition's electoral campaign strategies. They argue that in hybrid regimes where opposition parties can carry out sophisticated, energetic electoral campaigns, elections are more likely to trigger both political protests and leadership turnover.

Echoing these previous studies, this chapter posits conditional hypotheses about authoritarian elections' effects on turnover and protests. This research, however, contributes to the literature in two different and original ways. First, taking into account the costs and benefits of authoritarian elections, this chapter theoretically and empirically endogenizes the authoritarian leader's electoral manipulation calculations. Assuming that autocrats will decide strategically on a level of electoral manipulation that maximizes the informational benefits, I argue that autocrats will likely face post-electoral conflicts such as leadership turnover and protests when they miscalculate on the extent of electoral fraud. Second, I explain both leadership turnover and popular protests in a unified theoretical framework. Briefly, I argue that popular protests and leadership turnover both result from different types of mistakes that autocrats make at the ballot box.

The Electoral Dilemma in Authoritarian Regimes

According to the recent literature on authoritarian politics, political leaders and their potential opponents are more likely to lack reliable informational sources to know each other's strength and intention (Wintrobe 1998; Egorov et al. 2009). Since political rights and civil liberties are not institutionalized in authoritarian regimes, it is difficult for people to know to what extent the political leader is able and popular through reliable media outlets. In such circumstances, potential opponents are less likely to accurately estimate the strength of the autocrat. Such misinformation may increase the likelihood that a conflict accidentally occurs between an autocrat and potential opponents. Strengthening the military is a frequently used strategy by which an autocrat can credibly demonstrate her power. Yet, history suggests that a heavy reliance on the sword risks an autocrat's tenure by giving the military too much power (Svolik 2012). Therefore, strengthening the security apparatus is not a perfect solution.

On the other hand, the political leader also faces difficulties in knowing what people think in authoritarian regimes, because people have an incentive to conceal their preferences fearing tortures and repression by the government (Kuran 1991; Wintrobe 1998). This is problematic because if she is not familiar with the distribution of popular support, it is more difficult to govern the country efficiently. Strengthening domestic surveillance may be an available option to the autocrat. Yet, such methods do not always garner high-quality information, because in such situations people will falsify their true preferences in the public fearing possible sanctions by the government, as previous studies acutely pointed out (Wintrobe 1998).

Recent studies of authoritarian politics see elections as an important institution to overcome this information shortage. According to the current literature, authoritarian elections enable political leaders to (1) demonstrate their strength via large-scale electoral mobilization to potential opponents (e.g. Magaloni 2006; Geddes 2006; Simpser 2013) and (2) acquire information on the distribution of popular support for both the opposition and incumbent politicians—both of whom may turn against the political leader (e.g. Magaloni 2006; Cox 2009; Blaydes 2011). When autocrats call elections, however, they face a serious trade-off between the certainty of gaining an overwhelming victory and the credibility of election results (Higashijima 2013). Authoritarian leaders can stay in power by winning through ballot-stuffing, repression, intimidation, and the manipulation of election rules and institutions. Resorting to serious electoral manipulation, authoritarian leaders can effectively deter opposition parties from winning. Yet, at the same time, excessive electoral manipulation makes elections meaningless or even harmful to their authoritarian rule for two reasons. First, extremely pro-regime election results make it difficult for autocrats to convey a credible signal of their regime's strength to potential opponents because the more manipulated elections are, the less election results reflect the autocrat's real popularity. In such predetermined plebiscite elections, citizens tend to be indifferent or cynical about the electoral process and its results as in the Soviet Union (e.g. White 1988: 13; Tedin 1994). Therefore, the signaling effect of elections will be significantly reduced in heavily manipulated elections. The second problem is that if elections are just a façade, autocrats can no longer obtain accurate information about the popularity of potential opponents among ruling elites and opposition leaders. Obviously, electoral manipulation biases election results in favor of the autocrat, so that election results will suffer nonnegligible noises on electoral information. Deteriorated electoral information makes it very difficult for autocrats to maintain their authoritarian rule efficiently. This is because autocrats need to govern the country without the reliable information that would have been obtained if the political system had been more transparent (Wintrobe 1998; Egorov et al. 2009).

Therefore, although the electoral benefits that autocrats might want to exploit differs across countries, they all have incentives to open the electoral field and introduce some degree of competition via electoral reforms. This is what happened, for example, in the Soviet Union during the perestroika era (White 1988), in village-level elections in Communist China (Shi 1999), and in Mexico during the PRI's heyday (Eisenstadt 2004, 32–44). That being said, it does not necessarily mean that relatively free and fair elections are always good for autocrats. Given the strategic interactions between the autocrat and potential opponents under the electoral dilemma, if autocrats make elections too transparent, then they are more exposed to risks and may fail to obtain electoral victory with a large margin, thereby revealing their weaknesses. This may give an opportunity for potential opponents to challenge the political leader. On the other hand, excessive electoral manipulation deteriorates the information problems that I mentioned above, which makes efficient communication between the autocrat and opponents more difficult. Under the constraint of the electoral dilemma, autocrats need to decide the level of electoral manipulation while considering likely responses from potential opponents, in such a way that autocrats can balance the credibility and the certainty of election results.

Backfiring at the Ballot Box

When an autocrat wins an election by an overwhelming margin, the total number of votes that she obtains consists of "clean" and "dirty" parts. The "clean" part is the total number of real votes from her supporters. These citizens vote for the dictator after positively evaluating her economic and policy performance. In particular, previous studies suggest that authoritarian leaders' popular support depends on the breadth their distribution of economic favors to the citizenry (e.g. Magaloni 2006; Greene 2007, 2009). For example, nontax revenues, like natural resource wealth or foreign aid, significantly enrich state coffers and thus enable increased public spending without having to levy taxes on their citizens (e.g. Ross 2001; Desai et al. 2009; Morrison 2009; Wright, Frantz and Geddes 2013). Even if state revenue is raised by taxation, autocrats can buttress public support by selectively collecting taxes from opposition loyalists and using it to benefit regime supporters, as is the case in many authoritarian regimes (Levitsky and Way 2010, 10–11, Chapters 5–7). Gaining voluntary support is therefore costly because governments must invest large amounts of financial resources to satisfy their citizens. Therefore, an election victory upheld by costly mobilization of citizens' support makes election results a credible way of knowing the autocrat's strength and popularity. In this chapter, I refer to citizens' voluntary support for the political leader through economic and policy performance as the leader's "mobilization power."

The second, "dirty" part is the total number of votes resulting from various kinds of electoral manipulation. In this chapter, electoral fraud is defined as a series of illegal measures that bias election results in favor of the political leader (Lehoucq 2003), including election violence, election cheating, and undemocratic restrictions on electoral law. Election violence is physical intimidation exercised largely by incumbent parties during elections (Straus and Taylor 2012; Hafner-Burton et al. 2012). Using electoral violence against opposition leaders and anti-regime supporters, autocrats can undermine oppositions' effective campaigns and decrease opposition supporters' turnout. Cheating also allows autocrats to affect the electoral result with nonviolent but still illegal measures, such as undermining of the oppositions' freedom to campaign, media bias, ballot-stuffing, vote-buying, and nonviolent intimidation (Kelley 2012). Restrictions on electoral laws refer to a series of regulations that prevent citizens and electoral candidates from effectively participating in elections, including limits on voting rights based on certain social characteristics such as gender and ethnicity, flaws in the complaints procedures, high thresholds for new parties to get registered and gain seats, constraints on the right to run for office such as language and educational requirements, and so on (Kelley 2012). All three fraud techniques, though different, contribute to an electoral victory with a margin that could not be achieved without these techniques.

Making full sense of her mobilization power, if the autocrat can tactfully match the level of electoral fraud with her strength, she can exploit as much informational benefit as possible while maintaining an overwhelming majority. When this is the case, elections contribute to authoritarian stability. In fact, authoritarian regimes with substantial financial resources and a weak opposition tend to have lower levels of electoral fraud (Higashijima 2013), suggesting that authoritarian leaders strategically manipulate elections based on their ability to cultivate voluntary popular support. When the autocrat fails to adequately deal with the electoral dilemma, the elections are more likely to backfire. More specifically, autocrats fail to deal with the electoral dilemma in two ways.

First, stability may not be achieved when authoritarian leaders are over-confident about their popularity, hold multiparty elections, and then lose a supermajority (or even an electoral victory). Researchers have provided substantial anecdotal evidence and noted that autocrats' overconfidence unexpectedly paves the way for democratization and leadership change—e.g. in Brazil (1974), Pinochet's Chile (1988), Marcos's Philippines (1986), Myanmar (1990) and Algeria (1992) (Huntington 1991, 174–178; Diamond 2008, 53–54). In Poland, for example, the authoritarian government held multiparty elections in 1989 without using serious electoral fraud. The incumbent government did not doubt its popularity, and the opposition Solidarity party also did not expect its eventual electoral triumph (Olson 1993, 425). Nevertheless, after the vote count, Solidarity scored a sweeping electoral victory, which resulted in Poland's transition to democracy. Algeria's 1991 election exhibited similar characteristics to Poland's;

however, elections there did not result in democratization. Algeria's president did decide to hold multiparty elections with a free and fair electoral process. In the first round of elections, the opposition Islamic Salvation Front emerged victorious with 87.7 percent of the total seats decided (Bouandel 1993, 13). Fearing the rise of the radical Islamists, the army annulled the election results and removed the president from power in a military coup. This military intervention then led to the civil war between the government and Islamist rebel groups. These Polish and Algerian cases suggest that when an autocrat does not increase electoral fraud up to the level that her de facto weakness demands, election results can credibly reveal her regime's true weakness to potential opponents and lead to a leadership change. Revealed weakness in an election is most likely to result in leadership turnover via electoral victory of opposition parties and hence democratization, as in the cases of Poland and Chile. Or like Côte d'Ivoire and Algeria, such a dictator's weakness may encourage ruling coalitions to then change their leader via a military coup or civil war.

Hypothesis 1: When an autocrat underuses electoral fraud relative to her power, political turnover is more likely to occur after an election.

Second, autocrats may likely face another type of political conflict—popular protests—after they use excessive electoral fraud. When the autocrat excessively rigs elections, potential opponents are more likely to think that election results will be largely driven by political manipulation, rather than voluntary popular support. Therefore, the signals conveyed to potential opponents by the elections are more mixed when it comes to knowing an autocrat's true popularity and strength. In particular, previous studies suggest that "sticks" (blatant electoral fraud) without sufficient accompanying "carrots" (economic favors) encourage potential dissidents to speculate that the regime is now too weak to hold up its anti-regime collective action. As Bunce and Wolchik (2010, 38) put it, "while signals in the admittedly murky political environment of mixed regimes are always hard to read, repression can also be read as an indication that political leaders have become increasingly nervous about their hold on power." In fact, various studies show that both harsh repression and excessive election cheating without much patronage distribution fuel the escalation of protests in authoritarian regimes. Bratton and van de Walle (1997) and Wood (2000) argue that African autocracies (when failing to provide goods to citizens) have faced anti-regime popular mobilization after adopting harsh state repression. Investigating the experiences of South Asian countries during the Cold War era, Goodwin (2001) also asserts that political revolution is more likely to occur in the countries where the government has relied on indiscriminate violence against anti-government forces. Color Revolutions in post-Soviet countries were all preceded by rigged elections (Tucker 2007). In the "Tulip Revolution" in Kyrgyzstan, violence perpetrated by state police and electoral fraud exercized by incumbents fueled opposition forces' grievances, which activated anti-regime mobilization against the Akayev regime (Jones 2007). Therefore, I hypothesize that after being exposed to excessive electoral fraud, anti-government popular protests are more likely to be observed.

> Hypothesis 2: When an autocrat overuses electoral fraud relative to her power, post-election popular protests are more likely to occur.

Research Design

Data and Modeling Strategies

Cross-national statistical analysis is used to test the two hypotheses empirically. The *unit of analysis* is country–election year in an authoritarian country between 1977–2004. I limit my sample to authoritarian countries using a binary classification of political regime by Cheibub et al. (2010), a frequently used dataset to identify authoritarian regimes in the literature.

To measure the gap between the degree of electoral fraud and the autocrat's mobilization power, I adopt a two-stage model. In the first-stage, I use Ordinary Least Squares (OLS) to regress a series of predictors on electoral fraud, which is continuously measured with values ranging between 0 (no fraud) and 15 (most fraudulent) from Kelley's (2012) Quality of Elections (QOE) dataset. The electoral fraud variable includes five subcomponents that bias election results in favor of the incumbent: (1) pre-electoral election violence (0–3); (2) election-day electoral violence (0–3); (3) pre-electoral election cheating (0–3); (4) election-day election cheating (0–3); and (5) restrictions on electoral participation and electoral law (0–3). 0 indicates no fraud, whereas 3 represents for serious fraud. To measure the dictator's power of mobilization, the first model is based largely on Higashijima (2013), which is described below in detail. In addition to a series of variables measuring mobilization power, I also include other variables that are seen as relevant in the study of electoral manipulation. I then calculate the gap between predicted values in this first-stage model and real values of electoral fraud. In the second stage, I regress this gap variable (predicted values—real values) and other relevant controls on the two dependent variables – leadership turnover and popular protests. Capturing this gap enables us to see how well dictators match the level of electoral fraud with powers of mobilization. In other words, adopting this two-stage estimation, we can empirically assess how successfully the electoral dilemma is resolved. If the gap variable takes more positive values, then it suggests that the dictator manipulates elections more blatantly than he needs. My theoretical expectation is that excessively manipulated elections should be associated with a higher probability of popular protests, while having a lower likelihood of political turnover. When the variable takes more negative values elections are excessively transparent in light of the autocrat's strength. Therefore, I expect that political turnover is more likely to follow such elections.

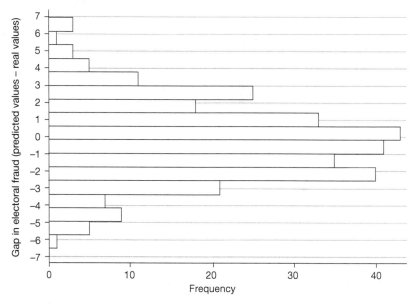

FIGURE 4.1 The gap in electoral fraud under dictatorship

The First Model Specification: A Mobilization Model

The dependent variable of the first model is electoral fraud. To measure the main explanatory factor, the autocrat's power to mobilize popular support, I focus on two factors (Higashijima 2013). The first is to what extent autocrats possess the ability to efficiently distribute economic favors to a wide range of citizens. To do so, they need to have (1) substantial financial resources and (2) strong political organizations to discipline ruling elites (and hence streamline economic distribution). As discussed before, the importance of financial resources to buy popular support has been established by previous studies. Without abundant public resources, autocrats cannot buy off popular support through public goods provision to a sufficient extent (see, e.g. Ross 2001; Morrison 2009). To make economic distribution to the citizenry efficient, disciplinary organizations are also necessary because such organizations can deter ruling elites from engaging in exploiting state resources. To measure the financial resources that autocrats control, I use Ross's (2011) oil-gas value per capita in constant 2000 dollars. This variable is calculated by multiplying a country's total oil and gas production by the current oil and gas price and then dividing this amount by the total population. The oil-gas value per capita variable is interacted with (1) a dominant-party regime dummy (Geddes et al. (2014)) and (2) the size and cohesiveness of politically dominant ethnic groups[3] (from Cederman et al.'s (2009) "Ethnic Power Relations

Dataset"*). Making long lasting power-sharing possible between the autocrat and ruling elites (Magaloni 2008; Svolik 2012) and thus preventing ruling elites' myopic appropriation of state resources, dominant-party regimes contribute to reducing the need for election fraud by increasing the efficiency of economic distribution. Coherent, large politically dominant ethnic groups[4] make it easier for the autocrat to monitor ruling elites' behavior (Fearon and Laitin 1995) while facilitating public goods provision to a large portion of citizens (e.g. Alesina et al. 1999; Habyarimana et al. 2007). Thus, such dominant ethnic groups help dictators to streamline economic distribution. I expect the negative impact of natural resource wealth on electoral fraud will be magnified when authoritarian regimes have dominant parties and/or less fractionalized, large dominant ethnic groups.

A second way to measure an autocrat's mobilization power is the extent to which clear opposition exists. In authoritarian regimes, challenging an autocrat is an extremely costly political behavior because in most cases anti-regime protests are brutally repressed (Davenport 2007). On the flip side, once initiated, this costly action would result in credibly showing the authoritarian leader that a considerable number of people are unsatisfied with the regime and strong opposition does exist at both national and local levels (e.g. Zimbabwe's Movement for Democratic Change during the 2000s) (Kuran 1991; Weiss 2012). To measure anti-government collective action, I follow the previous literature like Bueno de Mesquita and Smith (2010) and Howard and Roessler (2006: 372) and use indicators counting the number of demonstrations, riots, and strikes from Arthur Banks' (2014) *Cross-National-Time-Series Data Archive*. Summating the total numbers of these three collective actions, it turned out that the mean was just 1. Therefore, if the country experienced at least one riot, demonstration, or strike at (t–1) year, then the variable is coded as 1, otherwise 0.

Besides these variables measuring the autocrat's power of mobilization, I also add control variable: political competitiveness (measured by Polity IV), election administrative capacity (using Kelley's (2012) QOE), logged GDP per capita (using World Development Indicators (WDI) and Maddison 2011), GDP growth (WDI), trade openness (measured by sum of exports and imports relative to GDP, using Penn World Tables), rural population (WDI), type of election (presidential vs. parliamentary elections, Kelley 2012), the presence of domestic and international election monitoring (Kelley 2012), and decade dummies.

In Table 4.1, I show statistical results of the first stage model. As I expected, the oil-gas value is negatively associated with electoral fraud when autocrats have dominant parties or more coherent, larger dominant ethnic groups. The collective action variable is positively correlated with the level of electoral fraud. These results suggest that stronger dictators with mobilization power tend to refrain from using a series of manipulation techniques. R-squared is 0.446, suggesting that the first model explains more than 40 percent of total variation in electoral fraud. Based on this result, I compute predicted values of electoral fraud.

TABLE 4.1 Predicting electoral fraud

	Fraud
Oil-gas value per capita (US$ 100s)	0.025
	(0.02)
Collective action (t−1)	0.929★★
	(0.417)
Party-based regime	−0.259
	(0.419)
Party-based regime ★ oil-gas	−0.04★★★
	(0.013)
Ethnic organizational power	0.652
	(0.854)
Ethnic power ★ oil-gas	−0.176★
	(0.101)
Polity IV	−0.303★★★
	(0.039)
Election administrative capacity	0.25
	(0.208)
Logged GDP per capita (t−1) year	−0.16
	(0.430)
Economic growth (t−1) year	−0.029
	(0.027)
Trade (t−1) year	−0.006
	(0.005)
Rural population (t−1) year	0.009
	(0.019)
Parliamentary elections	−0.263
	(0.266)
Domestic election monitoring	0.183
	(0.636)
International election monitoring	0.874
	(0.529)
1980s	0.571
	(0.650)
1990s	2.513★★★
	(0.733)
2000s	3.324★★★
	(0.792)
Constant	3.618
	(4.217)
Observations	255
F-value	15.65★★★
R-squared	0.446

Note: Decade dummies are included. Clustered robust standard errors in parentheses. ★★★ $p < 0.001$, ★★ $p < 0.01$, ★ $p < 0.05$.

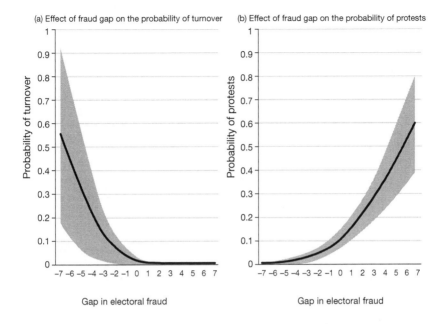

FIGURE 4.2 Predicted probabilities of turnover and protests

Note: Shaded areas are 90 percent confidence interval. The graph (a) and (b) are based on Models 1 and 3, respectively.

The Second Model Specification: Models of Leadership Turnover and Popular Protests

To measure the dependent variable for the Hypothesis 1, *leadership turnover*, I use a variable capturing broadly defined post-electoral leadership turnover from Hyde and Marinov (2012). This variable is coded as 1 if the incumbent leader is replaced after the election, 0 otherwise (NELDA39). It includes all types of post-election leadership change including turnover brought by hereditary successions and nomination of the next leader by the current ruler before an election. As these types of leadership change do not relate to an incumbent's electoral performance, I remove them from the sample by referring to another variable (NELDA23), which measures whether a successor assumes power after elections. I also found nine additional cases where leadership change occurred because of pre-electoral successions within ruling parties—rather than turnover as consequences of election results. I exclude these cases and re-run the model to check the robustness of empirical results.[5] Further, in both models, I do not include cases that experienced political turnover as a result of large-scale popular protests because these political turnover cases are not driven by election results but by protests (e.g. the 2003 Georgian election and the 2000 election in Côte d'Ivoire).

My second dependent variable, *popular protests*, is also measured by using the NELDA dataset. NELDA includes a variable indicating whether there were riots and protests after the election (NELDA29). If either riots or protests occur after the election, then the variable is coded as 1. As a robustness check, another variable including only riots and protests over electoral fraud is also used (NELDA30).

I calculate an election fraud gap using predicted values from a model calculating the difference between predicted and real values of fraud (predicted values—real values). Figure 4.1 shows the distribution of the gap. Using the gap variable as the main independent variable, I estimate probit models to empirically test my theoretical expectations. My empirical tests consist of two parts—a protest model and a turnover model. Regarding controls, I include the same set of control variables for the protest and turnover models. I add political competition (t–1 year lagged, measured by Polity IV), GDP per capita (t–1 year lagged, WDI and Maddison 2011), economic growth (t–1 year lagged, WDI), trade openness (measured by Penn World Tables), rural population (WDI), types of elections (from Kelley 2012, presidential vs. parliamentary elections), presence of domestic and international election monitoring (Kelley 2012), election administrative capacity (Kelley 2012), election boycotts (Hyde and Marinov 2012), military spending (t–1 year lagged, Correlates of War Project), leader's age (Goemans et al. 2009), leader's tenure length (Goemans et al. 2009), logged population (t–1 year lagged, WDI) and violent conflict incidence (t–1 year lagged, from PRIO's Armed Conflict Dataset, Harbom and Wallensteen 2009). I also control for regional and time specific heterogeneities by employing regional and decade dummies. To deal with possible temporal dependence, duration of peace years and three cubic splines are also included in all models (Beck et al. 1998).

Results

Table 4.2 reports results of the probit analysis. In Model 1 where the dependent variable is political turnover, the fraud gap is statistically significantly negative at the .01 level. This suggests that if autocrats fail to increase the level of electoral fraud despite their need to do so, they are more likely to experience political turnover after elections. Model 2 limits the sample by excluding the nine cases where political turnover was driven by pre-electoral leadership succession, and the fraud gap variable has the same negative and statistically significant effect on the likelihood of post-electoral turnover. Based on Model 1, Figure 4.2(a) graphically illustrates how a predicted probability of turnover changes as the fraud gap variable increases. When the gap variable takes the value of more than 0, the predicted probability is not distinguishable from 0. Yet, when the variable becomes more negative (between −1 and −7), the probability of turnover

TABLE 4.2 Post-electoral turnover and protests in dictatorship

Dependent variable	Model 1 Turnover	Model 2 Turnover	Model 3 Protests	Model 4 Protests (over fraud)
Fraud gap	−0.328★★★	−1.277★★★	0.219★★★	0.224★★★
	(0.08)	(0.43)	(0.05)	(0.05)
Duration of peace	−0.401★★	−2.904★★	−0.349★★★	−0.211★
	(0.20)	(1.43)	(0.13)	(0.13)
Polity IV (t−1)	0.217★★★	1.712★★	−0.0678★★	−0.132★★★
	(0.044)	(0.750)	(0.034)	(0.041)
Logged GDP per capita (t−1)	−0.286	−0.103	0.576★★	0.675★★
	(0.373)	(0.561)	(0.262)	(0.266)
Economic growth (t−1)	0.0604★★★	0.332★★	0.0092	0.0207
	(0.023)	(0.151)	(0.013)	(0.013)
Trade (t−1)	−0.0301★★★	−0.441★★	0.0021	0.00293
	(0.009)	(0.193)	(0.005)	(0.006)
Rural population (t−1)	0.0344★★	0.428★★	0.0209★★	0.0103
	(0.013)	(0.190)	(0.010)	(0.010)
Parliamentary elections	−0.605★	−0.81	0.00855	−0.0249
	(0.353)	(0.587)	(0.216)	(0.234)
Domestic election monitoring	1.654★★★	14.14★★	−0.18	−0.0096
	(0.443)	(5.664)	(0.312)	(0.335)
International election monitoring	1.022★★	4.617★★★	0.827★★★	0.903★★★
	(0.410)	(1.438)	(0.266)	(0.315)
Election administrative capacity	−0.750★★★	−8.885★★	0.14	0.135
	(0.226)	(3.655)	(0.110)	(0.113)
Election boycott	−0.609	−5.872★★	0.663★★	0.560★★
	(0.394)	(2.341)	(0.264)	(0.261)
Military spending (t−1)	0.002	−0.0588	0.0378	0.0126
	(0.052)	(0.166)	(0.029)	(0.037)
Leader age	0.0237	−0.112★	0.00355	−0.00956
	(0.019)	(0.058)	(0.015)	(0.016)
Leader tenure	−0.002	−0.0734	−0.0246	−0.0406★★
	(0.019)	(0.060)	(0.017)	(0.017)
Logged population (t−1)	−0.539★★★	−8.233★★	0.243★	0.227
	(0.207)	(3.373)	(0.136)	(0.139)
Violent conflict incident (t−1)	−0.077	−1.703	−0.398	−0.257
	(0.475)	(1.449)	(0.288)	(0.307)
Constant	6.886	121.9★★	−12.43★★★	−15.88★★★
	(4.653)	(49.24)	(4.027)	(4.351)
Observations	214	205	268	271
Log Pseudolikelihood	−40.65	−17.05	−85.19	−72.47
Pseudo R squared	0.6261	0.8179	0.2976	0.3291
Wald Chi^2	103.62★★★	51.16★★★	76.72★★★	993.93★★★

Note: Decade dummies, regional dummies and three cubic splines are all included in the probit models. Robust standard errors are in parentheses. ★★★$p < 0.001$, ★★ $p < 0.01$, ★$p < 0.05$.

exponentially increases in a statistically significant way. When the variable is −1, the probability of turnover is no more than 3 percent, whereas the probability increases to 55 percent when the gap variable is −7. These results support Hypothesis 1. Closely looking at the data, countries such as Sri Lanka (1977), Bolivia (1980), Honduras (1981), Guatemala (1982), Uruguay (1984), Zambia (1991), Azerbaijan (1992), Haiti (1995, 2000), Liberia (1997), and Niger (1999) underused electoral fraud in their elections, resulting in political turnover.

Then, Models 3 and 4 estimate the fraud gap's impact on the likelihood of popular protests. In Model 3, the fraud gap has a positive coefficient, which is statistically significant at the .01 level, meaning that when elections are more exposed to excessive electoral manipulation relative to dictators' mobilization power, they are more likely to face protesters in the aftermath of elections. In Model 4 where I focus only on protests clearly over the government's electoral fraud, a similar, positive and significant effect of fraud gap is confirmed. Using estimation results of Model 3, Figure 4.2(b) shows how the probability of protests will change with the values of fraud gap. When the gap variable is negative between −7 and −4, its impact is not distinguishable from 0. Yet, as the variable gets more positive and bigger, the impact of the fraud gap also tends to increase. For instance, when the gap variable is 0, the probability of protests is no more than 10 percent, whereas when the gap variable is 7, the probability rises up to 60 percent. Some examples in which overused electoral manipulation induced post-electoral protests include Haiti (1984), Senegal (1988), Kenya (1992, 1997), Mauritania (1992), Cameroon (1992), Togo (1994), Indonesia (1997), Algeria (1999), and Côte d'Ivoire (2000).

Robustness Checks

To make sure of the extent to which the results are robust, I conduct the following four robustness checks.[6] First, I include variables like leader's age, leader's tenure and a lagged dependent variable (the level of electoral fraud in the previous election) in the first model to take into account possible serial correlations as well as the fact that autocrats' calculation over electoral fraud may be influenced by their tenures and ages. Second, I use two alternative datasets, Boix, Miller and Rosato (2012) and Polity IV, to identify authoritarian countries and then re-run all the models using new samples of authoritarian countries.[7] Third, one may think that the results in the second-stage model might be unstable depending on the model specifications of the first model. To minimize this concern, I alternatively use the electoral fraud variable per se as a main independent variable and I regress it on the dependent variables with the same sets of controls.[8] Finally, I try every possible combination of control variables in the second models to see if results may change according to model specifications in the second stage estimation. As a result of these robustness checks, I find that most results are virtually the same as the ones that I reported above, except for the following two. First, probit regression in one turnover model does not compute standard errors because variations are perfectly explained by the independent variables included.[9] Second, in a sample filtered by Polity IV, the fraud gap variable in a turnover model does not reach a 10 percent statistical significance level. Yet, other than these two exceptions, all the additional analyses confirm the robustness of the results.

Conclusions

This chapter explores the conditions under which elections contribute to political conflict in authoritarianism—specifically leadership turnover and popular protests. Pointing to the fact that authoritarian leaders face a trade-off between the certainty of winning an overwhelming majority and the credibility of election results, I argue that when autocrats fail to match their electoral fraud to their de facto power balance with political elites, elections are more likely to be followed by political conflict. A cross-national statistical analysis of 72 authoritarian countries from 1977 to 2004 renders empirical support for my theoretical predictions. The theory and empirical analysis of this chapter suggest that elections are a double-edged sword for authoritarian leaders: elections may provide a good chance for autocrats to improve information shortage inherent in authoritarian regimes, yet the failure of choosing an appropriate level of fraud backfires on authoritarian leaders themselves. Recognizing this election paradox and preventing autocrats from flexibly manipulating elections via international pressures and foreign policies, the international community and domestic opposition may be able to transform authoritarian elections into the window of opportunity to achieve democratization.

Acknowledgments

I would like to thank Eric Chang, Takayuki Ito, Tolgahan Kinay, Peter Penar, and the editors for their helpful comments and suggestions on earlier versions of this chapter. This research is financially supported by the National Science Foundation (SES #1323671), the Suntory Foundation, and the Konosuke Matsushita Memorial Foundation.

Notes

1   Following Svolik (2012), I define an authoritarian regime as "an independent country that fails to satisfy at least one of the following two criteria for democracy: (1) free and competitive legislative elections and (2) an executive that is elected either directly in free and competitive presidential elections or indirectly by a legislature in parliamentary systems" (Svolik 2012, 22). I use the terms autocracy and authoritarian regime interchangeably and refer to the heads of these countries' governments as autocrats and authoritarian leaders.

2   Data range in time from 1977 to 2004 and are compiled using Hyde and Marinov's (2012) *National Elections in Democracy and Autocracy* (NELDA) and Kelley's (2012) *Quality of Elections* (QOE).

3   This variable is measured by multiplying the fractionalization index of politically dominant ethnic groups by the proportion of the dominant groups relative to total population.

4   Here politically dominant ethnic groups refer to ethnic groups that have access to political posts at the executive level in the country.

5   The nine cases are the Tanzania 1995 elections (both parliamentary and presidential), the Algerian 1999 elections (presidential), the Mozambique 2004 elections (both parliamentary and presidential), the Namibia 2004 elections (both parliamentary and presidential), and the Zambia 2001 elections (both parliamentary and presidential).

6   The results are available from the author upon request.

7   Boix, Miller and Rosato (2012) give an alternative, binary measure of political regimes (democracy vs. nondemocracies) covering 1800–2007. Regarding Polity IV (which ranges from −10 to 10), I use a conventional threshold of Polity2 score = 6 to empirically identify nondemocracies. If a country's Polity2 score is less than 6, then the country is seen as an authoritarian country. As Polity2 score covers countries that are exposed to civil war, we are able to avoid possible bias in estimation that we might have by using Cheibub et al. (2010)'s binary measure, which excludes countries under civil war.

8   From the theoretical point of view, using the electoral fraud variable per se does not necessarily represent the idea of the "fraud gap." However, a correlation between the fraud gap and the electoral fraud variable is very high, 0.80.

9   This happened when I included a lagged dependent variable, which ended up dropping many observations (about 40 percent of observations) from the first model and thus could not have enough observations in the second model.

References

Alesina, Alberto, Reza Baqir, and William Easterly. 1999. "Public Goods and Ethnic Division." *Quarterly Journal of Economics* 114: 1243–1284.

Ames, Barry. 1970. "Bases of Support for Mexico's Dominant Party." *American Political Science Review* 64 (1): 153–167.

Banks, Arthur S. and Kenneth Wilson. 2014. "Cross-National Time-Series Data Archive." Databanks International. Jerusalem, Israel. Available at: www.databanksinternational.com (accessed December 2, 2014).

Beck, Nathaniel, Jonathan Katz, and Richard Tucker. 1998. "Taking Time Seriously." *American Journal of Political Science* 42–4: 1260–1288.

Blaydes, Lisa. 2011. *Elections and Distributive Politics in Mubarak's Egypt.* Cambridge University Press.

Bouandel, Youcef. 1993. "Algerian National Popular Assembly Election of December 1991." *Representation* 32: 117, 10–14.

Boix, Carles and Milan Svolik. 2013. "The Foundations of Limited Authoritarian Government: Institutions, Commitment, and Power-Sharing in Dictatorships." Forthcoming in *The Journal of Politics*.

Boix, Carles, Michael Miller, and Sebastian Rosato. 2012. "A Complete Data Set of Political Regimes, 1800–2007." *Comparative Political Studies* 46–12: 1523–1554.

Bratton, Michael and Nicholas van de Walle. 1997. *Democratic Experiments in Africa: Regime Transitions in Comparative Perspective.* New York: Cambridge University Press.

Brownlee, Jason. 2009. "Portents of Pluralism: How Hybrid Regimes Affect Democratic Transitions." *American Journal of Political Science* 53(3): 515–532.

Bunce, Valerie and Sharon Wolchik. 2010. *Defeating Authoritarian Leaders in Post-Communist Countries*. Cambridge University Press.

Cederman, Lars-Erik, Brian Min, and Andreas Wimmer. 2009. "Ethnic Power Relations Dataset." Available at: www.epr.ucla.edu/ (accessed May 24, 2013).

Cheibub, Antonio, Jeniffer Gandhi and James Vreeland. 2010. "Democracy and Dictatorship Revisited." *Public Choice* 143–2: 67–101.

Cox, Gary. 2009. "Authoritarian Elections and Leadership Succession, 1975–2004." Unpublished manuscript.

Davenport, Christian. 2007. *State Repression and the Domestic Democratic Peace*. Cambridge: Cambridge University Press.

Desai, Raj, Anders Olofsgard, and Tarik Yousef. 2009. "The Logic of Authoritarian Bargains." *Economics and Politics* 21: 93–125.

Diamond, Larry. 2002. "Elections without Democracy: Thinking about Hybrid Regimes." *Journal of Democracy* 13–2: 21–35.

Diamond, Larry. 2008. *The Spirit of Democracy: The Struggle to Build Free Societies throughout the World*. New York: Holt.

Donno, Daniela. 2013. "Elections and Democratization in Authoritarian Regimes." *American Journal of Political Science* 57(3): 703–716.

Egorov, Georgy, Sergei Guriev, and Konstantin Sonin. 2009. "Why Resource-poor Dictators Allow Freer Media: A Theory and Evidence from Panel Data." *American Political Science Review* 103(4): 645–668.

Eisenstadt, Todd. 2004. *Courting Democracy in Mexico: Party Strategies and Electoral Institutions*. New York: Cambridge University Press.

Fearon, James and David Laitin. 1995. "Explaining Interethnic Cooperation." *American Political Science Review* 90(4): 715–735.

Gandhi, Jennifer and Adam Przeworski. 2007. "Authoritarian Institutions and the Survival of Autocrats." *Comparative Political Studies* 40(11): 1279–1301.

Gandhi, Jennifer. 2008. *Political Institutions under Dictatorship*. New York: Cambridge University Press.

Gandhi, Jennifer and Lust-Okar, Ellen. 2009. "Elections under Authoritarianism." *Annual Review of Political Science* 12: 403–422.

Gandhi, Jennifer and James Vreeland. 2004. "Political Institutions and Civil War: Unpacking Anocracy." Unpublished manuscript.

Geddes, Barbara. 1999. "What Do We Know about Democratization after Twenty Years?" *Annual Review of Political Science* 2: 115–144.

Geddes, Barbara. 2006. "Why Parties and Elections in Authoritarian Regimes." Working paper.

Geddes, Barbara, Joseph Wright, and Erica Frantz. 2014. "New Data on Autocratic Regimes." Forthcoming in *Perspective on Politics*.

Goemans, Hein, Kristian Skrede Gleditsch, and Giacomo Chiozza. 2009. "Introducing Archigos: A Data Set of Political Leaders." *Journal of Peace Research* 46(2): 269–283.

Goodwin, Jeff. 2001. *No Other Way Out: States and Revolutionary Movements, 1945–1991*. Cambridge: Cambridge University Press.

Greene, Kenneth. 2007. *Why Dominant Parties Lose: Mexico's Democratization in Comparative Perspective*. New York: Cambridge University Press.

Greene, Kenneth. 2009. "The Political Economy of Authoritarian Single-Party Dominance." *Comparative Political Studies* 43(7): 807–834.

Habyarimana, James, Macartan Humphreys, Daniel Posner and Jeremy Weinstein. 2007. "Why Does Ethnic Diversity Undermine Public Goods Provision?" *American Political Science Review* 101(4): 709–725.

Hafner-Burton, Emilie, Susan Hyde, and Ryan Jablonski. 2012. "When Do Governments Resort to Election Violence?" *British Journal of Political Science* 44(1): 149–179.

Harbom, Lotta and Peter Wallensteen. 2009. "Armed Conflict, 1946–2008." *Journal of Peace Research* 46(4): 577–587.

Howard, Marc and Phillip Roessler. 2006. "Liberalizing Electoral Outcomes in Competitive Authoritarian Regimes." *American Journal of Political Science* 50(2): 365–381.

Higashijima, Masaaki. 2013. "Beat Me If You Can: The Fairness of Elections in Dictatorship." Paper Prepared for the 2013 Pre-APSA Workshop on Electoral Integrity, Chicago.

Huntington, Samuel. 1991. *The Third Wave: Democratization in the Late Twentieth Century.* Norman, OK: University of Oklahoma Press.

Hyde, Susan and Nicholai Marinov. 2012. "Which Elections Can be Lost?" *Political Analysis* 20(2): 191–210.

Jones, Kevin. 2007. *The Dynamics of Political Protests: A Case Study of Kyrgyz Republic.* PhD dissertation, University of Maryland.

Kalandadze, Katya and Mitchell A. Orenstein. 2009. "Electoral Protests and Democratization Beyond the Color Revolutions." *Comparative Political Studies* 42(11): 1403–1425.

Kelley, Judith. 2012. *Monitoring Democracy: When International Election Observation Works, and Why It Often Fails.* Princeton, NJ: Princeton University Press.

Kim, Wonik and Jennifer Gandhi. 2010. "Coopting Workers under Dictatorship." *Journal of Politics* 72(3): 646–658.

Kuhn, Patrick. 2012. "Elections, Information, Fraud and Post-Electoral Protest." Working paper.

Kuntz, Philipp and Mark Thompson. 2009. "More Than Just the Final Straw: Stolen Elections as Revolutionary Triggers." *Comparative Politics* 41(3): 253–273.

Kuran, Timur. 1991. "Now Out of Never: The Element of Surprise in the East European Revolution of 1989." *World Politics* 44(1): 7–48.

Lehoucq, Fabrice. 2003. "Electoral Fraud: Causes, Types, and Consequences." *Annual Review of Political Science* 6: 233–256.

Levitsky, Steven, and Lucan Way. 2010. *Competitive Authoritarianism: Hybrid Regimes after the Cold War.* New York: Cambridge University Press.

Lindberg, Staffan I. 2009. *Democratization by Elections: A New Mode of Transition.* Baltimore, MD: Johns Hopkins University Press.

Lust-Okar, Ellen. 2004. *Structuring Conflict in the Arab World: Incumbents, Opponents, and Institutions.* New York: Cambridge University Press.

Maddison, Angus. 2011. "The Maddison Project Database." Available at: www.ggdc.net/maddison/maddison-project/home.htm (accessed May 24, 2013).

Magaloni, Beatriz. 2006. *Voting for Autocracy: Hegemonic Party Survival and Its Demise in Mexico.* New York: Cambridge University Press.

Magaloni, Beatritz. 2008. "Credible Power-sharing and the Longevity of Authoritarian Rule." *Comparative Political Studies* 41: 715–741.

Malesky, Edmund and Paul Schuler. 2010. "Nodding or Needling: Analyzing Delegate Responsiveness in an Authoritarian Parliament." *American Political Science Review* 104(3): 482–502.

Mesquita, Bueno de and Alastair Smith. 2010. "Leader Survival, Revolutions and the Nature of Government Finance." *American Journal of Political Science* 54(4): 936–950.

Miller, Michael. 2012. "Elections, Information, and Policy Responsiveness in Autocratic Regimes." Working paper.

Morrison, Kevin. 2009. "Oil, Nontax Revenue, and the Redistributional Foundations of Regime Stability." *International Organization* 63: 107–138.

Olson, David. 1993. "Compartmentalized Competition: The Managed Transitional Election System of Poland." *The Journal of Politics* 55(2): 415–441.

Roessler, Philip and Marc Haward. 2009. "Post-Cold War Political Regimes: When Do Elections Matter?" in Staffen Lindberg Ed. *Democratization by Elections*, Baltimore, MD: The Johns Hopkins University Press, pp. 101–127.

Ross, Michael, 2001. "Does Oil Hinder Democracy?" *World Politics* 53: 325–361.

Samaraweera, Vijaya. 1977. "Sri Lanka's 1977 General Election: The Resurgence of the UNP." *Asian Survey* 17(12): 1195–1206.

Schedler, Andreas Ed. 2006. *Electoral Authoritarianism: The Dynamics of Unfree Competition.* Boulder, CO: Lynne Rienner.

Shi, Tianjian. 1999. "Village Committee Elections in China: Institutionalist Tactics for Democracy." *World Politics* 51(3): 385–412.

Simpser, Alberto. 2013. *Why Governments and Parties Manipulate Elections: Theory, Practice and Implications.* New York: Cambridge University Press.

Straus, Scott and Charlie Taylor. 2012. "Democratization and Electoral Violence in Sub-Saharan Africa, 1990–2008." In *Voting in Fear: Electoral Violence in Sub-Saharan Africa*, Ed. Dorina Bekoe. Washington, DC: United States Institute of Peace, pp. 15–38.

Svolik, Milan. 2012. *The Politics of Authoritarian Rule.* New York: Cambridge University Press.

Tedin, Kent. 1994. "Popular Support for Competitive Elections in the Soviet Union." *Comparative Political Studies* 27: 241–271.

Teorrel, Jan and Alex Hadenius. 2009. "Elections as Levers of Democratization: A Global Inquiry." In Staffan Lindberg, Ed. *Democratization by Elections: A New Mode of Transition.* Baltimore MD: The Johns Hopkins University Press, pp. 77–100.

Tucker, Joshua A. 2007. "Enough! Electoral Fraud, Collective Action Problems, and Post-Communist Colored Revolutions." *Perspective on Politics* 5(3): 535–551.

Weiss, Jessica Chen. 2012. "Authoritarian Signaling, Mass Audiences, and Nationalist Protest in China." *International Organization* 67(1): 1–35.

White, Stephen. 1988. "Reforming the Electoral System." *Journal of Communist Studies* 4(4): 1–17.

Wintrobe, Ronald. 1998. *The Political Economy of Dictatorship.* New York: Cambridge University Press.

Wood, Elizabeth. 2000. *Forging Democracy from Below: Insurgent Transitions in South Africa and El Salvador.* New York: Cambridge University Press.

PART II

Catalyzing and Preventing Electoral Violence

5

DO CONTENTIOUS ELECTIONS TRIGGER VIOLENCE?

Patrick M. Kuhn

In theory, elections ought to be a peaceful mechanism of leadership selection, which make governments accountable to citizens and thereby discourage corruption and rent seeking. Yet, the introduction of elections in countries where their complementary democratic institutions, such as the rule of law and a free and independent media, remain weak, has left the behavior of competing candidates unconstrained, resulting in contentious contests marred by irregularities, such as vote buying, ballot fraud, and voter intimidation (Collier 2009).

That contentious elections may trigger violence has long caught scholarly attention. Early studies treated electoral violence[1] as a side effect of democratization or just another manifestation of the political instability generally associated with hybrid regimes (e.g. Huntington 1968; Dahl 1971; Huntington 1991). For them, intimidation and violence around elections are the regrettable, yet ultimately unavoidable "birth pangs" associated with political liberalization, which will eventually disappear as countries become fully democratic or slide black into autocracy.

More recent studies, however, suggest that electoral violence is not a by-product of political liberalization, but a strategic tool in the competition for office (Austin 1995; Laakso 1999; Klopp and Zuern 2007; Laakso 2007; Hickman 2009; Höglund and Piyarathne 2009; Boone 2011; Bekoe 2012a). Based on this insight, a small but sophisticated theoretical literature on violence as an illicit campaign strategy has formed (e.g., Chaturvedi 2005; Robinson and Torvik 2009; Collier and Vicente 2012). These theoretical models suggest that violence can be used to rig elections in countries lacking the institutional capacity to effectively mediate conflict over political power and ensure a level playing field among candidates.

A rapidly growing body of quantitative studies has recently emerged on the causes of electoral violence. For example, Wilkinson (2004) and Wilkinson and

Haid (2009) show that state and local electoral incentives explain a large part of the observed variation in Hindu–Muslim riots between Indian states. Arriola and Johnson (2012) find that clientelistic corruption inhibits pre-electoral violence in competitive electoral autocracies—the set of regimes most susceptible to such violence. Clientelism, as an informal mechanism of political bargaining, provides elites with an alternative for arriving at mutually beneficial outcomes, which lowers the electoral stakes and reduces the candidates' incentives to recourse to violence. Hafner-Burton, Hyde, and Jablonski (2013) find that when institutionally unconstrained incumbents have information suggesting that they will lose the election, they become more likely to engage in pre-electoral violence. Finally, Taylor, Pevehouse, and Straus (2013) find that in Sub-Saharan Africa most violence takes place before elections and is committed by incumbents seeking re-election. They also demonstrate that pre-existing social conflict and the quality of founding elections shape pre-vote violence, while the stability of democratic institutions and weaker economic growth shape post-vote violence.

While these institutional, economic, and election-specific differences are doubtlessly important, very little attention has been given to the disparities between social contexts in which these elections take place. This chapter addresses this gap by systematically investigating the relationship between ethnic voting and pre-electoral violence. Drawing on the civil war, ethnic conflict, and electoral violence literatures, I argue that a high level of ethnic voting increases electoral competition and reduces the effectiveness of other campaign instruments, which in turn creates strong incentives for candidates to use violence and intimidation in order to increase their electoral chances. Using 54 nationally representative surveys from 19 different countries in Sub-Saharan Africa and four different measures of pre-electoral violence, the study demonstrates a robust positive association between a country's level of ethnic voting and the use of violence during election campaigns. This result provides an explanation for the persistent cross-national differences in electoral violence across Sub-Saharan Africa.

The remainder of this chapter is organized as follows. The next section reviews the related literature and derives the main prediction. Thereafter, I present the data, measurements, and empirical strategy used to empirically evaluate the relationship between ethnic voting and pre-electoral violence. Section 4 presents the regression results and assesses their sensitivity and robustness towards alternative explanations. The final section concludes, discusses the results' implications, and suggests avenues for future research.

The Relationship Between Ethnic Voting and Pre-Electoral Violence

Much research suggests that democratization may affect the risk of conflict both between (e.g., Mansfield and Snyder 1995; Ward and Gleditsch 1998, Snyder 2000) and within states (e.g., Gleditsch 2002; Mansfield and Snyder 2007;

Cederman, Hug and Krebs 2010). The link between democratization and conflict relies on two mechanisms. First, it is argued that ethnic affiliation often dominates other cleavages in post-authoritarian political environments. Especially in institutionally weak states with ethnically heterogeneous societies, where the provision of local public goods and access to state resources are politically contentious issues, ethnicity tends to increase in salience with political competition (e.g., Breton 1964; Mann 2005). The second mechanism focuses on the incentives political competition creates among political elites to strengthen their ethnic clientele by inciting hostility towards other groups. The resulting ethnic outbidding in political mobilization raises tensions and the risk of violence (e.g., Rabushka and Shepsle 1972; Mansfield and Snyder 1995; 2007).

Although democratization is about much more than elections alone, competitive elections play a prominent role in democratic governance and most definitions of democracy (Schumpeter 1942; Dahl 1989; Alvarez et al. 1996). As Bratton (1998, 52) pointed out: "While you can have elections without democracy, you cannot have democracy without elections." The arguments above are closely linked to the role of elections as the event inciting political competition and thereby exacerbating the risk of conflict. Several empirical studies find evidence that elections increase the risk of conflict, violence, and social unrest (Collier and Rohner 2008). Mansfield and Snyder (2007) and Strand (2005; 2007) all show that elections in hybrid regimes increase the likelihood of conflict breaking out. Looking more precisely at the ordering of elections and distinguishing between different types of conflict, Cederman, Gleditsch, and Hug (2013) find that post-electoral violence and ethnic civil wars are particularly likely to erupt after first and second elections following periods of no polling. Focusing on competitive elections in developed countries, Anderson and Mendes (2006) explore the link between electoral losses and protest behavior and find that political minorities in countries with less democratic experience are more prone to resort to violence after elections. Finally, Brancati and Snyder (2011) provide evidence that elections held soon after the end of a conflict, when political institutions are still weak, increase rather than decrease the likelihood of a return to violence.

These claims, however, are not uncontroversial. Other scholars have challenged this negative view on empirical grounds. Birnir (2007), for example, argues that democratic elections tend to stabilize ethnic politics. This stabilizing effect may be sustained through inclusive representation of all ethnic groups in the government process. Lindberg (2009) presents a similar argument. Examining all competitive elections in Sub-Saharan Africa, he finds evidence of democratic learning through repeatedly held competitive elections, which thereby contribute to successful transitions. Finally, Cheibub, Hays, and Savun (2012) argue that elections may be a response to anticipated conflict and thereby prevent violent conflict in democratizing states. They find that once this potential endogeneity concern is taken into account, the relationship between elections and conflict is, in fact, negative.

Finally, there is a voluminous literature on constitutional design that has looked at the relationship between elections and violence in ethnically heterogeneous societies. Two schools of thought predominate. The scholarly orthodoxy, most closely associated with Arend Lijphart (1977; 1984; 1999) and the consociational model of democracy, has long argued that some form of proportional representation (PR) is needed in cases of deep-rooted ethnic divisions to prevent violence and civil unrest. Proponents of this view argue that party-list PR is the best choice, as it enables all significant ethnic groups, including minorities, to "define themselves" into ethnically based parties and thereby gain representation in parliament in proportion to their size in society. This allows them to voice their concerns and settle disputes within the political institutions rather than violently outside the political process. In contrast to this orthodoxy, critics, led by Donald Horowitz (1985; 1990), argue that the best way to mitigate destructive patterns of divided societies is to discourage the formation of ethnic parties through the use of majoritarian electoral systems that encourage cooperation and accommodation among rival groups, and therefore work to reduce the salience of ethnicity, rather than replicating existing ethnic divisions in the legislature. They advocate electoral rules that promote reciprocal vote pooling, electoral bargaining, and accommodation across group lines.

The empirical evidence tends to support the consociationalist prediction. Cohen (1997), Sisk and Reynolds (1998), Saideman et al. (2002), and Schneider and Wiesehomeier (2008) all find that proportional electoral systems are associated with less violence. Furthermore, Birch (2007) finds that single-member districts are more likely to result in electoral misconduct, which previous studies (e.g., Tucker 2007; Hafner-Burton, Hyde and Jablonski 2013; Borzyskowski 2014) have found to significantly increase the risk of post-electoral protests and violence. But the causal mechanism through which PR reduces violence is unclear. Huber (2012) finds that contrary to the consociationalist claim, PR is associated with less ethnicization of electoral behavior. The main reason seems to be that by allowing relatively easy party formation, PR allows parties to form that appeal on bases other than ethnic identity, with the result being that voters from the same ethnic group often divide their support across a number of parties, often non-ethnic ones. Moreover, Norris (2013) shows that there is no monotonic relationship between the type of electoral system and majority–minority differences in political support. In particular, she finds no evidence for the proposition that PR party-list systems are directly associated with higher levels of support for the political system among ethnic minorities.

Overall the existing literature on the relationship between elections and violence is somewhat inconclusive, in part because it looks at different types of contentious politics (e.g., protests, demonstrations, ethnic conflict, and civil war) and does not directly account for the politicization of ethnicity. This chapter circumvents these issues by focusing on a specific type of violence and looking specifically at the degree to which ethnicity is politicized. First, I focus on pre-electoral violence—that is, violence committed during the campaign period in order to suppress turnout of certain groups of voters. Second, rather than relying on some apolitical measure of a country's ethnic diversity, I focus on the degree of ethnic voting, which measures the ethnicization of electoral behavior. Ethnic voting is generally seen as an instrumental action that is part of an ongoing exchange between politicians and voters. Politicians mobilize voters along ethnic lines promising targeted provision of state resources in exchange for votes and voters use ethnicity as cue to gauge the credibility of these promises as well as past patterns of patronage distribution (e.g., Bates 1983; Chandra 2004; Posner 2005; Ferree 2006). The ethnic voting measure captures the closeness of the relationship between vote choice and ethnic group identity. It measures the role of ethnicity in relation to a political activity and is therefore conceptually distinct from the commonly used measures of ethnic diversity, which are based exclusively on the relative size of the various groups.

How is the degree to which ethnicity determines vote choice associated with pre-electoral violence? I argue that there is a positive relationship between ethnic voting and pre-electoral violence. Two potential mechanisms explain why. First, if group identity determines vote choice perfectly, then elections degenerate into head counts and campaigning becomes highly ineffective (Chandra 2004). Programmatic appeals no longer work in convincing citizens to switch their vote, since they generally concern public policies that cannot be targeted towards a specific group. Even patronage, which can be targeted towards specific groups, is ineffective, as according to the instrumental logic of ethnic voting described above, promises will not be credible if coming from a candidate of a party with a different ethnic support base. Hence, faced with losing the election, candidates have strong incentives to resort to the only instrument left: violence. By sending thugs to suppress turnout of the competitor's supporters through violence and intimidation in competitive districts, candidates are able to increase their vote share and secure electoral victory.

The second mechanism is complementary, but focuses on electoral competition rather than the ineffectiveness of nonviolent campaign strategies. The higher the degree of ethnic voting, the fewer politically unaffiliated voters there are that can be influenced. The fewer undecided voters there are, the greater electoral competition, since the value of each additional vote increases. Rather than engaging in a costly electoral battle over the few unaffiliated voters, candidates may be tempted to deter those voters from casting their ballot and thereby save resources and energy. Thus, as before a higher degree of ethnic voting creates strong incentives for candidates to engage in pre-electoral violence.

Research Design

Why Sub-Saharan Africa?

Although the theoretical arguments above are sufficiently general to apply to all competitive elections in developing countries, I limit the empirical evaluation of the connection between ethnic voting and pre-electoral violence to Sub-Saharan Africa for two reasons. First, many Sub-Saharan African counties made the transition towards more competitive electoral regimes in the early 1990s, going through a historically similar transition period (Bratton and Van de Walle 1997; Lindberg 2006). Regular multiparty elections are now held in almost all African countries (with the exception of Eritrea, Somalia, and Swaziland), but the integrity of these contests is often questionable (e.g., Bratton 1998; Basedau, Erdmann and Mehler 2007). Most importantly, these elections vary considerably with regard to pre-electoral violence. Figure 5.1 shows the percentage of elections with significant campaign violence for three different measures of pre-electoral violence, which are discussed in greater detail below.

Overall the maps for the different measures look very similar. While countries such as Benin, Burkina Faso, Botswana, or Mozambique experienced no election campaigns with significant violence, states like Ivory Coast, Nigeria, Kenya, or Zimbabwe had significant per-electoral violence in more than half of their elections in the first two decades since the end of the Cold War.

Second, Sub-Saharan Africa is currently the only region for which a sufficiently large number of comparable and nationally representative surveys with sufficiently fine-grained information on both the respondent's ethnicity and vote intensions exists. This is necessary in order to generate the ethnic voting measure.[2] A substantial literature in African politics shows a broad correspondence between voters' ethnicity and vote choice (e.g., Melson 1971; Horowitz 1985; Posner 2005), but also notes that there is considerable cross-national variation in the degree to which ethnicity determines vote choice (e.g., Norris and Mattes 2003; Dowd and Driessen 2008; Dunning and Harrison 2010). In fact, as illustrated below, Sub-Saharan Africa is the ideal testing ground for this proposition, since the cross-national variation in ethnic voting is particularly large.

Data

Pre-electoral violence is measured by four distinct election-specific measurements. The first measure is taken from Lindberg (2009), who offers an ordinal measure of violence during the campaign period and on election day for all multiparty elections between 1990 and 2007. He distinguishes between peaceful elections, those with isolated incidents, and those with systematic and widespread violence. His classification is based on country-specific academic research, reports from international news agencies, such as the British Broadcasting

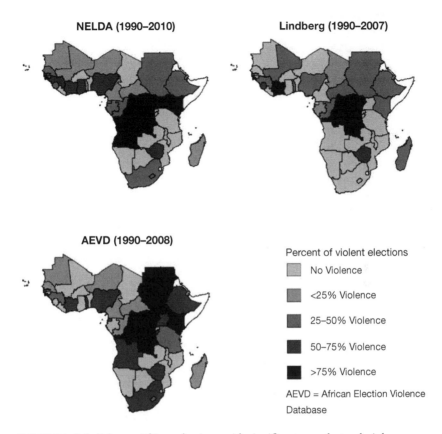

NELDA (1990–2010)

Lindberg (1990–2007)

AEVD (1990–2008)

Percent of violent elections

No Violence

<25% Violence

25–50% Violence

50–75% Violence

>75% Violence

AEVD = African Election Violence
Database

FIGURE 5.1 Sub-Saharan African elections with significant pre-electoral violence

Corporation (BBC) or the Agence France-Presse (AFP), and local newspapers assessed via AllAfrica.com.[3]

The second measure comes from the African Election Violence Database (AEVD) (Straus and Taylor 2012) and is also an ordinal measure of pre-electoral violence, covering all multiparty elections between 1990 and 2008. It distinguishes between non-violent, violent harassing, violent repressive, and highly violent campaigns. Violent harassment refers to incidents of party supporters brawling in the streets, the police and security forces breaking up rallies, the confiscation of opposition newspapers, and the disqualification of certain opposition candidates. Violent repression refers to incidents of high-level assassinations, long-term high-level arrests of party leaders and the consistent use of violent intimidation and harassment. Finally, an election campaign is considered highly violent, if repeated widespread physical attacks occurred, leading to a substantial number of deaths over time. The coding is based on the U.S. State Department's annual *Country Reports on Human Rights Practices*, which are written by the U.S. embassy personnel in those countries, Amnesty International's annual Human Rights Watch reports, and the journalistic coverage in *Africa Report*.[4]

The third measure of electoral violence is taken from the National Elections Across Democracy and Autocracy (NELDA) dataset (Hyde and Marinov 2012). The dichotomous variable NELDA33 indicates whether there was significant violence involving civilian deaths during an election between 1945 and 2010. Similar to the previous two measures, the coding is based on news reports, archives, and country reports from the library of congress and the U.S. State Department. Unlike the previous two measures, which focus explicitly on pre-electoral violence, this measure is not limited to the campaign period. Relying on additional variables from NELDA (i.e., NELDA29 and NELDA31) and the case notes in the dataset, I cleaned the measure of pure post-electoral violence cases. According to the codebook, the measure includes no specific threshold of deaths, but violence must be 'significant' and at least one civilian must have been killed.

The final measure of pre-electoral violence is derived from the Social Conflict and Africa Database (SCAD) (Hendrix and Salehyan 2013), which codes all forms of social conflict in Africa between 1990 and 2011. Following Daxecker (2013), I count the number of election-related violent events six months prior to election day.[5] A higher number of events indicates more pre-electoral violence. The SCAD event coding is based on AFP reports in Lexis-Nexis.

The four country-level measures of pre-electoral violence are positively correlated ranging from 0.60 to 0.81, indicating that they capture a similar phenomenon, although they were coded independent of each other by different research teams and rely on different coding schemes and sources. Hence, finding a consistent effect of an independent variable across these different indicators provides robust empirical evidence, as the association cannot easily be dismissed due to coding error or bias of a specific source.

A country's degree of ethnic voting is measured using Huber's (2010) index of ethnic voting (EV). The index captures the extent to which knowledge of a voter's ethnicity predicts his/her vote intent. The EV index is based on Gallagher's (1991) disproportionality index normalized by the number of ethnic groups in a country, so that it ranges from zero to one, where higher values indicate a higher degree of ethnic voting. To better understand what this index measures, consider a country with two ethnic groups A and B and two political parties. If all members of group A vote for one party and all members of group B vote for the other party, then ethnicity is a perfect predictor of individual voting behavior and the EV index will be one. But as more and more members—up until half of all members of the two ethnic groups—switch their alliance from one party to the other, ethnicity becomes an increasingly worse predictor of an individual's vote choice and the value of the EV index drops towards zero.[6]

The construction of the EV index requires a list of relevant ethnic groups and representative surveys with questions on respondents' ethnicity and vote intent. Fortunately, the Afrobarometer Surveys (Round 3 and later) provide this information[7] for a total of 20 different Sub-Saharan African countries. To identify a country's relevant ethnic groups, I use the group list of the Ethnic Groups in Power dataset 2.0 (EPR-ETH) (Cederman, Wimmer, and Min 2010). This list identifies all politically relevant ethnic groups at the national level between 1946 and 2009,[8] where ethnicity is broadly defined as any group based on linguistic, religious, racial, and caste identities. A group is considered politically relevant if it is either discriminated against by the state or political elites make ethnic claims on behalf of it. Political relevance and thereby temporal variation are the main two differences between the EPR-ETH and the Fearon (2003) group list, which Huber (2010) uses. As previous research recommends focusing on politically relevant ethnic groups when studying ethnic politics (e.g., Posner 2004), I opted for the EPR-ETH list.[9] For each country answers to the ethnicity question in the surveys were matched to the EPR-ETH group list. In the vast majority of country-election years (27 out of 43) matching the ethnic groups in the surveys to the groups in the EPR-ETH list was perfect. In the remaining 16 country-election years the largest EPR-ETH group I was unable to match, made up less than 2 percent of the country's population and the total proportion of unmatchable groups in a country never exceeded 4 percent of a country's population. Overall, the surveys are pretty representative of the ethnic composition of a country, as the high correlation (r = 0.91) between the ethnic fractionalization scores from the EPR-ETH database and the surveys indicate. These surveys are therefore an appropriate data source to examine ethnic behavior across countries.

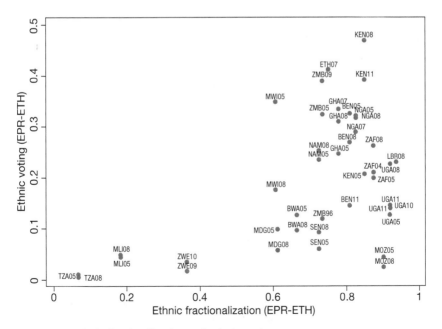

FIGURE 5.2 Ethnic fractionalization and ethnic voting

Figure 5.2 presents a scatter plot between ethnic fractionalization and ethnic voting. The result clearly indicates that the EV index is different from ethnic fractionalization and cannot be explained exclusively by the underlying levels of ethnic diversity. With the exception of Mali (MLI), Tanzania (TZA), and Zimbabwe (ZWE), African countries generally have quite high ethnic fractionalization scores and among highly fractionalized countries there is considerable variation in the degree of ethnic voting. Countries with an ethnic fractionalization index between 0.8 (Benin (BEN)) and 0.9 (Mozambique (MOZ)) have EV scores ranging from 0.024 (Mozambique (MOZ08)) to 0.469 (Kenya (KEN08)). In addition, Sub-Saharan African countries cover a large part of the empirical spectrum of ethnic voting, making them the ideal testing ground to study the impact of ethnic voting on campaign violence. While countries such as Mozambique (MOZ08) (EV = 0.024), Senegal (SEN05) (EV = 0.06), and Botswana (BWA08) (EV = 0.096) exhibit virtually no ethnic voting, others such as Kenya (KEN08) (EV = 0.469), Ethiopia (ETH07) (EV = 0.412), and Nigeria (NGA08) (EV = 0.321) exhibit high levels of ethnic voting.

The main set of control variables include the political regime as measured by the Polity IV index (Marshall, Gurr, and Jaggers 2010), the level of economic development (Heston, Summers, and Aten 2013), and the degree of ethnic fractionalization (Cederman, Wimmer, and Min 2010). Previous studies (e.g., Arriola and Johnson 2012; Hafner-Burton, Hyde, and Jablonski 2013) have found that established democracies have less violent elections and it is widely held that the politicization of ethnicity is particularly likely in the early stages of democratic development (e.g., Birnir 2007; Lijphart 2002, 38). Similarly, low levels of economic development are commonly associated with violence and conflict (e.g., Collier and Hoeffler 2004) and could increase the political salience of ethnicity in politics as different ethnic groups struggle for access to state resources. If political and economic development reduces campaign violence, the Polity and GDP per capita variable should have negative coefficients. Finally, since previous research has found that fractionalization of politically relevant groups is positively associated with conflict (e.g., Cederman and Girardin 2007) and Figure 5.2 points towards a positive, but low correlation with the degree of ethnic voting, I also include the ethnic fractionalization index. If more ethnically fractionalized countries are, in fact, prone to more violence during election campaigns, this coefficient should be positive.

Aside from these main controls, a series of country- and election-specific control variables (e.g., conflict and electoral history of a country, the electoral system, or the degree of geographic isolation of ethnic groups) are also considered. They are discussed in greater detail during the analysis.

The necessary individual-level data to construct the EV index restricts the number of Sub-Saharan African countries included in the analysis. In the following analysis I use data on 54 election-years in 19 different countries throughout Sub-Saharan Africa between 2004 and 2011.

Empirical Strategy

The small number of observations also restricts the available statistical techniques to isolate the association between the degree of ethnic voting and pre-electoral violence. I therefore regress the EV index on different measures of campaign violence with a limited set of controls (i.e., Polity, GDP per capita, and ethnic fractionalization) and then stepwise include a series of measures associated with alternative explanations to account for potential selection issues.

Linear probability models are estimated using the Lindberg, AEVD, and NELDA measures of pre-electoral violence and a negative binominal regression is run on the SCAD count data to account for over-dispersion. Because the dataset includes multiple surveys per country and election year, all regressions are weighted by the inverse of the observations frequency and the standard errors are clustered at the country-level.

Empirical Analysis

Bivariate Relationships

Figure 5.3 illustrates the bivariate relationships between ethnic voting and the four measures of pre-electoral violence, after excluding the Zimbabwean elections, which have been identified as outliers.[10] Based on the theoretical discussion above, I expect a positive association between the degree of ethnic voting and pre-electoral violence.

The upper two plots indicate that there is a discontinuous relationship between ethnic voting and the Lindberg and AEVD measures of pre-electoral violence. The degree of ethnic voting in countries with peaceful elections is not significantly different from countries with low levels of campaign violence, but once ethnic voting passes a certain threshold, a country is significantly more likely to experience high levels of pre-electoral violence. Hence, any positive association between ethnic voting and violence will be driven by the significant difference between the highest and all lower categories, which is why I dichotomized both measures. Doing so makes the two measures identical in my subset of Sub-Saharan African countries, so that they are treated as a single dependent variable in the subsequent analysis.

The plot in the lower-left corner presents the relationship between the NELDA measure of electoral violence and ethnic voting. There is a positive relationship, but it is not as strong as in the upper two plots, which may be due to the different violence thresholds. While any violence with civilian deaths is coded as significant in the NELDA dataset, both Lindberg (2009) and the AEVD (Straus and Taylor 2012) are more restrictive, requiring not only deaths, but also the systematic and widespread use of violence during an election campaign. It is

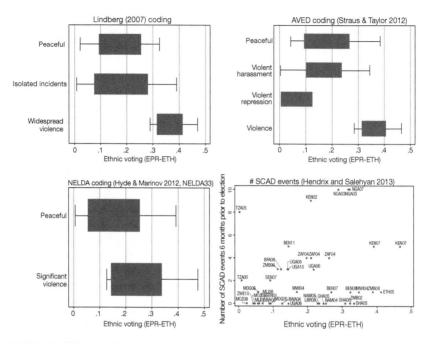

FIGURE 5.3 Ethnic voting and pre-electoral violence

therefore not surprising that the election campaigns coded as violent by Lindberg and the AEVD are a subset of those coded as violent by NELDA.

Finally, note the overall positive association between the number of violent events in the six months prior to an election and the level of ethnic voting. The 2005 Tanzanian general elections seem to be a prominent outlier: although Tanzania has a low level of ethnic voting, it had almost as many violent incidents during the campaign period as Kenya in 2002 or Nigeria in 2007. A closer inspection reveals that the vast majority of those events occurred in Zanzibar, two islands (Pemba and Unguja) off the coast of Tanzania, whose small population is more ethnically divided (i.e., mainland Africans versus people of Arab origin),[11] considerably poorer than the mainland Tanzanians (i.e., $220 versus $600 GDP per capita), and whose past multiparty elections in 1995 and 2000 have been marred by accusations of fraud and violence (Laakso 2007, 237–238; Bekoe 2012b, 132). Hence, if we were able to divide Tanzania into Tanganyika (i.e., mainland Tanzania) and Zanzibar, the two cases would nicely fit the overall positive association: Tanganyika would have a very low level of ethnic voting and very few violent events, whereas Zanzibar would have a higher degree of ethnic voting and a high number of violent campaign events.

Multivariate Relationships

Table 5.1 presents the regression results for the different measures of electoral violence on ethnic voting. As indicated earlier in Figure 5.3, there is a positive association between ethnic voting and electoral violence across all measures of pre-electoral violence. The association remains statistically significant and the coefficient even increases by roughly 50 percent for the NELDA and SCAD measures after adding the main set of control variables. Moreover, the association between ethnic voting and electoral violence is substantively important: an increase of the ethnic voting index by 0.1 (i.e., slightly less than one standard deviation) increases the probability of significant pre-electoral violence between 18 and 30 percentage points or more than doubles the number of violent incidents during the campaign period. The majority of the estimates for the control variables point in the expected direction: more ethnically fractionalized, less democratic, and less developed countries experience more violence during election campaigns, but most of those coefficients are statistically insignificant. This may be due to the similarity of the countries, especially after controlling for Zimbabwe. Finally, the positive and (in most models) highly significant coefficient of the Zimbabwe dummy supports the notion that Zimbabwean elections are

TABLE 5.1 The effects of pre-electoral violence on ethnic voting

	(1) AEVD/ Lindberg Dummy	(2) AEVD/ Lindberg Dummy	(3) NELDA Violence	(4) NELDA Violence	(5) # SCAD Events	(6) # SCAD Events
Ethnic voting	1.904*	1.820*	2.053*	3.082***	5.512*	8.268**
	(1.020)	(0.880)	(1.061)	(0.535)	(3.214)	(4.078)
Ethnic fractionalization		0.858		1.034		9.753
		(0.792)		(1.227)		(6.276)
Polity IV (lagged)		0.021		−0.091***		−0.035
		(0.021)		(0.020)		(0.107)
GDP p.c. (log, lagged)		−0.103		−0.026		0.334
		(0.081)		(0.115)		(0.539)
Zimbabwe	1.258***	1.636***	0.889**	0.690	2.824***	8.441**
	(0.157)	(0.498)	(0.341)	(0.740)	(0.729)	(3.842)
Constant	−.306	−0.324	0.060	−0.360	−0.563	−11.858
	(0.181)	(0.667)	(0.364)	(1.531)	(0.797)	(7.943)
Weighted N	32	32	32	32	32	32
Clusters	10	10	10	10	10	10

Notes: Estimates in columns 1–4 come from linear probability models, estimates in columns 5 and 6 from negative binomial regressions. All regressions are frequency weighted and standard errors are clustered at the country level. The standard errors are reported in parentheses and estimates statistically significant at the 0.05 (0.10, 0.01) level are marked with ** (*, ***).

outliers: they are significantly more violent than the average African election, although ethnicity is a very weak predictor of individual vote choice.

Robustness

To assess the robustness of the association between ethnic voting and pre-electoral violence, I stepwise add a series of country-specific variables to the regression models. Table 5.2 presents the results of the regressions with additional country-specific control variables.

Conflict, especially ethnic conflict, may strengthen ethnic cleavages and thereby contribute to ethnic voting and create a "culture of violence" (Omotola 2010), which makes violence an excepted way to resolve arguments and social tensions. As a result, the association between ethnic voting and campaign violence

TABLE 5.2 The effects of pre-electoral violence on ethnic voting with country-specific controls

	(1)	(2)	(3)	(4)	(5)
		Additional Control Variables			
	Peace years	Conflict history	Current conflict	Federalism	Geographic isolation
Panel A: AEVD/Lindberg Dummy					
Ethnic voting	1.486**	2.284***	1.908*	1.739*	1.913*
	(0.623)	(0.629)	(0.883)	(0.940)	(1.032)
Additional control	0.037**	−0.184	−0.750	0.227	0.672
	(0.015)	(0.132)	(1.045)	(0.412)	(1.227)
Panel B: NELDA Violence					
Ethnic voting	2.922***	2.355**	3.145***	3.189***	3.274***
	(0.572)	(0.846)	(0.626)	(0.572)	(0.642)
Additional control	0.018	0.288	−0.535	−0.301	1.381*
	(0.011)	(0.170)	(0.623)	(0.310)	(0.631)
Panel C: # SCAD Events (6 months)					
Ethnic voting	4.574*	7.779**	9.358**	7.126***	8.763
	(2.401)	(3.559)	(3.687)	(2.597)	(6.211)
Additional control	0.134***	0.410	−4.811**	2.167***	4.025
	(0.039)	(0.939)	(2.309)	(0.457)	(17.460)
Weighted N	32	32	32	32	32
Clusters	10	10	10	10	10

Note: Estimates in panels A and B come from linear probability models, estimates in panel C from negative binomial regressions. All regressions include the following control variables: ethnic fractionalization from the EPR-ETH dataset, Polity IV (lagged), GDP p.c. (log, lagged) and a dummy for Zimbabwe. All regressions are frequency weighted and standard errors are clustered at the country level. The standard errors are reported in parentheses and estimates statistically significant at the 0.05 (0.10, 0.01) level are marked with ** (*, ***).

may be due to the countries' different conflict histories. To check for this, columns 1–3 in Table 5.2 include three different conflict related measures: the number of peace years (i.e. years since last conflict), number of past conflicts since independence, and a dummy variable indicating whether a country was involved in a conflict with at least 25 conflict-related deaths during the election year. All measures are taken from the UCDP/PRIO Armed Conflict Dataset (Themnér and Wallensteen 2011). The positive association between ethnic voting and pre-electoral violence remains both statistically and substantively significant, independent of the measure of electoral violence and the conflict control. Interestingly, time since last conflict is positively related to pre-electoral violence, suggesting that campaign violence is a distinct phenomenon that does not just occur in and right after conflicts. Conflict history is positively related to pre-electoral violence, supporting the notion that repeated fighting might strengthen ethnic cleavages, but fails to reach conventional levels of statistical significance. Finally, current conflict involvement has a negative coefficient estimate that reaches statistical significance in the negative binomial regression, suggesting that the measures—and especially the SCAD count variable—does in fact capture election-specific violence and not just incidents occurring during an election campaign, but that are unrelated to the electoral process.

Next, I consider the impact of decentralization. Scholars have widely argued that decentralization can politicize ethnic identities, although there is no agreement on how this works (Brancati 2009). Ethnic voting might therefore be more prevalent in decentralized political systems. At the same time, electoral competition in federal states may be more peaceful, as power is divided between the states and the federal government, which reduces the electoral stakes at the national level. To see whether the results regarding ethnic voting are robust when controlling for decentralization, I add a dummy variable indicating whether a country has a federal structure. The variable is taken from Treisman (2002) and supplemented by my own research for missing cases.[12] The impact of ethnic voting remains strong and there seems to be no clear relationship between federalism and pre-electoral violence across the three measures.

As a last country-level control, I consider the role of geographic concentration. If individuals from the same ethnic group tend to live in the same region and are therefore exposed predominantly to members of their own group with little exposure to members of other groups, then they might form group-specific viewpoints and interests, and thus vote together with their own ethnic kin. Moreover, if these regions are electorally equally strong and vary in other politically relevant aspects, then elections may have particularly high stakes, creating incentives for electoral violence and other forms of electoral manipulation. To account for this potentially omitted variable, I include a measure of geographic isolation used by scholars studying residential segregation. It captures the extent to which members of an ethnic group are exposed only to one another and can theoretically range from 0 to 1, where 1 indicates perfect isolation (Massey and

Denton 1988, 288).[13] To calculate this measure, I use the region variable of the same surveys that were used in the EV calculation. The region variable refers to the highest subnational administrative unit (e.g., the states in federal systems and provinces in centralized systems). The relationship between ethnic voting and pre-electoral violence remains statistically significant in two of the three measures. Only in the count model does the coefficient estimate fail to reach conventional levels of statistical significance. The coefficient of the geographic isolation index is generally positive, suggesting that countries with high ethnic segregation are more likely to experience violent election campaigns.

Conclusions

This chapter explores the relationship between the degree of ethnic voting and pre-electoral violence. I argue that higher levels of ethnic voting should increase the likelihood of violent election campaigns, since it increases electoral competition and renders other campaign tactics, such as programmatic appeals and patronage, ineffective. To evaluate this prediction empirically, I use data on 54 election years in 19 different countries in Sub-Saharan Africa between 2004 and 2011. Overall, the analysis suggests that there is a robust positive association between ethnic voting and pre-electoral violence. It survived the inclusion of various additional controls that account for alternative explanations.

The chapter contributes to two related literatures. First, it adds to the broader literature on elections and violence by offering a more nuanced view on the relationship between ethnicity, elections, and violence. In the vast majority of regression models ethnic factionalization had no significant impact on pre-electoral violence, while the ethnic voting index is significantly related to campaign violence. Hence, at least with regard to pre-electoral violence, not ethnic diversity per se, but the politicization of ethnicity for electoral purposes increases the risk of violence. Second, with regard to the more specialized literature on electoral violence, the chapter highlights the importance of the social structure and behavior of the electorate next to the institutional and economic factors emphasized in previous research. Given that the degree of ethnic voting does not change much over time, this chapter points towards an additional explanatory factor for the persistent cross-country differences in electoral violence across Sub-Saharan Africa.

Although the empirical scope of the paper is limited to Sub-Saharan Africa, the theoretical arguments are general and not limited to any specific region. Different degrees of ethnic voting may therefore also explain differences in electoral violence in other parts of the world. Unfortunately, survey data on ethnicity and vote choice is still limited for most other regions, but with the sixth wave of the World Value Survey being released soon, a wider range of comparable and nationally representative surveys will become available, allowing researchers to replicate this study in other parts of the world plagued by electoral violence, such as South East Asia and the Caribbean.

Future research should also expand the empirical analysis within Sub-Saharan Africa, which remains in many ways preliminary due to data limitations. With the Afrobarometer Wave 5, it will become possible to create a country–election year panel dataset on ethnic voting, allowing us to look more precisely at the causal connection between the degree of ethnic voting and the extent of pre-electoral violence.

Notes

1 Electoral violence differs from other forms of political violence in its timing and motivation. For the purpose of this chapter, I define electoral violence as any harm or threat of harm against voters during the election process. This is narrower than the IFES (2013) definition of electoral violence, which includes candidates, property, and the electoral process itself as targets. Electoral violence may occur at three distinct periods during the election process: between the beginning of the campaign period and election day, on election day, and between closing of the polls and the inauguration of the newly elected body (Höglund 2009). This chapter focuses on pre-electoral violence; that is the election related violence occurring during the campaign period up until election day.

2 Other cross-national surveys containing the necessary information are the World Value Survey (WVS) and the Comparative Studies of Electoral System Surveys (CSES). But most of the countries included in these surveys are consolidated democracies, which differ in various aspects from developing countries and generally have free, fair, and nonviolent elections. Moreover, they tend to vary little and have low levels of ethnic voting.

3 Elections after 2007 were coded by the author following Lindberg's coding rules and using only the sources he listed.

4 As before, I expand the AEVD coding for elections after 2008, relying only on the sources they listed and following their coding rules.

5 In order to check the robustness of my findings with regard to the somewhat arbitrarily chosen six-month time period, I have also coded the number of events in the three months period up to election day. The two measures are highly correlated ($r = 0.977$) and all findings are qualitatively identical, suggesting that the choice of time frame does not matter.

6 Formally, a country's degree of ethnic voting is equal to:

$$EV = \frac{1}{\sqrt{\frac{G-1}{2G}}} \sum_{g=1}^{G} \left(EV_g * s_g \right) = \frac{1}{\sqrt{\frac{G-1}{2G}}} \sum_{g=1}^{G} \left(\sqrt{\frac{1}{2} \sum_{p=1}^{P} \left(V_g^p * V^p \right)} * s_g \right)$$

where G is the total number of ethnic groups in a country, EV_g is a group g's degree of ethnic voting, which is based on the adapted Gallagher index with V_g^p indicating the proportion of individuals in that group supporting party p and V^p indicating the proportion in society supporting party p, P denotes the number of political parties, and s_g the proportion of group g in the country's population. Birnir (2007) offers an alternative index of ethnic voting based on the volatility of electoral support for political parties, based on the assumption that higher levels of ethnic voting result in less volatility. The problem with her measure is that it does not only capture ethnic voting, as various other factors may also affect electoral volatility. Brancati (2008) offers another alternative, focusing on the vote share of regional parties, which is often ethnic based. While some regional parties are in fact ethnic (e.g., the Basque National party in Spain), other ethnic parties are not regional (e.g., the Bharatiya Janata Party (BJP) in India), rendering this measure problematic. In fact, Huber (2010, 11) shows that it is only weakly correlated with his ethnic voting index.

7 The ethnicity question is phrased "What is your tribe? You know your ethnic or cultural group?" and the vote-intent question is worded "If a presidential election was held tomorrow, which party's candidate would you vote for?"

8 For the two elections in 2011 in my dataset, I extend their coding using the same sources and following their coding rules.

9 Empirically, there is little difference in the EV index between the two group lists. In my dataset, the EV values based on the lists are highly correlated ($r = 0.976$) and all reported results below are qualitatively similar across the two lists.

10 Zimbabwe is the poorest and most autocratic country in the dataset, is ethnically relatively homogenous (i.e., the EPR-ETH ethnic fractionalization index is 0.37), and displays little ethnic voting (i.e., $EV = 0.025$), but generally has very violent elections (see Figure 5.1). Country-specific factors, such as Mugabe's highly autocratic and repressive regime, his lack of popularity throughout most of the country, the militarized youth wing of the regime party ZANU-PF, the empty state coffers, and the dismal state of the country's economy account for the high level of campaign violence in the absence of ethnic voting (Meredith 2002; Boone and Kriger 2012).

11 Unfortunately, the number of respondents in Afrobarometer Surveys from the islands of Zanzibar is too small to calculate a reliable ethnic fractionalization and EV score.

12 The Sub-Saharan African countries with a federal structure in my dataset are Benin, Ethiopia, Madagascar, Nigeria, and South Africa.

13 The country-level measure is defined as follows:

$$I = \sum_{g=1}^{G} \left(\sum_{r=1}^{n} \left(\frac{p_g^r}{p_g} \frac{p_g^r}{T_r} \right) \frac{P_g}{T} \right),$$

where r is a region, n is the total number of regions, g is an ethnic group, G is the total number of ethnic groups, p_g^r is the population of group g in region r, P_g is the total population of group g in the country, T is the total population of a country, and T_r is the total population in the region r. The greater the index I, the more geographically isolated are the ethnic groups in a country.

References

Alvarez, Michael R., José Antonio Cheibub, Fernando Limongi, and Adam Przeworski. 1996. "Classifying political regimes." *Studies in Comparative International Development* 31(2): 3–36.

Anderson, Christopher J. and Silvia M. Mendes. 2006. "Learning to lose: Election outcomes, democratic experience and political protest potential." *British Journal of Political Science* 36(1): 91–111.

Arriola, Leonardo and Chelsea Johnson. 2012. "Election violence in democratizing states." Working Paper. Department of Political Science, University of California, Berkeley, CA.

Austin, Dennis. 1995. *Democracy and Violence in India and Sri Lanka*. Royal Institute of International Affairs: Council on Foreign Relations Press.

Basedau, Matthias, Gero Erdmann, and Andreas Mehler. 2007. *Votes, Money and Violence: Political Parties and Elections in Sub-Saharan Africa*. Nordiska Afrikainstitutet: Kwazulu-Natal Press.

Bates, Robert. 1983. "Modernization, ethnic competition, and the rationality of politics in contemporary Africa." In *State Versus Ethnic Claims: African Policy Dilemmas*, edited by Donald S. Rothchild and Victor A. Olorunsola, pp. 152–171. Boulder, CO: Westview.

Bekoe, Dorina A. 2012a. *Voting in Fear: Electoral Violence in Sub-Sahara Africa*. Washington, DC: United States Institute of Peace.

Bekoe, Dorina A. 2012b. *Postelection Political Agreements in Togo and Zanzibar: Temporary Measures for Stopping Electoral Violence?* Washington, DC: United States Institute of Peace, Chapter 5, pp. 117–145.

Birch, Sarah. 2007. "Electoral systems and electoral misconduct." *Comparative Political Studies* 40(12): 1533–1556.

Birnir, Johanna K. 2007. "Divergence in diversity? The dissimilar effects of cleavages on electoral politics in new democracies." *American Journal of Political Science* 51(3): 602–619.

Boone, Catherine. 2011. "Politically allocated land rights and the geography of electoral violence: the case of Kenya in the 1990s." *Comparative Political Studies* 44(10): 1311–1342.

Boone, Catherine and Norma Kriger. 2012. *Land Patronage and Elections: Winners and Losers in Zimbabwe and Côte d'Ivoire*. Washington, DC: United States Institute of Peace, Chapter 4, pp. 75–116.

Borzyskowski, Inken. 2014. "Sore losers? International condemnation and domestic incentives for post-election violence." Forthcoming in *International Organization*.

Brancati, Dawn. 2008. "The origins and strengths of regional parties." *British Journal of Political Science* 38(01): 135–159.

Brancati, Dawn. 2009. *Peace by Design: Managing Intrastate Conflict through Decentralization*. Oxford: Oxford University Press.

Brancati, Dawn and Jack L. Snyder. 2011. "Rushing to the polls: The causes of premature postconflict elections." *Journal of Conflict Resolution* 55(3): 469–492.

Bratton, Michael. 1998. "Second elections in Africa." *Journal of Democracy* 9(3): 51–66.

Bratton, Michael and Nicolas van de Walle. 1997. *Democratic Experiments in Africa: Regime Transitions in Comparative Perspective*. Cambridge: Cambridge University Press.

Breton, Albert. 1964. "The economics of nationalism." *Journal of Political Economy* 72: 376–386.

Cederman, Lars-Erik and Luc Girardin. 2007. "Beyond fractionalization: Mapping ethnicity onto nationalist insurgencies." *American Political Science Review* 101(1): 173–185.

Cederman, Lars-Erik, Simon Hug, and Lutz Krebs. 2010. "Democratization and civil war." *Journal of Peace Research* 47(4): 377–394.

Cederman, Lars-Erik, Kristian Skrede Gleditsch, and Simon Hug. 2013. "Elections and ethnic civil war." *Comparative Political Studies* 46(3): 387–417.

Cederman, Lars-Erik, Andreas Wimmer and Brian Min. 2010. "Why do ethnic groups rebel?: New data and analysis." *World Politics* 62(1): 87–119.

Chandra, Kanchan. 2004. *Why Ethnic Parties Suceeed: Patronage and Ethnic Headcounts in India*. Cambridge, MA: Cambridge University Press.

Chaturvedi, Ashish. 2005. "Rigging elections with violence." *Public Choice* 125(1–2): 189–202.

Cheibub, Jose Antonio, Jude Hays, and Burcu Savun. 2012. "Elections and civil war in Africa." Unpublished manuscript, Department of Political Science, University of Illinois at Urbana-Champaign, IL.

Cohen, Frank S. 1997. "Proportional versus majoritarian ethnic conflict management in democracies." *Comparative Political Studies* 30(5): 607–630.

Collier, Paul. 2009. *Wars, Guns, and Votes: Democracy in Dangerous Places.* New York, NY: Harper.

Collier, Paul and Anke Hoeffler. 2004. "Greed and grievance in civil war." *Oxford Economic Papers* 56(4): 563–595.

Collier, Paul and Dominic Rohner. 2008. "Democracy, development, and conflict." *Journal of the European Economic Association* 6(2–3): 531–540.

Collier, Paul and Pedro C. Vicente. 2012. "Violence, bribery, and fraud: The political economy of elections in Sub-Saharan Africa." *Public Choice* 153(1–2): 117–147.

Dahl, Robert A. 1971. *Poliarchy: Participation and Opposition.* Vol. 54. New Haven, CT: Yale University Press.

Dahl, Robert A. 1989. *Democracy and its Critics.* New Haven, CT: Yale University Press.

Daxecker, Ursula. 2013. "All quiet on election day? International election observation and incentives for violent manipulation in African elections." Working paper, Department of Political Science, Free University of Amsterdam, Amsterdam.

Dowd, Robert A. and Michael Driessen. 2008. "Ethnically dominated party systems and the quality of democracy: Evidence from Sub-Saharan Africa." Afrobarometer Working paper #92.

Dunning, Thad and Lauren Harrison. 2010. "Cross-cutting cleavages and ethnic voting: An experimental study of cousinage in Mali." *American Political Science Review* 104(1): 21–39.

Fearon, James D. 2003. "Ethnic and cultural diversity by country." *Journal of Economic Growth* 8(2): 195–222.

Ferree, Karen E. 2006. "Explaining South Africa's racial census." *Journal of Politics* 68(4): 803–815.

Gallagher, Michael. 1991. "Proportionality, disproportionality and electoral systems." *Electoral Studies* 10(1): 33–51.

Gleditsch, Kristian Skrede. 2002. *All International Politics is Local: The Diffusion of Conflict, Integration, and Democratization.* Ann Arbor, MI: University of Michigan Press.

Hafner-Burton, Emilie M., Susan D. Hyde, and Ryan S. Jablonski. 2013. "When do governments resort to election violence?" *British Journal of Political Science* First View Article: 1–31.

Hendrix, Cullen S. and Idean Salehyan. 2013. "Social conflict in Africa database (SCAD)." Available at: https://strausscenter.org/scad.html (accessed May 2013).

Heston, Alan, Robert Summers, and Bettina Aten. 2013. "Penn World Table, Version 7.2." Center for International Comparisons at the University of Pennsylvania.

Hickman, John. 2009. "Is electoral violence effective? Evidence from Sri Lanka's 2005 presidential election." *Contemporary South Asia* 17(4): 429–435.

Höglund, Kristine. 2009. "Electoral violence in conflict-ridden societies: Concepts, causes, and consequences." *Terrorism and Political Violence* 21(3): 412–427.

Höglund, Kristine and Anton Piyarathne. 2009. "Paying the price for patronage: Electoral violence in Sri Lanka." *Commonwealth and Comparative Politics* 47(3): 287–307.

Horowitz, Donald L. 1985. *Ethnic Groups in Conflict.* Berkley, CA: University of California Press.

Horowitz, Donald L. 1990. "Comparing democratic systems." *Journal of Democracy* 1(4): 73–79.

Huber, John D. 2010. "Measuring ethnic voting: Do proportional electoral laws politicize ethnicity?" Presented at the Conference in Honor of Prof. G. Bingham Powell, Jr. at the University of Rochester.

Huber, John D. 2012. "Measuring ethnic voting: Do proportional electoral laws politicize ethnicity?" *American Journal of Political Science* 56(4): 986–1001.

Huntington, Samuel P. 1968. *Political Order in Changing Societies.* New Haven, CT: Yale University Press.

Huntington, Samuel P. 1991. *The Third Wave: Democratization in the Late Twentieth Century.* Norman, OK: University of Oklahoma Press.

Hyde, Susan D. and Nikolay Marinov. 2012. "Which elections can be lost?" *Political Analysis* 20(2): 191–210.

International Foundation for Electoral Systems (IFES). 2013. 'Voting undeterred.' IFES Borchure on Electoral Violence.

Klopp, Jacqueline M. and Elke Zuern. 2007. "The politics of violence in democratization: Lessons from Kenya and South Africa." *Comparative Politics* 39(2): 127–146.

Laakso, Liisa. 1999. "Voting without choosing: State making and elections in Zimbabwe." *Acta Politica* 11.

Laakso, Liisa. 2007. "Insights into electoral violence in Africa." In *Votes, Money and Violence. Political Parties and Sub-Saharan Africa,* edited by Matthias Basedau, Gero Erdmann, and Andreas Mehler, pp. 224–252, Uppsala: NAI.

Lijphart, Arend. 1977. *Democracy in Plural Societies.* New Haven, CT: Yale University Press.

Lijphart, Arend. 1984. *Democracies: Patterns of Majoritarian and Consensus Government in Twenty-one Countries.* New Haven, CT: Yale University Press.

Lijphart, Arend. 1999. *Patterns of Democracy: Government Forms and Performance in 35 Countries.* New Haven, CT: Yale University Press.

Lijphart, Arend. 2002. "The wave of power-sharing democracy." In *The Architecture of Democracy: Constitutional Design, Conflict Management, and Democracy,* edited by Andrew Reynolds, pp. 37–54. Oxford: Oxford University Press.

Lindberg, Staffan I. 2006. *Democracy and Elections in Africa.* Baltimore, MD: The Johns Hopkins University Press.

Lindberg, Staffan I. 2009. "Elections and democracy in Africa 1989–2007." STATA File, Department of Political Science, University of Florida.

Mann, Michael. 2005. *The Dark Side of Democracy: Explaining Ethnic Cleansing.* New York, NY: Cambridge University Press.

Mansfield, Edward D. and Jack Snyder. 1995. "Democratization and the danger of war." *International Security* 20(1): 5–38.

Mansfield, Edward D. and Jack Snyder. 2007. "Democratization and civil war." Unpublished manuscript, University of Pennsylvania and Columbia University, New York.

Marshall, Monty G., Ted R. Gurr, and Keith Jaggers. 2010. "Polity IV Project, political regime characteristics and transitions, 1800–2010." Center for Systemic Peace and Center for Global Policy, University of Maryland, Baltimore, MD.

Massey, Douglas S. and Nancy A. Denton. 1988. "The dimensions of residential segregation." *Social Forces* 67(2): 281–315.

Melson, Robert. 1971. "Ideology and inconsistency: The 'cross-pressured' Nigerian worker." *American Political Science Review* 65(1): 161–171.

Meredith, Martin. 2002. *Mugabe, Power and Plunder in Zimbabwe.* New York, NY: Public Affairs.

Norris, Pippa. 2013. "Ballots not bullets: Testing consociational theories of ethnic conflict, electoral systems, and democratization." Working paper, Kennedy School of Government, Harvard University.

Norris, Pippa and Robert B. Mattes. 2013. "Does ethnicity determine support for the governing party?" In *Voting and Democratic Citizenship in Africa*, edited by Michael Bratton. Boulder, CO: Lynne Rienner Publishers.

Omotola, Shola. 2010. "Explaining electoral violence in Africa's `new democracies." *African Journal of Conflict Resolution* 10(3): 51–73.

Posner, Daniel N. 2004. "Measuring ethnic fractionalization in Africa." *American Journal of Political Science* 48(4): 849–863.

Posner, Daniel N. 2005. *Institutions and Ethnic Politics in Africa*. New York, NY: Cambridge University Press.

Rabushka, Alvin and Kenneth A. Shepsle. 1972. *Politics of Plural Societies: A Theory of Democratic Instability*. Columbus, OH: Merrill.

Robinson, James A. and Ragnar Torvik. 2009. "The real swing voter's curse." *American Economic Review: Papers and Proceedings* 99: 310–315.

Saideman, Stephen M., David J. Lanoue, Michael Campenni, and Samuel Stanton. 2002. "Democratization, political institutions, and ethnic conflict: A pooled time-series analysis, 1985–1998." *Comparative Political Studies* 35(1): 103–129.

Schneider, Gerald and Nina Wiesehomeier. 2008. "Rules that matter: Political institutions and the diversity-conflict nexus." *Journal of Peace Research* 45(2): 183–203.

Schumpeter, Joseph A. 1942. *Capitalism, Socialism and Democracy*. New York, NY: Harper.

Sisk, Timothy D. and Andrew Reynolds. 1998. *Elections and Conflict Management in Africa: Exploring the Nexus*. Washington, DC: US Institute of Peace Press.

Snyder, Jack. 2000. *From Voting to Violence: Democratization and Nationalist Conflict*. New York: W.W. Norton & Company

Strand, Håvard. 2005. "A theory of democratic elections and armed conflict onset." Presented at the Annual Norwegian Political Science Conference, January.

Strand, Håvard. 2007. "Political regimes and civil war revisited." PhD diss. University of Oslo.

Straus, Scott and Charlie Taylor. 2012. *Democratization and Electoral Violence in Sub-Saharan Africa, 1990–2008*. Washington, DC: United States Institute of Peace, Chapter 2, pp. 15–38.

Taylor, Charles, Jon Pevehouse and Scott Straus. 2013. "Perils of pluralism: Electoral violence and competitive authoritarianism in Sub-Saharan Africa." Working paper, Department of Political Science, University of Wisconsin—Madison.

Themnér, Lotta and Peter Wallensteen. 2011. "Armed conflict, 1946–2010." *Journal of Peace Research* 48(4): 525–536.

Treisman, Daniel. 2002. "Defining and measuring decentralization: A global perspective." Department of Political Science, University of California, Los Angeles.

Tucker, Joshua. 2007. "Enough! Electoral fraud, collective action problems, and post-communist colored revolutions." *Perspectives on Politics* 5(3): 535–551.

Ward, Michael and Kristian Skrede Gleditsch. 1998. "Democratizing for peace." *American Political Science Review* 92: 51–61.

Wilkinson, Steven I. 2004. *Votes and Violence: Electoral Competition and Ethnic Riots in India*. Cambridge, MA: Cambridge University Press.

Wilkinson, Steven I. and Christopher J. Haid. 2009. "Ethnic violence as a campaign expenditure: Riots, competition, and vote swings in India." Working paper, Department of Political Science, Yale University.

6

DO REFERENDUMS RESOLVE OR PERPETUATE CONTENTION?

Katherine Collin

One of the most controversial and potentially contentious types of contest concerns separatist referendums involving popular participation in issues of nationalism and independence. An example comes from the experience of Timor-Leste. "If you want independence, six months from now you will be eating rocks" (Nevins 2005, 6). That Indonesian language graffito in Dili, the capital of Timor-Leste, was prophetic. On August 30, 1999, the United Nations administered a referendum (with Indonesia providing security) offering a choice to the East Timorese: either independence or autonomous status within Indonesia. Contention marked the lead-up to the vote, but it was the post-polling violence that destroyed the territory. Pro-integration militias rampaged through the province immediately following the referendum's announced results on September 4, 1999. By September 8, the United Nations Mission in East Timor (UNAMET) began to evacuate its international staff. In the following three weeks, out of a population of just over one million people over 1,000 were killed and over 250,000 were displaced. The infrastructure suffered greatly, with 70 percent of it destroyed, including virtually all of the water and electricity systems (Martin and Mayer-Reickh 2005). True to the promise of the graffito, when UN electoral workers re-entered Timor on September 20, 1999 to assist international peacekeepers, they had to carry in bags of rice.

The 1999 popular consultation in East Timor has been described as "the most damaging form of democratic legitimation—a yes or no vote on the peace deal in a plebiscite or referendum" (Reilly 2008, 236). Moreover, East Timor experienced a long transition from Indonesian to United Nations (UN) administrations and then a return to conflict following the withdrawal of international peacekeepers. In terms of democratic governance, according to Freedom House and Polity, Indonesia has experienced greater improvements than East Timor since

1999. East Timor's experience might appear to paint a picture of the dangers of direct democracy—the risks (e.g. referendum-related violence) are high while the victory (what is won at the polls) may end up being pyrrhic. However, this perspective ignores the fact that the decades-long civil conflict over East Timor was brought to an end by this referendum and that those involved report that there were no alternatives for achieving the goal of independence. Indeed, South Africa (1992), Northern Ireland (1998), and New Caledonia (1998) provide contemporary counter examples that further demonstrate the power of direct democracy to definitively affect conflict. Yet at the same time, the use of popular referendums by pro-Russian forces in Crimea and Eastern Ukraine may well have fuelled separatist tensions and cross-border disputes with Russia. In short, the question remains: do referendums have the power to make peace, or are the attendant risks of violence too high in contentious contests?

Since the close of the Cold War, peacemakers have mandated and held a growing number of referendums similar to East Timor and Northern Ireland in efforts to address the causes of armed conflicts. These referendums seek to create a foundation on which to build peace. Such "peacemaking referendums" are a tool that is increasingly used but little understood.

Despite the potential for violence and polarization, peacemaking referendums also have the potential power to end intractable conflicts when peace negotiations cannot. Peacemaking referendums are held in the context of national conflict and designed to make peace by changing basic state sovereignty structures: borders, membership, center-periphery relations. Furthermore, these types of referendums are mandated and conducted in the context of multiparty input into the process. In other words, parties to an existing or potential conflict agree to use a referendum to attempt to change a sovereign structure that is a source of contention.

This chapter explores the conditions under which referendums successfully contribute to peace. First, the chapter clarifies the key terms, the types of referendums under consideration, the risks associated with contentious referendums in conflict transitions, and the mechanisms that link referendums to peace-promoting outcomes. Second, the chapter develops a typology of peacemaking referendums that indicates under which conditions they are employed. Third, levels and types of risk are linked to these types of referendums, indicating varied conditions for success.

Sovereignty, "Stateness," and Peacemaking

Peacemaking referendums are sovereignty referendums in a conflict context. They are designed to forge peace in intractable conflicts by transforming state structures. They do this by addressing *stateness* issues at the core of many conflicts: territory, citizenship, and basic governance structures (Linz and Stepan 1996; Sambanis 2001; Sarkees and Wayman 2010; Themner and Wallensteen 2011), what Dahl (1989,

207) referred to as the "rightfulness of the unit." Many contemporary conflicts relate to borders, membership, or fundamental founding principles of the state (Fearon and Laitin 2003; Gurr 2000). While these conflicts are generally analyzed in terms of ethno–nationalist conflict, in many cases they are expressed, at least in part, in claims made for changes to structures of state authority. Peacemaking referendums direct these ethno–nationalist claims to the institutional forms of the state, and therefore in terms of analyzing peacemaking referendums, it is more useful to frame issues in terms of *stateness* rather than ethno-nationalism.

Successful peacemaking referendums change and delimit the status of state authority affecting, for example, partition, unification, international or internal borders, state to sub-state relations, state membership and citizenship rights, peace plan endorsement or enactment, or some combination thereof. These changes are proposed through referendums in response to a perceived or actual *stateness* problem at the root of conflict. Peacemakers identify such a problem and refer

TABLE 6.1 Peacemaking referendums: question, year, and impact

Stateness-type question	*State or territory holding a peacemaking referendum*	*Year held (or mandated)*	*Successful?*
Partition	Algeria	1961	Yes
	Western Sahara	(1991)	No
	East Timor	1999	Yes
	Bougainville	*Before 2020*	TBD
	South Sudan	2011	Yes
Unification	Cyprus	2004	No
International border	Egypt (Sinai, Camp David Accords)	1979	Yes
settlement	Argentina/Chile	1984	Yes
	Belize/Guatemala	*2013*	TBD
Internal border	Abyei	(2005)	No
settlement	Kirkuk and Iraqi disputed territories	(2005)	No
Changed federal	Jaffna	(1984)	No
structure and	Northern Ireland	1998	Yes
devolution	Darfur	(2006/2011)	No
Expanded citizen-	South Africa	1992	Yes
ship rights	Guatemala	1999	No
Peace plan	Algeria	1962	Yes
endorsement	Egypt	1979	Yes
	Northern Ireland and Ireland	1998	Yes
	New Caledonia	1988/1998/*2020*	Yes
	Guatemala	1999	No
	Cyprus	2004	No
	Algeria	2005	Yes

Note: Several referendums are listed twice, as their questions fit more than one category. Referendums mandated but not held have the year of the mandate in parentheses. Referendums due to be held have the year in italics.

either its solution or a process for identifying or enacting a solution to a peacemaking referendum. Table 6.1 summarizes peacemaking referendums: the question posed, when it was held or mandated, and it resulted in peacemaking.

The Population of Cases

The population of cases under consideration was selected by examining the history of self-determination referendums and plebiscites following civil conflict, beginning at the Peace of Versailles, when the international norm of self-determination and the break-up of empires increased the use of plebiscites for peacemaking. The time frame has been limited to those mandated since 1990 due to the dramatic increases in internal wars over *stateness* issues and the prevalence of negotiating peace since the end of the Cold War. The unit of analysis is a mandate, or legalization, for a referendum. Unilateral referendums held by the victors of war (e.g. Eritrea) and single-party states (e.g. Transneistria) have been excluded.

Peacemaking referendums are sovereignty referendums, as opposed to policy or constitutional type referendums. Adapting LeDuc (2003) and Sussman (2011), *policy referendums* are those that create new laws or policies, and *constitutional referendums* amend or enact constitutions. *Sovereignty referendums* address basic state structures and generally require a specific legalizing mandate. The soviet member states' referendums on exiting the Soviet Union, Canada's referendums on Quebec's and Nunavut's status, and Scottish and Welsh referendums on devolution are therefore sovereignty referendums. In post-conflict contexts, constitutional referendums are commonly held during a transitional process, as in Rwanda, Iraq, or the Democratic Republic of Congo. However, I argue that the context, impact, and politics surrounding post-conflict constitutional referendums differ strikingly from sovereignty referendums, and are not included in the universe of cases under analysis.[1]

By *mandated* I refer to the legalization of the referendum. Peacemaking referendums are mandated through special legislation, bilateral treaties, United Nations Security Council resolutions, and peace agreements. A mandated referendum is one that has been agreed to by the parties involved, and it is not unusual for a peacemaking referendum's mandate to remain outstanding while the polls are not held, as in Kashmir or Western Sahara. Of the 13 peacemaking referendum mandates since 1990, four have been blocked from being held. This commonality implies that the most common cause of referendum failure is not from rejection by voters but instead rejection by political elites. Defining the unit of analysis as a referendum that has been legalized includes the dogs that don't bark, such as Western Sahara, in the universe of cases.

There are also *unilateral referendums* that are organized by one side of a conflict as a means of seeking legitimacy rather than an effort at state transformation. In this way they are similar to "Bonapartist" referendums used in authoritarian states

(Butler and Ranney 1994). Separatists (such as the Sri Lankan Tamils, former Yugoslav states, Nagorno-Karabakh, Transneistria, or Somaliland) sometimes organize these referendums. Occasionally, states organize similar referendums to assert the strength of their positions vis-à-vis separatist movements, such as the Russians in Chechnya (2003) and the British in Northern Ireland (1973) (Bogdanor 1994). Unilateral referendums, however, do not alleviate conflict—they neither establish consent nor force change—and they are organized for broadcasting or legitimizing the organizers' position. The international community rarely views them as legitimate and neither do the relevant dissenting populations. Therefore none of the peacemaking mechanisms discussed below has an impact in this context.

Furthermore, conflict is now normally brought to an end not through military victory but by negotiation (Call 2012; Toft 2010). International norms of negotiating the ends of conflicts, the self-determination of peoples (Hannum 1990), and border fixity (Atzili 2012; Fabry 2010) act together to promote demand for sovereign changes while reducing opportunities for bringing these about. With increasing frequency, peacemaking referendums are mandated to reconcile these conflicting norms.[2]

Over the last century, referendums have been associated with democratization and the self-determination of peoples (Qvortrup 2012; Wambaugh 1933). This association was forged through conflict and facilitated by intergovernmental organizations. Following World War I, the League of Nations oversaw a series of plebiscites[3] used to determine sovereign status for territories throughout Europe and the former Ottoman Empire (Butler and Ranney 1994; Qvortrup 2012; Sussman 2011; Wambaugh 1933). The post-war promotion of democracy and self-determination brought together these two norms through direct democracy.[4]

The involvement of the UN in settling the status of nonself-governing territories and the inclusion of the right of self-determination of peoples in the UN charter has deepened the association between state transformation, self-determination, and the use of referendums. The UN began its use of referendums for self-determination in the management of the decolonization of nonself-governing territories. Colonial powers also employed self-determination referendums during de-colonization, often in the context of conflict, in the mid-twentieth century. This practice was associated with British and, more closely, French decolonization.[5] Peacemaking in Algeria was punctuated by referendums. Other notable cases touching on conflict contexts include Mongolia (1945) and United States-administered territories, including the Trust Territories of the Pacific, which touched off conflict in Palau. There have been referendum-related failures to legitimately settle territorial status, leading to or promoting conflict, such as Kashmir (mandated in 1947 by the United Nations Security Council) and West Irian (mandated by the UN and administered by Indonesia in 1969).

Following the end of the Cold War, direct democracy and self-determination have become associated less with decolonization and increasingly with peacemaking. The 1970s and 1980s saw some experimentation with referendums mandated to consolidate peace or stave off conflict, such as Egypt's 1979 referendum approving the Camp David Accords,[6] a referendum in Chile and Argentina (1984) settling a territorial dispute in Tierra del Fuego after a papal intervention, and the 1987 Indo-Lankan Accords which mandated a referendum (never held) on devolution for the Tamil-majority Jaffna state in Sri Lanka. These cases tried to use referendums to reshape state structures for peacemaking purposes. This is the type of referendum that is now mandated with increasing frequency as an element of peace plans. Since 1990, there have been 13 peacemaking referendum mandates.

Referendum Risks

There has been increasing attention given to referendums in international perspective (Butler and Ranney 1978, 1994; LeDuc 2003; Qvortrup 2002; Rourke, Hiskes, and Zirakzadeh 1992; Walker 2003) and direct democracy and separatism (Bogdanor 1981; Goodhart 1981; Lee and McGinty 2012; Loizides 2009; Qvortrup 2012; Reilly 2008; Sussman 2011). Nevertheless the literature examining peacemaking sovereignty referendums is limited. Some scholars have a negative view of the use of referendums in divided societies, regarding them as easily manipulated and potentially polarizing (Lee and MacGinty 2012; Reilly 2008). Furthermore, peacemaking referendums are held without the mitigation strategies built into representative democracy, and therefore the polarizing impacts of post-conflict elections could be maximized in referendums.

Referendums are notoriously subject to manipulation. As LeDuc (2003, 169) puts it, "When a governing party opts for a referendum strategy, it generally does so in the expectation that it will win." Referendums' potential to promote a pre-determined result relates to the *control* of the referendum process, which in turn refers to how a referendum is initiated, legalized, administered, and campaigned (Bogdanor 1981; Qvortrup 2002; Rourke, Hiskes and Zirakzadeh 1992; Smith 1975). The greater a government's influence over the process the more likely a government-favored result is. Furthermore, public information efforts and campaigns for referendums can be captured and distorted by interest groups.

The risk is great that a referendum might become a distorted or manipulated process, useful to particular factions and subject to multiple nodes of control at which intervention might sway the result. Direct democracy, in established and transitional states, poses challenges for electoral integrity. At the same time, however, referendums can bypass intransigent political forces blocking publicly preferred changes to the status quo.

Additionally, significant referendum-related violence operates in ways similar to election-related violence. Many of the cases of peacemaking referendums have had some level of violence. East Timor, South Africa, Northern Ireland, and Southern Sudan all experienced some form of intimidation and violence intended to influence or overturn the outcome of the referendum. Referendum-related violence is instrumental or strategic and used to influence the outcome of the polls; takes place throughout the electoral cycle; is frequently associated with the spoiler effect; and is instigated during the campaign or subsequent to the results by those who risk being disempowered by the outcome.

However, referendum-related violence is distinct from violence associated with regular elections. Post-election violence is more common in the cases under consideration (e.g. East Timor, South Africa, South Sudan). This tends not to be protests about an election's integrity, but rather an attempt to overturn results. Threats from spoilers are enhanced. Finally, the spoilers in question are more frequently drawn from forces associated with state power structures (e.g. East Timor, South Africa, Cyprus, Western Sahara) as well as extremists challenging the status quo (e.g. Northern Ireland, South Africa). While referendum results do have a disciplining impact on these groups, this effect can be delayed, and that threat of violence may linger.

Unlike elections, and despite serious outbreaks of armed conflict, violence has never undermined the outcome of a peacemaking referendum or prevented its implementation. This is generally because peacemaking referendum results are accorded a high level of legitimacy. In turn, the international community has vigorously defended peacemaking referendums when necessary.

Peacemaking Mechanisms

Several mechanisms account for the power of peacemaking referendums to make peace. These are distinct from those associated with elections, which displace violent contention for power with electoral competition. Referendums can remove contention and parties do not return to conflict. The outcomes of peacemaking referendums have never been overturned. Outcomes are supported and defended by domestic coalitions and international sponsors. The resulting change in the sovereign status quo undermines and delegitimizes spoilers.

Peacemaking referendums incentivize the creation of political coalitions that bridge conflict cleavages.

> Referendums entail political risks for incumbent leaders and can divide ethnic constituencies internally between peacemakers and hardliners supporting the "yes" and "no" camps respectively. On the other (hand), referendums could create new cross-cutting cleavages, including a shared political vision of the future among supporters of the 'yes' vote transcending ethnic and communal boundaries.
>
> (Loizides 2009, 7–8)

This was the case in South Africa, in which the referendum allowed for the eventual inclusion of whites in the ANC (Loizides 2009, 7–8). As Sussman (2011) describes, governments sometimes call referendums when they are unable to pass policy through their own party or government. In other words, a mandate for a referendum can reflect a breakdown in consensus (Björklund 1982). Governments can lose referendums unless they mobilize broad coalitions.

There is a venerable debate over the use of elections systems for peace-making and whether majoritarian or proportional systems improve transitional outcomes (Blanc, Hylland, and Volland 2006; Diamond and Plattner 2006; Horowitz 1985, 1991; Lijphart 1999; Reilly 2008; Reynolds and Carey 2011, 2012). Advocates of proportional representation systems hypothesize that pro-portional systems require governing parties to build post-election coalitions, moderating extremism (Sisk 2009; Reilly 2011). Similarly, coalitions built around peacemaking referendums bring together political rivals within and between communities. Examples are in evidence in the National Congress for Timorese Reconstruction (CNRT) in East Timor, in the South African case, in cross-community organizing within Northern Ireland in support of the Good Friday Agreements, in the unification of South–South differences in the preparation for the Southern Sudan referendum, and even potentially in the early formation of cross-community organizing currently taking place in Cyprus. Lee and McGinty (2012) argue that the lack of similar organizing in indigenous communities in Guatemala contributed to the defeat of the 1999 referendum. These referendum-related coalitions improve the context of conducting peacemaking referendums and of working within new state structures the referendums bring about.

Peacemaking referendums build coalitions that include powerful actors within the international community. These include interested third parties, such as the United States in Northern Ireland, or South Sudan and Australia in East Timor; colonial powers, such as France in New Caledonia; and intergovernmental organizations, such as the UN in East Timor, South Sudan, and Western Sahara and the European Union in Cyprus. International participation in coalitions mandating, controlling, administering, and securing peacemaking referendums have frequently pushed forward a process that might otherwise have been blocked, have guaranteed that a referendum result is respected, and addressed or deterred post-referendum violence. East Timor and South Sudan demonstrate that violent challenges to the results of peacemaking referendums provoke powerful inter-national defense. Unlike elections, and despite serious outbreaks of armed conflict, violence has never undermined the outcome of a peacemaking referendum or prevented its implementation. This indicates the legitimacy accorded to the exercise as well as appropriate, relatively swift, and strong reactions mobilized by the international community.

Given that successful peacemaking referendums lock in their outcomes, potential spoilers are forced to adjust their strategies and tactics. Thereby, an important source of violence and destabilization in post-conflict and transitional elections is removed through the use of direct democracy. Bogdanor (1981) and Loizides (2009) explore path dependence and the related de-legitimation of spoilers.

Settlement, once decided through an exercise in direct democracy, has a political reality that all sides must come to terms with. Potential spoilers, such as the Real Irish Republican Army, lose credibility if they continue to fight about an issue that has already been settled for the community the spoiler claims to represent (Bogdanor 1981). Loizides (2009) points out that this path dependence increases the durability of peace agreements. Using Northern Ireland and South Africa as examples, he shows how both peace processes energized the opposition; however, the referendum's outcome changed the rules of the game, and ultimately spoilers were forced to acknowledge the new status quo and either adjust their focus or discontinue their activities.

The legitimacy granted to peacemaking referendums creates path dependence. As South Sudanese political leaders attest, there are no alternatives to a referendum that would not risk a return to conflict.[7] Either the referendum would proceed or the country would return to war. This logic helps explain why states might allow a referendum to move ahead when the predictable result is the loss of territory.

Success and Failure

The 13 cases of peacemaking referendums mandated since 1990 include several types of questions, processes, and interventions. New Caledonia (1998, second in a series), Northern Ireland and Ireland (1998), Guatemala (1999), and Cyprus (2004) voted on peace plans at various stages of completion.[8] Western Sahara (mandated in 1991 but not held), East Timor (1999), South Sudan (2011), and Bougainville (pending) held or have mandates for referendums on independence. The territories of Abyei[9] and Kirkuk have mandates for referendums to decide to which territory or country they will adhere. South Africa held a 1992 referendum on whether to continue with negotiations to dismantle apartheid, in the form of a vote of confidence for the government. Darfur is mandated to have a referendum involving state restructuring and devolution, first mandated in 2006. Belize and Guatemala were slated for holding simultaneous referendums on their border dispute in October 2013.

TABLE 6.2 Peacemaking referendum success and failure

Status quo changed	Status quo change rejected at polls	Referendum mandated but not held as of 2013	To be determined (as of 2013)
New Caledonia 1988/1998	Guatemala 1999	Western Sahara 1991	Guatemala and Belize
South Africa 1992	Cyprus 2004	Kirkuk 2005	Bougainville before
Northern Ireland and Ireland 1998		Darfur 2006/2011	2020
East Timor 1999		Abyei 2011	
South Sudan 2011			

Referendums risk provoking outbreaks of violence but end wars. A successful peacemaking referendum is one in which the referendum was held, the initiative was approved at the polls, the status quo was altered, and parties did not return to war. Paths to failure are more diverse. Political deadlock during preparation is the most common source of failure. Voters occasionally reject proposals at the polls. Of the 13 cases, five have succeeded, six have failed, and two are (as of 2013) still in process.[10] In each case of success, the referendum succeeded in transforming the conflict and diminishing violence and militarization over the medium term. In no case since 1990 has a referendum passed and the results were not implemented or the conflict was rekindled over a period of two to five years.[11] In other words, once a referendum achieves an outcome the results stick and are viewed as legitimate, and militarized conflicts are diminished. Conflicts continue in cases in which referendums are mandated but not held or are rejected at the polls. The cases of failure have resulted in frozen conflicts (Western Sahara, Cyprus), polarized societies (Cyprus, Guatemala), and unresolved, hot conflicts (Kirkuk, Darfur, Abyei).

A Typology of Peacemaking Referendums

Two referendum-design elements underpin referendums' successes and risks: peace-process integration and ballot-question type. A referendum is held in the context of a broader peace process, as in Northern Ireland, or may stand alone, as in East Timor. Ballot questions either endorse a process or decide the outcome. For example, Belize and Guatemala will hold process referendums on whether to refer their border dispute to the International Court of Justice. In contrast, the Southern Sudan referendum determined the country's independence. When a peace process is possible, a referendum is less risky and used to lock-in continuation of the process. When a peace process is impossible, a referendum is a unique tool for implementing a legitimate solution, but risks violence. Process orientation and indirect ballot questions reduce risks. However, stand-alone events with high-stakes questions are sometimes indispensable for conflict transformation.

Peacemaking referendums can either enact *stateness* transformations negotiated through peace processes or act as the sole mechanism for affecting change. Referendums most closely associated with peace processes maximize and legitimize consensus between the electorate, political elites, and the international community. Those that are held in conflicts without peace processes force intransigent political elites to recognize a consensus position held by the electorate, decision-makers from one side of a conflict, and the international community. These bring about change when conflict cannot and negotiations are impossible.

For example, the peace and decolonization process in New Caledonia has been moved forward by three referendums, each spaced at least 10 years apart. The referendums have validated the process of negotiating governance structures and the status of sovereignty at its various stages, which have moved the territory from colonial status to local autonomy while demilitarizing the conflict. Mandates for future referendums keep the process moving forward. New Caledonia, which began its peace process in 1988, will vote on final status later this decade. Similarly, Northern Ireland's devolved autonomy was delivered through the Good Friday Agreements. This solution to the conflict was more acceptable because it is couched in transitional terms. Incorporated into the process is a possibility of future changes to the sovereign status of the territory, achieved via referendum.

In contrast, the referendum in East Timor was conceived, negotiated, organized and held in a matter of months within a firm, short timeframe. Indonesia's transitional president wanted the issue settled within his mandate. The brief moment of his administration and Indonesia's own process of *reformasi* after Suharto's fall was viewed by all parties as a unique opportunity for East Timor to exercise self-determination. Although the dangers inherent in the lack of consensus between the East Timorese leadership and the Indonesian regime, the provision of security, and the process of demilitarizing the province were perceived by on all sides.

Additionally, a referendum can pose a question to an electorate on the outcome of the *stateness* question, as in whether the electorate votes for independence, or pose a question on whether the process of peacemaking should be furthered. Orienting a peacemaking referendum towards a process empowers negotiators and requires that concrete action continues toward certain goals. For instance Belize and Guatemala have agreed to hold simultaneous referendums on whether to refer their border dispute to the International Court of Justice; voters endorse the peacemaking mechanism, but the Court will decide whether and where the border will be changed (Shelley 2013). Alternately, before the end of the decade, Bougainville is mandated to hold a referendum on whether to maintain its autonomous status within Papua New Guinea or become independent. In this event, voters will decide the sovereign status outcome, whether the territory will secede.

These two design elements—peace process integration and ballot question orientation—establish a matrix with which it is possible to identify the conditions that underpin success and the risks associated with the process. Referendums that are fully process-oriented, in that they are integrated into larger negotiations and ask voters to endorse that process rather than decide outcomes tend to be more successful and reduce risks of referendum-related violence. Referendums that are fully outcome-oriented take place without the context of broader peace negotiations and interventions and ask voters to decide sovereign outcomes. Outcome orientation produces more mixed results in terms of successful transformation of *stateness* problems and the risks of referendum-related violence. However, most peacemaking referendums are outcome-oriented because this is what the conditions allow, and there are advantages to definitively addressing *stateness* problems.

TABLE 6.3 Typology of peacemaking referendums

	Integrated in a peace process	*Stand alone*
Process ballot question	*Process maximizing* New Caledonia 1988 and 1998 – passed Northern Ireland 1989 – passed	*Process mandating* *Guatemala and Belize – 2013?* South Africa 1992 – passed
Outcome ballot question	*Process concluding* Guatemala 1999 – failed at polls South Sudan 2011 – passed Abyei (2011) – blocked Darfur (2012) – blocked Bougainville (by 2020)	*Outcome maximizing* Western Sahara (1991) – blocked East Timor 1999 – passed Cyprus 2004 – passed in the north/failed at polls in the south Kirkuk (2007) – blocked

Process Maximizing Referendums

These are fully identifiable *ex ante* by their mandate and are integrated with a larger peace process and pose process questions. These are intended to punctuate and legitimize peace plans that implement interim and transitional measures. They build on pre-existing consensus and therefore have a good chance of success with low risks for referendum-related violence. The Good Friday Agreements in Northern Ireland and the Matignon and Noumea Accords in New Caledonia are examples.

Outcome Maximizing

These referendums are stand-alone events with definitive, outcome-oriented ballot questions. These leverage the referendum process to get to a solution. For example, the 2004 Cyprus referendums on the Annan Plan to reunify the island divided since 1974 were legalized only weeks before the referendums were held, and the ballot asked whether or not voters approved of a plan that included the entire structure of the state, complete with a constitution and 9,000 pages of legal framework in an annex (Hannay 2005; Ker-Lindsay 2005). Leaders in the south and north had not previously signed off on the plan; approval was entirely left to the voters. Although there were lengthy negotiations leading up to the referendums, what was referred to the electorate was not whether this process should continue and was not accompanied by any confidence building measures or other efforts to build peace. The referendums addressed the *stateness* conflict with immediacy, enhancing chances that the referendum would increase opportunistic uses of political violence or polarization by creating a zero-sum, high-stakes game. It also allowed for the total transformation of the state, a "virgin birth" as it was called by the UN team, taking advantage of a unique moment in which voters might be more inclined to opt for unification prior to entry to the European Union (Hannay 2005; Martin 2006). The referendum was designed to bypass obstructive leadership in the north with the assumed cooperation of southern leaders. However, elections in both north and south, precipitated in the Turkish Republic of Northern Cyprus by massive street protests in anticipation of the referendums, changed the leaders of both parts of the island in the year before EU accession. Members of negotiating teams in both north and south report that, ironically, the traditional positions of both sides switched with the governments.[12] The outcome-oriented referendum succeeded in the north but was rejected by voters in the south upon the urging of the new Cypriot president, Tassos Papadopolous.

Process Concluding

These referendums ask definitive questions after an extended transitional process has prepared the groundwork for the event. In South Sudan, for instance, the Southern Sudanese had *de jure* control of their territory and had set up much of their state functions between the transitional 2010 elections, the referendum, and formal independence. It also allowed for mitigation plans to be implemented, for instance in assisting internally displaced persons.

Process Mandating

Described by Loizides 2009, these referendums mandate the initiation or continuation of a peace process, asking questions that do not in themselves transform the status quo, endorse a solution and/or approach to a conflict. For instance, the 1992 South African referendum mandated President De Klerk to continue negotiating with the African National Congress on opening the South African constitution to multiparty competition. The referendum itself was a vote of confidence for the De Klerk government, and it passed.

Determinants of Referendum Design

The alignment of consensus between voters, political elites, and international actors is a key element in determining referendum design. A strong consensus between each level indicates that a more conservative, process-maximizing model can be used. In these circumstances, an effective peace process is more likely to be possible. In the Northern Ireland and New Caledonia cases, the referendums enact compromises previously reached by political elites and international sponsors (Bogdanor 1994; O'Leary 2006; Reilly 2008).

A lack of consensus between levels or between key actors within levels indicates that a referendum design would be employed with the ability to force an outcome that is undesirable to important stakeholders, such as in East Timor or Cyprus. In some cases like South Africa, Guatemala, or Southern Sudan, consensus exists for the referendum mandate but not necessarily for the preferred or pre-negotiated outcome. In these cases, the process-mandating and process-concluding models were used to either build confidence in the interim between the mandate and the polls or to mandate an otherwise controversial political outcome.

Another factor in designing peacemaking referendums is the role of international sponsors. Most peacemaking referendums are mandated and carried out with significant support from international actors, including the UN and bilaterally significant partners, such as Australia in East Timor, the United States and the Republic of Ireland in Northern Ireland, France in New Caledonia, or the European Union and Turkey in Cyprus. International peacemaking efforts and activities in monitoring, funding, and sometimes in administering peacemaking referendums increases the likelihood that the polls will be carried out and the proposed outcome will be popularly endorsed. The UN's involvement made it possible to carry out the referendums in East Timor, Cyprus, and Southern Sudan. International actors enhance both the consensus and the force aspects of peacemaking referendums.

Finally, peacemaking referendum design is shaped by its timing. Outcome-maximizing referendums take advantage of unique moments of opportunity and change in global alignment. As stated above, East Timor's referendum depended on several changes to the international system. The end of the Cold War allowed for greater international support for East Timorese self-determination. The war in the former Yugoslavia increased Indonesian concern for effectively addressing their breakaway provinces to avoid "Balkanization." The 1998 Asian financial crisis toppled the Suharto regime in Jakarta and brought in B.J. Habibie, who initiated a dramatic change in Indonesia's East Timor policy (Greenlees and Garran 2003). Similarly, the Cyprus referendums were designed to take advantage of European Union accession and were held in the weeks just prior to joining (Martin 2006). Peace negotiators in South Sudan report that the National Congress Party in Sudan agreed to the Comprehensive Peace Agreement, which mandated referendums in Southern Sudan and Abyei, because the Khartoum regime feared the threat of a more extreme United States position toward its fundamentalist regime in the wake of the attacks of September 11, 2001 in New York and the invasion of Iraq.

Risks of Each Type

Peacemaking referendums incur three primary risks: referendum-related violence; the risk that the referendum does not appropriately address the *stateness* problem,

TABLE 6.4 Typology of referendums: risks

	Integrated in a peace process	*Stand alone*
Process ballot question	*Process maximizing*	*Process mandating*
	> Risk of violence	< > Risk of violence
	> Impact on stateness problem	< > Impact on stateness problem
Outcome ballot question	*Process concluding*	*Outcome maximizing*
	< > Risk of violence	< Risk of violence
	> Impact on stateness problem	< Impact on stateness problem
	< Risk of unfulfilled mandate	< Risk of unfulfilled mandate

Note: > increases; < decreases; <> cases where violence could increase or decrease.

and that, therefore, over time the conflict will re-emerge; and the risk that the referendum will fail to progress. These risks are distributed unevenly across the typology of referendums, with outcome-maximizing referendums posing the greatest risk of violence and of unfulfilled mandates and process-maximizing referendums risking the re-emergence of conflict due to a lack of *stateness* transformation.

Outcome-maximizing referendums conform to expectations that posing existential questions to divided societies risks incentivizing violence and intimidation as a strategy for influencing the polls. This type risks the highest levels of violence, as in East Timor. However, all types risk causing some violence. For example, in Northern Ireland a spoiler group (the Real IRA) splintered off of the Irish Republican Army and continued to act as a source of terrorist threat. Additionally, the largest stumbling blocks to the process of devolved government came from Sinn Fein's resistance to decommissioning weapons and increased support after 1998 for the Democratic Unionist Party, which was opposed to some of the governance provisions. In South Africa, the period between the 1992 referendum and the first open elections in 1994 was marked by increased violence between forces opposing reform and also among anti-apartheid groups. The post-referendum militarization and conflict in the Sudans has been discussed above.

The risk that conflict will re-emerge due to the peacemaking referendum failing to appropriately or sufficiently address the *stateness* problem is similarly shared by all peacemaking referendums, but is most closely associated with process-oriented referendums that by design do not bring about a definitive solution to the conflict. In Northern Ireland and New Caledonia, the long-term approach risks the re-emergence of spoilers. As stated above, this has taken place in Northern Ireland and threatened the devolved governance in Belfast. In New Caledonia, rumors that certain political groups have been bolstering their number of voters between referendums typify this risk. Finally, the interconnected problems in the Sudans demonstrate the importance of rightness of fit for the referendums.

Most failed referendums fail due to governments blocking a mandate's fulfillment, as in Western Sahara, Abyei, and Darfur (and perhaps Guatemala and Belize). These risks should be expected to occur most commonly in outcome-oriented referendums where parties that are reluctant to change the status quo retain more power to stymie a process through lack of cooperation.

Conditions for Success

Peacemaking referendums are successful (they bring about status quo change) given two sets of conditions. First, they reflect an alignment of consensus between voters, political leaders, and peacemakers. This is evidenced by the polling outcome, the state's support, and levels of international attention and physical and monetary support. In these conditions, peacemaking referendums will be process-oriented, as peace negotiations will most likely be possible and productive. However, these conditions risk spoilers re-emerging, violence continuing, or political elites defecting. These risks are due to the lessened impact of the referendum on the *stateness* conflict, when a process-oriented referendum will not directly address the root causes of the conflict.

Alternately, a consensus can form between voters, some (but not all) political elites, and the international community. In these conditions, the international community's strong support is more important. Referendum mandates will be outcome-oriented and substitute for negotiated settlements. Referendums are used to bypass intransigent elites to get to a result preferred by both voters and international sponsors. In Cyprus, the use of dual referendums was intended to bypass the political leadership of the Turkish Republic of North Cyprus, as it was assumed that President Rauf Denktash would never support a solution that would unify the island. The referendum allowed social movements to change the power structures in the north, and it was successful. However, in the south, political leaders appealed directly to voters to reject the UN-sponsored peace plan, and voters duly rejected unification in the south. In Southern Sudan, strong support for the referendum (and its likely outcome) existed among the southern Sudanese voters, the SPLM, and the international sponsors of the CPA. Given the UN's support (primarily in referendum logistics and funding) the Southern Sudanese were able to hold the referendum while bypassing the Khartoum regime.[13]

Conclusions

This chapter suggests that peacemaking referendums are a unique and powerful peacemaking tool used to end some of the world's most intractable conflicts. Similar to other transitional elections, the risk of referendum-related contention is high–including the strategic use of violence and other forms of intimidation to affect the poll results, the emergence of spoilers seeking to undermine the legitimacy of the vote, and post-referendum violence intended to send a variety of messages. However, also similar to regular elections, in most cases there are few, if any, acceptable alternatives to peacemaking referendums, other than negotiated settlements, and they mitigate risk by delegitimizing spoilers, building cross-cleavage coalitions, and investing powerful external sponsors in the results.

Not all of these referendums are designed to maximize the majoritarian and existential characteristics that accompany risk. By posing ballot questions that endorse a peace process and integrating referendum mandates into long-term peace processes, peacemaking referendums are frequently designed to build on (and build up) consensus. Process maximizing referendums are not accompanied by high risk of referendum related violence. Alternatively, referendums can be used to force certain parties to cede territory or position when other methods of changing a sovereign status quo at the center of conflict have failed. Although these outcome-maximizing referendums hazard polarization and violence, these referendums are used because they are the only method for transforming the conflict. Parties on the ground report that the risks related to the referendum are seen as acceptable compared with the risk of returning to war.

Notes

1　I include certain cases that are both constitutional and sovereignty determining, such as Cyprus and Guatemala, since these are directly redressing *stateness* conflicts. These cases, though, demonstrate the pitfalls of conflating these two categories, as both complex documents were rejected at the polls, in the case of Guatemala with a low voter turnout.

2　For example, the only new state between 1948 and 1990 was Bangladesh. Since 1990, there have been 32 new states (including unions of formerly partitioned states, such as Germany and Yemen, as well as the independence of constituent members of several large states such as the Trust Territories of the Pacific, the Soviet Union, and Yugoslavia), of which 21 processes have been associated with referendums (either peacemaking or not).

3　*Plebiscite* means the decree of the people, and was the term used and internationalized by France following the French Revolution. It has become generally associated with sovereignty consultations and with nonbinding or advisory results, as was the case for several of the League of Nations administered plebiscites in Europe, the results of which were interpreted and occasionally broken down in a variety of ways (i.e. by sub-territorial districts, thereby allowing the partition of certain territories).

4　France, Italy, Norway, Romania, Switzerland, Canada, and Australia all used referendums in the creation of their nation states. Napoleon would frequently legitimize territorial acquisition by the use of a plebiscite. Hence the term "Bonapartist" referendum for one that is put to autocratic ends without a true exercise of free and fair balloting. For good reviews of the history of nationalism and referendums, see Wambaugh (1920, 1933); Sussman (2011); Qvortrup (2012).

5　France held referendums (of varying quality) on status preference in all of its colonies in 1958, with the passage of the new constitution via referendum. Peacemaking in Algeria was driven and punctuated by referendums. The first pair in 1961, in France and in Algeria, on Algerian self-determination, approved transitional autonomy leading to independence. The second pair, held in 1962 on the Evian Accords in both France and Algeria, approved independence with a slate of measures encouraging peace between the two countries.

6 Sadat garnered roughly 99 percent approval in this referendum. It is a good example of a Bonapartist exercise.
7 Dr. Kuyok Abol Kuyok unpublished data 7/20/2013 (personal interview); Hon. Chaan Rec Madut, unpublished data 7/23/2013 (personal interview).
8 Guatemala's referendum was on the constitutional amendments that came out of their extended peace negotiations. Cyprus's referendum was on the Annan Plan (V), which included the blueprint for a complete new state, including an entire legal framework in annexes over 9,000 pages long, a flag, a national anthem, and employees including a cleaning staff.
9 The 2005 Comprehensive Peace Agreement (CPA) for Sudan included mandates for referendums in South Sudan and Abyei. Critics have claimed that the war in the border area is due to the incomplete fulfillment of the CPA mandates and advocate for a comprehensive settlement for the several continuing conflicts in Sudan.
10 In 2008, Guatemala and Belize signed a bilateral treaty in which the states agree to submit their territorial dispute to the International Court of Justice, and idea mooted and promoted by the Secretary General of the Organization of American States. The simultaneous referendums were set to be held in October 2013. In April 2013, Guatemala pulled out of the referendums, and the next month further confidence-building measures were established. As of writing, the date has not been re-set, but the confidence-building measures are moving forward.
11 South Sudan's referendum is very recent and difficult to judge by these criteria.
12 Kudret Ozersay 05/24/2013 (personal interview); Michaelis Papapetrou 05/22/2013 (personal interview).
13 Under the terms of the CPA, the Khartoum government was responsible for funding the Southern Sudan referendum. However, Khartoum never came through with any significant funding. International donors made up the difference in the final months of referendum preparation.

References

Atzili, Boaz. 2012. *Good Fences, Bad Neighbors: Border Fixity and International Conflict*. Chicago: University of Chicago Press

Björklund, Tor. 1982. "The Demand for Referendum: When Does It Arise and When Does It Succeed?" *Scandinavian Political Studies* 5(3): 237–260.

Blanc, Jarret, Aanund Hylland, and Kåre Vollan. 2006. *State Structure and Electoral Systems in Post-Conflict Situations*. Washington, D.C.: International Foundation for Election Systems.

Bogdanor, Vernon. 1981. "Referendums and Separatism II." In *The Referendum Device*, edited by Austin Ranney, pp. 143—158. Washington, DC: American Enterprise Institute.

Bogdanor, Vernon. 1994. 'Western Europe.' In *Referendums Around the World: The Growing Use of Direct Democracy*, edited by David Butler and Austin Rainey, pp. 24–97. Basingstoke: Macmillan.

Butler, David and Austin Ranney. 1978. "Theory." In *Referendums: A Comparative Study of Practice and Theory*, edited by David Butler and Austin Ranney, pp. 23–37. Washington, DC: American Enterprise Institute.

Butler, David and Austin Ranney, Eds. 1994. *Referendums Around the World: The Growing Use of Direct Democracy*. Washington, DC: American Enterprise Institute.

Call, Charles T. 2012. *Why Peace Fails: The Causes and Prevention of Civil War Recurrence*. Washington, DC: Georgetown University Press.

Carey, John M. and Andrew Reynolds. 2011. "The Impact of Election Systems." *Journal of Democracy* 2(4): 36–47.

Dahl, Robert A. 1989. *Democray and Its Critics*. New Haven, CT: Yale University Press.

Diamond, Larry and Marc F. Plattner. 2006. "Introduction." In *Electoral Systems and Democracy*, edited by Larry Diamond and Marc F. Plattner, pp. ix–xxvi. Baltimore, MD: Johns Hopkins University Press.

Fabry, Mikulas. 2010. *Recognizing States: International Society and the Establishment of New States Since 1776*. Oxford: Oxford University Press.

Fearon, James, and David Laitin. 2003. "Ethnicity, Insurgency and Civil War." *American Political Science Review* 97(1): 75–86.

Greenlees, Donald and Robert Garran. 2003. *Deliverance: The Inside Story of East Timor's Freedom*. Sydney: Allen & Unwin.

Goodhart, Philip. 1981. "Referendums and Separatism I." In *The Referendum Device*, edited by Austin Ranney, pp. 138–142. Washington, DC: The American Enterprise Institute.

Gurr, Ted Robert. 2000. *Peoples Versus States: Minorities at Risk in the New Century*. Washington, DC: Institute of Peace Press.

Hannay, David. 2005. *Cyprus: The Search for a Solution*. New York: I.B. Tauris.

Hannum, Hurst. 1990. *Autonomy, Sovereignty, and Self-Determination*. Philadelphia, PA: University of Pennsylvania Press.

Horowitz, Donald L. 1985. *Ethnic Groups in Conflict*. Berkeley, CA: University of California Press.

Horowitz, Donald L. 1991. "Making Moderation Pay: The Comparative Politics of Ethnic Conflict Management." In *Conflict and Peacemaking in Multiethnic Societies*, edited by Joseph V. Montville, pp. 451–476. New York: Lexington Books.

Ker-Lindsay, James. 2005. *EU Accession and UN Peacemaking in Cyprus*. New York: Palgrave Macmillan.

Lee, Song Yong and Roger MacGinty. 2012. "Context and Postconflict Referendums." *Nationalism and Ethnic Politics* 18: 43–64.

LeDuc, Lawrence. 2003. *The Politics of Direct Democracy*. Ontario: Broadview.

Lijphart, Arend. 1999. *Patterns of Democracy: Government Forms and Performance in Thirty-Six Countries*. New Haven, CT: Yale University Press

Linz, Juan J. and Alfred Stepan. 1996. *Problems of Democratic Transition and Consolidation: South America, Southern Europe, and Post-Communist Europe*. Baltimore, MD: The Johns Hopkins Press.

Loizides, Nyophytos G. 2009. "Referendums in Peace Processes." Paper presented at the annual meeting of the International Studies Association, New York.

Martin, Harriet. 2006. *Kings of Peace, Pawns of War: The Untold Story of Peace-making*. New York: Continuum.

Martin, Ian and Alexander Mayer-Reickh. 2005. 'The United Nations and East Timor: From Self-Determination to State-Building.' *International Peacekeeping* 12(1): 125–145.

Nevins, Joseph. 2005. *A Not-So-Distant Horror: Mass Violence in East Timor*. Ithaca, NY: Cornell University Press.

O'Leary, Brendan. 2006. "Debating Partition: Justifications and Critiques." Working Paper. Institute for British-Irish Studies (University College Dublin).

Qvortrup, Matt. 2002. *A Comparative Study of Referendums: Government by the People*. New York: Manchester University Press.

Qvortrup, Matt. 2012. "The History of Ethno-Nationalist Referendums." *Nationalism and Ethnic Politics* 18: 129–150.

Reilly, Benjamin. 2008. "Democratic Validation." In *Contemporary Peacemaking*, edited by John Darby and Roger MacGinty, pp. 230–41. New York: Palgrave.

Reilly, Benjamin. 2011. "Understanding Elections in Conflict Situations." In *Elections in Dangerous Places*, edited by David Gillies, pp. 3–20. Ithaca, NY: McGill-Queen's University Press.

Reynolds, Andrew and John M. Carey. 2012. "Getting Elections Wrong." *Journal of Democracy* 23(1): 164–168.

Rourke, John T., Richard P. Hiskes, and Cyrus Ernesto Zirakzadeh. 1992. *Direct Democracy and International Politics: Deciding International Issues through Referendums*. Boulder, CO: Lynne Reinner.

Sambanis, Nicholas. 2001. "Do Ethnic and Nonethnic Civil Wars Have the Same Causes?" *The Journal of Conflict Resolution* 45(3): 259–283.

Sarkees, Meredith Reid and Frank Wayman. 2010. *Resort to War: 1816–2007*. Thousand Oaks, CA: CQ Press.

Shelley, Fred. 2013. *Nation Shapes: The Story behind the World's Borders*. Santa Barbara: ABC-CLIO.

Sisk, Timothy D. 2009. "Pathways of the Political: Electoral Processes after Civil War." In *The Dilemmas of Statebuilding: Confronting the Contradictions of Postwar Peace Operations*, edited by Roland Paris and Timothy D. Sisk, pp. 196–223. New York: Routledge.

Sisk, Timothy D. 2009. "Elections and Conflict Prevention: A Guide to Analysis, Planning and Programming." United Nations Development Programme.

Smith, Jeffrey W. 1975. "A Clear Test of Rational Voting." *Public Choice* 23: 55–68.

Sussman, Gary. 2011. "When the Demos Shapes the Polis – The Use of Referendums in Settling Sovereignty Issues." Report. Initiative and Referendums Institute.

Themnér, Lotta and Peter Wallensteen. 2011. "Armed Conflict 1945–2010." *Journal of Peace Research* 48(4): 525–536.

Toft, Monica Duffy. 2010. "Ending Civil Wars: A Case for Rebel Victory?" *International Security* 34(4): 7–36.

Walker, Mark Clarence. 2003. *The Strategic Use of Referendums: Power, Legitimacy, and Democracy*. New York: Palgrave.

Wambaugh, Sarah. 1933. *Plebiscites Since the World War*. Washington, DC: Carnegie Endowment for International Peace.

PART III

Conclusions

7

THE RISKS OF CONTENTIOUS ELECTIONS

Pippa Norris, Richard W. Frank, and Ferran Martínez i Coma

As illustrated by the cases in this volume, contentious elections occur, with varying degrees of severity, around the world. Multiple illustrations could be given, from Afghanistan to Cambodia and Bangladesh. The February 2014 general elections in Thailand exemplify this phenomenon, where a series of street protests reflecting deep divisions between the "red-shirts" (pro-government) and "yellow-shirt" (opposition) movements proved so destabilizing and tense in the run up to the election that buildings were blockaded, gun battles erupted on the streets of Bangkok, and only around 90 percent of districts could open polling stations to voters. The February contest generated inconclusive results, lack of a working majority in parliament, paralysis for the caretaker government led by Prime Minister Yingluck Shinawatra, legal challenges through the courts, and a series of continued mass rallies and opposition demonstrations prolonging uncertainty. A month later, the Constitutional Court annulled the results and called for a complete do-over. In May 2014, the National Anti-Corruption Commission (NACC) unanimously voted to indict Ms Yingluck. Thailand's Constitutional Court also ruled that the prime minister acted illegally when she transferred her national security head to another position in 2011, forcing her to step down.

To address concern about disputed elections, and puzzles about this phenomenon, this volume has brought together studies from a wide range of scholars, diverse cases, and multiple sub-fields. This conclusion seeks to integrate the main findings and to test some core propositions about the risks of contentious elections. In particular, this chapter compares the dangers of contentious elections associated at macro-level with three sets of factors: the type of regime, the characteristics of electoral institutions, and structural social conditions. To be able to generalize beyond single case studies, evidence is compared from over 60 countries worldwide, drawing upon new data derived from the expert survey of

Perceptions of Electoral Integrity. Contentious elections are measured by both peaceful protests and violent acts. The evidence leads us to conclude that the risks of contentious outcomes are gravest in hybrid regimes that are neither full-blown democracies nor dictatorships. The dangers are also highest in contests lacking fair procedures and impartial electoral authorities, as well as in some of the world's poorer societies. The conclusion summarizes the overall lessons of the book for both consensual and contentious elections and considers the implications for deepening theories of elections and for strengthening electoral integrity through the public policy agenda.

The Concept of Contentious Elections

As discussed in the book's introduction, this volume builds on the extensive literature seeking to understand the phenomenon of contentious politics, including research on social movements, protest demonstrations, revolutions, and civil wars, but applies the core ideas to understanding the nature of disputed elections (Tilly 1979; McAdam, Tarrow, and Tilly 2001; Tilly and Tarrow 2006). Chapters have sought to understand the underlying mechanisms which link together the causes and consequences of this phenomenon. Drawing ideas from this broad and rich research agenda, the concept of "contentious elections" has been defined throughout this book as *contests involving major challenges, with different degrees of severity, to the legitimacy of electoral actors, procedures, or outcomes*. In this understanding, contentious elections are apparent in contests experiencing popular disputes challenging either the authority of electoral *actors* (such as the impartiality, authority, and independence of electoral management bodies); the fairness of electoral *procedures* throughout the electoral cycle (including the rules of the game used to draw boundaries, register voters, candidates and parties, allocate elected offices, regulate campaigns, cast ballots, and translate votes into seats), and/or the legitimacy of *outcomes* and thus those winning office (including representatives and political parties). Successive chapters have used detailed cases and cross-national data to examine how far contentious elections have dampened civic engagement and voter turnout (Chapter 2), encouraged protest activism (Chapter 3), and even occasionally led to the overthrow of authoritarian leaders (Chapter 4), as well as sparking deadly violence (Chapter 5) and secession (Chapter 6).

Consensual and legitimate elections provide a constitutional mechanism to settle disputes in an orderly and peaceful manner, where contests channel democratic competition among rival visions of society, leaders and political parties. In its absence, ruling elites can govern through alternative mechanisms, including patronage (carrots) and coercion (sticks) (Svolik 2012). By contrast, this book contends that contentious elections are deeply problematic for regime stability, especially in hybrid regimes stuck in the process of transition from absolute autocracies, because they raise fundamental doubts about the legitimate authority of electoral authorities, actors, and the basic rules of the game.

The core concept of "contentious elections" becomes evident if there are one or indeed several symptoms, which we regard as inter-related in a descending slope of growing severity, including:

1. Low or declining trust and confidence and low public participation in elections.
2. Contests that result in peaceful mass demonstrations, opposition boycotts, or court challenges.
3. In the most serious cases, incidents of electoral violence during or after polling day and nonpeaceful protests involving the deployment of coercive tactics, the destruction of property, and/or physical harm to people. Electoral violence is defined by acts of physical coercion, or threats of such acts, involving any person or property at any stage of the long electoral cycle, including before, during, or after polling day.

Studies in this book have presented case-study evidence from diverse contexts and types of regimes which help to demonstrate the connections among each of these elements—with research utilizing public opinion surveys of confidence in elections and voter turnout, as well as expert perceptions of the existence of peaceful electoral demonstrations, and survey and aggregate data monitoring outbreaks of electoral violence. Thus, where it is widely believed that an election has experienced problems of electoral integrity, chapters demonstrate how this damages public trust and confidence in electoral authorities, procedures, and outcomes. In turn, lack of public trust in electoral authorities and procedures generates a climate of suspicion which opposition forces exploit to organize and mobilize challenges to the process and outcome, whether through peaceful mass protests, legal challenges through the courts or electoral authorities, or opposition boycotts of the polls, all of which characterize contentious elections. The national case studies presented in different chapters deepened our knowledge of the micro-level conditions that undermine confidence in elections, facilitate public demonstrations, and spark violence. But it is plausible that macro-level conditions also play an important role as part of the explanation for this phenomenon, and this issue requires further exploration through cross-national comparisons.

Theoretical Perspectives on Contentious Elections

What comparative evidence is available to assess the risks of contentious elections? Contributors to this volume have examined several key issues concerning different aspects of the research agenda but many important questions remain. In particular, building upon these foundations, the central question tackled by this conclusion is whether the risks of contentious elections are heightened by the existence of several macro-level conditions including, most importantly, *the type of regime in power*—with the risks of disputes rising in a curvilinear fashion in the middle category of hybrid regimes or "electoral autocracies," such as Cambodia, Ukraine, and Pakistan, which are neither full-blown dictatorships nor democracies. In addition, *electoral institutions and procedures* are expected to be important for reducing the risks of contention, notably the impartiality and capacity of the electoral authorities, and the fairness and administration of electoral procedures. Finally, *structural social conditions*, including deep-rooted poverty and ethnic heterogeneity, are also theorized to heighten the vulnerabilities to contention. Several of the core propositions which flow from the general theory can be tested in this chapter against new sources of empirical evidence.

The Risks of Hybrid Regimes

Recent years have seen growing interest in the intermediary category of "hybrid" regimes—also known as "electoral autocracies" and "competitive authoritarian" states (Diamond 2002; Levitsky and Way 2010a, 2010b). Hegre et al. (2001) have argued that a curvilinear relationship exists between the dangers of civil war and democratization, with hybrid regimes at greatest risk compared with dictatorships and democracies. Similarly, Mansfield and Snyder provide one of the most plausible structural arguments about regime types, associated with curvilinear patterns of democratization, with risks of violence and instability thought to rise during the initial stages of regime transitions from absolute autocracy, when multiple newly formed parties are believed to have strong incentives to emphasize ethno-nationalist, ethno-religious and ethno-linguistic identities in the battle to win votes and seats. Without a strong organization or ideological profile, party competition centers around issues of identity politics. Moreover the state's institutional capacity to use coercive control diminishes with liberalization. Over time, however, Mansfield and Snyder (2007) argue that if transitional regimes become consolidated democracies, with party competition institutionalized and democratic cultures deepened over a succession of elections, then the dangers of instability diminish.

This argument also receives further empirical support from research using the NELDA dataset, which confirms that the risks of electoral violence are typically relatively low in the most autocratic states, before rising during the intermediate "hybrid" regimes of "electoral autocracies," and then falling again in long-established democratic states (Norris 2014, Ch. 8).

Building upon these insights, our theory expects to observe a curvilinear relationship linking levels of democratization with contentious elections, as illustrated schematically earlier in Figure 1.2. Thus in the most repressive autocracies, such as Turkmenistan, Cuba, and Iran, mass challenges to elections are predicted to remain latent rather than becoming manifest, even if serious abuses of political rights and electoral malpractices are widespread and self-evident to citizens and opposition parties, and if elections are widely regarded as illegitimate and fraudulent. In such regimes, coercion and the brutal suppression of dissent by the courts, police, army, the intelligence services, partisan thugs, and criminal gangs serves to suppress outright criticism and mass demonstrations by opposition forces. Highly autocratic states are therefore expected to have relatively low levels of violence, since they characteristically maintain strong control by the security forces and leaders have few constraints in deploying coercion when suppressing attempted insurgencies and stamping out opposition protests. Autocratic states also exercise tighter control of the independent media.

If absolute autocracies transition to become "hybrid" regimes or "electoral autocracies," however, political conditions gradually liberalize through the initial stages of democratization. In this intermediate stage, where hybrid regimes such as Ukraine and Russia are located in the political spectrum somewhere in the grey zone between absolute autocracies and consolidated democracies, there are fewer limits on party competition, free speech, the independent media, and civic society organizations. State capacity for repression also often weakens as well, electoral institutions still remain poorly consolidated, and a culture of low trust in political authorities typically persists. In this context, elections are predicted to be more likely to witness heated and lively disputes over procedures and outcomes, involving public protests, lobbying, petitions, internet mobilization, legislative debate, and legal challenges. Where dispute resolution mechanisms remain weak, and the underlying quality of the contest reflects relatively poor international standards of electoral integrity, conflict is likely to spill over into violence. Thus the most violent forms of contentious elections are predicted to peak in states with hybrid regimes.

Finally, long-established democracies are characterized by greater respect for the rights of freedom of expression, mobilization, and dissent. Moreover stronger channels of legal redress through the courts and legislative debate provide opportunities to resolve partisan disputes about any contentious electoral malpractices through peaceful means. In democratic states that respect the rights to freedom of expression and rights to assembly, any public discontent with electoral procedures can be mobilized by opposition forces and freely expressed through public protests, peaceful demonstrations, and legal challenges through parliament and the courts, without recourse to violence. Thus, in the United States, heated partisan disputes divide Democrats and Republicans over the most appropriate electoral procedures, voter identification requirements, and registration processes in states such as Ohio, Texas, and Wisconsin, but at least these noisy and litigious battles end at the courtroom steps, rather than spilling over into worse forms of conflict.[1]

Electoral Institutions

Comparative research about democratization, regime transitions, and electoral systems, among scholars of political institutions, has long been interested in determining the most effective constitutional arrangements and regulatory procedures designed to mitigate electoral conflict. A long series of studies, building upon Lijphart's theories of consociational or consensus democracy, have emphasized the dangers of winner-take-all majoritarian electoral systems and the benefits of power-sharing institutions for new constitutional settlements (Sisk and Reynolds 1998; Kumar 1998; Reilly 2002; Norris 2004, 2008). The sequential timing of elections as part of the reconstruction and state-building process has also been regarded as important (Snyder 2000; Mansfield and Snyder 2007; Brancati and Snyder 2013; Bhasin and Gandhi 2013), as has the impact of international monitors in either containing or exacerbating tensions (Mulikita 1999; Daxecker 2012).

The role of election management bodies as effective dispute resolution mechanisms is receiving increasing attention, although the design of these bodies remains under-studied, with perhaps the most attention from practitioners rather than scholars. Nevertheless, the research literature has been growing, including the links between the electoral management bodies (EMBs) and public confidence in electoral procedures (López-Pintor 2000; Struwig, Roberts, and Vivier 2011; Ugues 2014). A comprehensive global database of EMBs by International IDEA has been widely used to classify types of bodies into those that are independent, those located within a government ministry, and a mixed model combining both elements, for example, at central and local levels (Wall et al. 2006). The authors of the IDEA report concluded that the de facto independence of electoral authorities from the ruling party is important for performance; those under direct control of the government, such as electoral authorities employed as civil servants located within a ministry, are thought more vulnerable to suspicions of partisan manipulation and favoritism. More autonomous bodies are freer to act in an impartial and fair manner as an 'ombudsman' above the partisan fray. Yet the de facto independence of the EMB does not necessarily mean de jure independence. Indeed independent EMBs may struggle to gain the human, technical, and financial resources necessary for running complex and large-scale electoral operations. The composition and appointment process may also be important, with EMBs composed of legal experts, judges, scholars, public figures, and other technical professionals often regarded as performing better than government officials (Balule 2008; Gazibo 2006). Moreover the evidence for this assumption is not well established and other studies suggest that the inclusiveness of the composition of the EMB, so that all political parties are represented within the organization, may be more effective for reducing conflict (Opitz, Fjelde, and Höglund 2013). A more cautious conclusion by Sarah Birch suggests that the design of the electoral management bodies is not "one-size-fits-all" since the involvement of political party representatives in EMBs has mixed results on different aspects of electoral manipulation (Birch 2011, Ch. 6).

In contributing towards this debate, we theorize that two aspects of the electoral cycle are likely to be particularly important for mitigating or exacerbating contentious elections, namely the characteristics and qualities of electoral authorities and electoral procedures. In particular, using the PEI-2 expert survey, these dimensions were measured by judgments of the impartiality, transparency and performance of *election authorities* (irrespective of their organizational structure and composition), as well as the management, transparency, fairness and respect for the legality of *electoral procedures*. Standardized 100-point indices were constructed from PEI for each of these characteristics.[2]

Structural Conditions

In addition, the risks of peaceful protests turning violent are expected to be exacerbated by the standard underlying societal conditions that are commonly associated with inter-communal conflict and civil war, including the existence of deep-rooted poverty, under-development, and socioeconomic inequality, levels of ethnic heterogeneity, the curse of natural resources, levels of corruption, and a recent history of prior armed conflict. Structural social conditions which are often thought to heighten the general risks of societal struggles, functioning as the "deep-drivers" of electoral violence. Theories about the role of structural explanations in civil wars have been developed most fully in a series of studies published for more than a decade by Paul Collier and Anke Hoeffler analyzing problems of armed rebellion and outbreaks of conflict (Collier and Hoeffler 1998, 2002, 2004; Collier, Hoeffler, and Sambanis 2005; Collier, Heffler, and Rohner 2009; Collier 2009). The Collier–Hoeffler model categorizes the causes of violence as either "greed" or "grievance," emphasizing societal characteristics such as ethnic heterogeneity and polarization, low levels of development and sluggish rates of economic growth, the role of geographic locations, the size of a country and its physical terrain, the persistence of socioeconomic inequality and endemic poverty, and the role of natural resources controlled by the state. Deep-rooted socioeconomic conditions in divided societies, used to explain the onset, persistence, or recurrence of civil wars, may be extended to help provide insights into outbreaks of electoral violence. Standard variables for all the social structural conditions are available for comparison, compiled from several sources, from the Quality of Government Dataset (2013).

Evidence for the General Theory

Does evidence tend to support this general argument and the specific propositions about the risks of contentious elections associated at macro-level with the type of regimes, electoral institutions, and structural social conditions? Case studies providing historical narratives of contentious elections occurring in single countries are abundant in the literature. To demonstrate the empirical evidence for the linkage mechanisms and building blocks underlying these relationships, several chapters within this book employ social surveys in different countries, as well as drawing broader cross-national comparisons.

To supplement these materials, this chapter draws upon evidence from a new resource, the expert survey of Perceptions of Electoral Integrity, developed by the Electoral Integrity Project (2014). The second release of the dataset (PEI-2) used in this study covers 73 elections held in 66 countries over an 18-month period from July 1, 2012 to December 31, 2013. The study sought assessments from around 40 domestic and international election experts per contest, achieving around a 30 percent response rate including the views of 855 experts. The questionnaire includes 49 individual indicators which are clustered into 11 stages of the electoral cycle, as well as generating an overall summary Perception of Electoral Integrity (PEI) 100-point index and comparative ranking. Upon further examination, the evidence has been found to display high levels of external validity, internal validity, and legitimacy (Norris, Martínez i Coma, and Frank 2014).

The relatively abstract notion of "contentious elections" is operationalized and monitored in this study using a range of empirical indicators available from the PEI survey. As proposed earlier, evidence for contentious elections is manifest typically at micro and macro-levels by *cultural indicators* (including low or declining levels of public trust and confidence in elections, as well as lack of civic engagement and participation in the electoral process); by *peaceful electoral challenges* (typically expressed through the repertoire of nonviolent collective acts such as demonstrations, internet mobilization, political strikes, opposition electoral boycotts, property occupations, signed petitions, legal challenges, and court cases); and, in the most serious cases, *by threats or actual outbreaks of electoral violence* (including riots, strikes, and armed confrontations, perpetrated by the regime, opposition forces, or other actors).

Accordingly contentious elections are operationalized and measured in this analysis using four selected survey items:

> Do you agree or disagree with the following statements?
> "The election led to peaceful protests."
> "The election triggered violent protests."
> "Parties/candidates challenged the results."
> "Some voters were threatened with violence at the polls."

Experts reported whether each of these occurred during the specific election they were asked to evaluate using a 5-point "strongly agree" to "strongly disagree" scale. These four items fell into a single consistent index when tested for reliability (Cronbach's Alpha = 0.876). Accordingly the items were combined to form a Contentious Election Index and a standardized 100-point scale was constructed, for ease of interpretation.

Explaining Contentious Elections

Which elections proved most the contentious elections, according to these indicators? Figure 7.1 describes the comparison across the 73 elections included

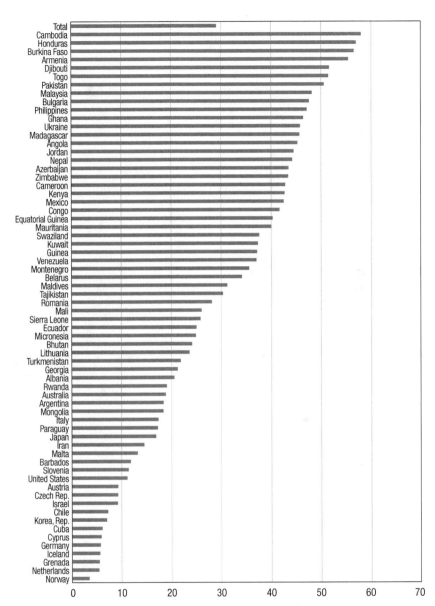

FIGURE 7.1 The distribution of contentious elections

Note: Contentious elections are operationalized and measured using a 100-point standardized scale by combining four items: "Some voters were threatened with violence at the polls;" "The election led to peaceful protests;" "The election triggered violent protests;" and "Parties/candidates challenged the results." These items fell into a single consistent scale when tested for reliability (Cronbach's Alpha = 0.892).

Source: Electoral Integrity Project 2014. *The Expert Survey of Perceptions of Electoral Integrity*, Release 2 (PEI_2)

in the expert survey. Thus, diverse cases from different world regions—such as Cambodia, Honduras, Burkina Faso, Armenia, Djibouti, Pakistan, and Malaysia—all suffered the worst levels of contentious elections.

The July 2013 Cambodian general elections, for example, were for the 123 seat House of Representatives (the lower house in the National Assembly). The elections used a closed party list proportional representation system. Under the leadership of Prime Minister Hun Sen, the ruling Cambodian People's Party has been the largest party in a coalition government with the royalist FUNCINPEC party ever since the 1993 elections following the UN-brokered peace accord. Elections are organized by the National Election Committee. The 2013 election saw the governing Cambodian People's Party win 49 percent of the vote and 68 seats, down from 90 seats in 2008. Under the leadership of Sam Rainsy, the opposition Cambodian National Rescue Party made considerable gains (+26) by winning all the remaining 55 seats with 44 percent of the vote. Five other parties failed to gain any representatives. Invited international observers from the International Conference of Asian Political Parties (ICAPP) and the Centrist Asia Pacific Democrats International (CAPDI) claimed that the process had been "free, fair and transparent." Nevertheless the election saw many complaints about voter registration processes and media biases, with ANFREL calling for an independent investigation. The opposition lawmakers refused to take their seats, demanding an investigation into alleged election irregularities. Anti-government forces staged several large protests over many months, accusing the prime minister of rigging the vote (Grömping 2013). Cambodia scored the fifth worst rating by PEI, especially poor in voting registration.

By contrast, several long-established Western democracies and affluent post-industrial societies were observed as less at risk from contentious elections, including Norway, the Netherlands, Iceland, and Germany. Mature democracies that have held a long succession of competitive elections over decades or even centuries, and seen a regular rotation of parties in government and opposition, can be expected to have developed consolidated institutions and democratic cultures. Affluent post-industrial societies also have the economic and human resources to invest in managing elections and a well-developed public sector with the professional capacity to do so. Yet the link between contentious elections and contemporary levels of democratization and development proved far from linear. Several newer democracies and middle-income economies also ranked relatively highly in consensual elections, notably Grenada, Chile, the Czech Republic, and Slovenia. Moreover, experts also saw several highly autocratic regimes as having relatively consensual elections, notably the communist state of Cuba.

To explore the links between contentious elections and the type of regime more systematically, and to make sense of the rankings, Figure 7.2 depicts the bivariate relationship between levels of contentious elections (monitored by the PEI Contentious Elections Index already discussed) and levels of democratization,

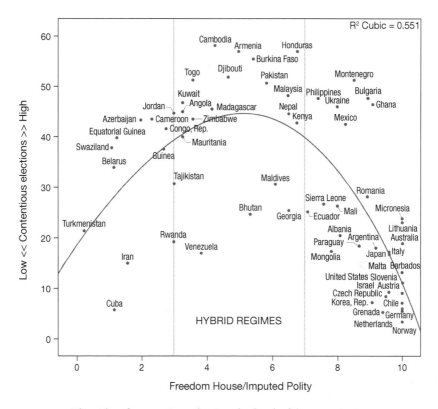

FIGURE 7.2 The risks of contentious elections by level of democratization

Note: Contentious elections are operationalized and measured using a 100-point standardized scale by combining four items: "Some voters were threatened with violence at the polls;" "The election led to peaceful protests;" "The election triggered violent protests;" and "Parties/candidates challenged the results." These items fell into a single consistent scale when tested for reliability (Cronbach's Alpha = 0.892).

Source: Electoral Integrity Project (2014); Quality of Government Cross-National Dataset (2013)

(monitored by the combined Freedom House/Imputed Polity IV scale constructed by Jan Teorell from the Quality of Government dataset). The observed results in Figure 7.2 show striking confirmation of the curvilinear pattern that was predicted theoretically in Chapter 1 (see Figure 1.2). Thus, as expected, there are relatively few explicitly contentious elections in highly autocratic states governed by some of the world's most repressive regimes, including Cuba, Iran, and Turkmenistan, as well as Belarus and Swaziland. In these regimes, competition for elected office is tightly controlled by the rulers and any public expression of dissent or street protests which pose a major threat to the legitimacy of the regime are likely to be repressed by the incumbent rulers.

At the opposite extreme, however, the risks of contentious elections also fall
once democratic institutions and cultures consolidate through repeated experience
of free and fair elections, as well as having relatively low risks in more developed,
affluent and well-educated societies, such as Chile, Norway, and Israel. Thus the
states that can be observed to be most at risk of contentious elections are many
of the hybrid regimes located in the middle of the distribution, which are neither
absolute dictatorships nor yet safely consolidated democracies. Thus elections in
countries such as Armenia, Pakistan, and Honduras regularly see relatively high
levels of disputes and protests around polling day. In Armenia, for example, in
the first round of the presidential elections, on February 18, 2013, the incumbent President Serzh Sargsyan of the Republican Party of Armenia defeated
former foreign minister Raffi Hovannisian of the Heritage Party, 57 to 36
percent. The previous Armenia presidential elections in 2008 saw protests over
accusations of fraud ending in police clashes and deadly violence. This election
was more peaceful but there was still concern about malpractices. Despite noting
"a lack of impartiality of the public administration, misuse of administrative
resources, and cases of pressure on voters," an OSCE observer mission issued a
largely positive preliminary statement, reporting that the "election was generally
well-administered and was characterized by a respect for fundamental freedoms."
Hovannisian, however, called the election rigged, sparking protests that attracted
thousands. After filing a number of complaints with the Central Electoral
Commission, he launched a hunger strike to pressure Sarkisian to resign. IFES
concluded that several problems occur in Armenia, "including voter cynicism
and mistrust, failure of prominent parties to field candidates, lack of issue-based
campaigns, and prevalence of individual personalities over party-based politics"
(Bowyer 2013). Despite improvements in electoral administration, "instances of
vote buying, misuse of state resources, intimidation and pressure on voters, reports
of ballot stuffing, and questionable turnout figures and voting results in some
precincts continued to mar the election environment" (Bowyer 2013). Armenia
ranks 53rd in PEI, flawed by problems of voter registration, campaign finance,
and announcement of the results.

To test the core propositions more systematically, and to make sure that the
observations were not spurious, Table 7.1 enters the type of regime, electoral
procedures and electoral authorities into successive OLS regression models which
also control for many of the standard variables associated in previous research
with risks of domestic conflict and civil war, including levels of economic
development (GDP per capita with purchase power parity), levels of religious
and linguistic fractionalization, geography (measured by latitude from the equator),
societies where Muslims are the predominant faith, and population size. The
comparison covers 60 nations. The results of the analysis confirm that out of all
the structural controls, only levels of economic development proved to be a
consistently significant predictor of contentious elections. Thus, as long suspected,
poorer societies such as Bangladesh, Pakistan, and Afghanistan are most at risk of

TABLE 7.1 Factors explaining contentious elections

	Model A: Type of regime				Model B: Electoral procedures index				Model C: Electoral authorities index			
	B	s.e.	Beta	Sig p.	B	s.e.	Beta	Sig p.	B	s.e.	Beta	Sig p.
POLITICAL CONDITIONS												
Highly democratic regime	-16.09	3.87	-.487	.000								
Highly autocratic regime	-7.98	4.31	-.186	.050								
Electoral procedures index					-.604	.113	-.588	.000				
Electoral authorities index									-.464	.110	-.462	.000
STRUCTURAL CONTROLS												
Economic development (GDP/capita)	.001	.000	-.435	.001	.000	.000	-.253	.040	.000	.000	-.344	.008
Linguistic fractionalization	-5.26	6.61	-.088	.430	-3.93	6.10	-.066	.522	-4.33	6.571	-.073	.513
Religious fractionalization	10.1	6.97	.144	.151	5.50	6.55	.078	.405	10.00	6.905	.142	.153
Geography (latitude)	-11.60	9.55	-.132	.230	-9.07	8.83	-.103	.309	-11.20	9.486	-.127	.243
Muslim religion	.046	.051	.094	.376	.037	.044	.077	.398	.062	.046	.127	.187
Population size	.000	.000	.068	.445	.000	.000	.054	.508	.000	.000	.068	.435
Constant	46.4	5.16			77.24	8.31			65.25	7.76		
Adjusted R-square	.576				.640				.584			

Note: OLS linear regression models with the models presenting the unstandardized Beta coefficients (b), the standard errors, the standardized Beta coefficients, and the statistical significance where the Contentious Elections Index is the dependent variable in 60 countries. All coefficients were checked to be free of problems of multicollinearity. Regimes were classified by their score on the Freedom House/Polity IV combined 10-point scale. Highly democratic regimes scored < 7.0; highly autocratic regimes scored < 3.0. The default category was hybrid regimes.

Source: Electoral Integrity Project (2014); Quality of Government Cross-National Dataset (2013))

contentious elections. After controlling for structural factors, however, the type of regime (in Model A), the quality of electoral procedures, and the quality of electoral authorities were all consistent predictors of contentious elections. Thus, the risks diminished for the most democratic and the most autocratic types of regimes, so that hybrid regimes were indeed the riskiest category. Moreover the impact of the strongly democratic regimes in reducing the risks of contentious elections was slightly stronger than the effects of economic development. Overall the risks of contentious elections diminish most sharply in contests where election procedures met international standards of electoral integrity, for example, where procedures were seen to be well-managed, transparent, fair, and in accordance with the law. This emerged as the single most powerful predictor diminishing the risks of contentious elections.

Conclusions and the Next Steps in the Research Agenda

Therefore chapters in this book have explored many aspects of the phenomenon of contentious elections. Contributors have demonstrated many of the underlying linkage mechanisms that we believe serve to produce contentious elections. Thus, at individual level, several chapters in the first section of the book employed in-depth surveys of particular countries and showed how citizen's attitudes towards the electoral process, especially public confidence in the integrity of elections, contributes towards feelings of trust and confidence in electoral authorities, as well as the propensity to turn out to vote or to engage in protest activism. These attitudes are usually found to be strongly related to whether citizens backed the winning or losing side of the contest, to direct experience and mediated knowledge of electoral malpractices, and to other standard social characteristics that commonly are associated with political attitudes and political participation, such as age, gender, and education. The studies in countries of Eastern and Central Europe certainly suggest that this approach could usefully be employed elsewhere to understand whether similar micro-level factors are associated, as we suspect, with a culture of contentious elections in many other regions of the world and diverse types of contexts. The growing body of cross-national surveys monitoring electoral integrity and political attitudes and behavior suggest that this is a promising area of future research.

In addition the second section analyzed many of the conditions associated with catalyzing and preventing electoral violence, the most serious and lethal symptom of contentious elections. The contributors found that ethnicity is an important condition for this phenomenon, at least in Sub-Saharan Africa, with a strong link between levels of ethnic voting and the use of violence in election campaigns. In addition although referendums are often held as part of the peace-building process, especially in cases of succession, the study presented in this book suggests that they are only partially successful in building the conditions for lasting peace and stability.

Overall the volume therefore contributes towards the larger literature in comparative politics, international relations, political behavior and other related sub-fields that have generated insights into the phenomenon of contentious politics. Instead of "sitting at separate tables," this book has sought to explore the links and overlaps among these separate sub-fields. Yet a substantial research agenda remains to expand insights into this phenomenon. In particular, we suggest that several issues deserve further attention in the future research agenda.

First, the phenomena of election protest, conflict, and outright violence are hardly novel; the historical roots are exemplified by such diverse events as the Chartist riots and protests seeking to expand the franchise and reform politics during the nineteenth century in Britain, the early suffragettes in the United States and the later civil rights movement mobilizing to expand voting rights for African-Americans during the 1950s and 1960s, and, even more recently, protests over the "color revolutions" in post-communist Europe, violence in many contests in places such as Nigeria, Afghanistan, and Bangladesh, and the "Arab uprisings" seeking regime change on the streets of Tunisia, Egypt, and Libya. Despite the widely acknowledged importance of contentious elections, the large body of literature on contentious social movements and a similar body on electoral protests and violence have largely moved along parallel tracks, instead of generating a fruitful interchange of ideas. Therefore the study of elections, protest activism, and public opinion needs to reengage with the larger agenda, especially to understand contentious elections in many developing countries and hybrid regimes.

In addition, there are many questions about this phenomenon in answer to which we have only scratched the surface. Who are the main perpetrators of protests and violence? When do these problems occur during the electoral cycle, and how does the timing relate to many other events during an election? In particular, are all problems of electoral integrity equally important for spurring contentious elections, or are some types of malpractices more serious flash points, such as evidence of vote miscounts, lack of security in polling places, or the imprisonment or harassment of opposition candidates? We need better evidence about the timing, perpetrators, victims, and conditions of contentious politics to make headway on these issues.

Finally, there is also a substantial need for policy-relevant research that could help to mitigate or control the factors associated with contentious elections. The international community and many domestic stakeholders are seeking answers about effective strategies which could ensure that elections are regarded as legitimate, trustworthy and fair, especially by the losers as well as the winners of any contest. There are many interventions designed to reduce electoral conflict but it remains unclear whether it is better to, say, retrain the security forces to handle demonstrations peacefully, to improve the quality of election management bodies so that the process is more efficient, transparent and effective, to reform electoral laws and procedures to reflect power-sharing principles, or to promote civic education and media training to expand understanding of the electoral procedures and outcomes. Evidence from this chapter certainly suggests that electoral procedures and electoral authorities are vitally important to legitimate and peaceful elections—especially in hybrid regimes which are most at risk from disputed contests—but it is not well established yet how to encourage contests to meet international standards of electoral integrity. Thus chapters within this book seek to add to the growing research agenda but better answers are needed both to understand this phenomenon more fully in the social sciences as well as to address this problem more effectively in the policy-making community.

Notes

1   See The Brennan Center (www.brennancenter.org/issues/voting-rights-elections).
2   The PEI survey asked experts to use 1–5 point scales to evaluate whether a specific election met the following criteria:
Electoral procedures
2-1 Elections were well managed
2-2 Information about voting procedures was widely available
2-3 Election officials were fair
2-4 Elections were conducted in accordance with the law
Electoral authorities
11-1 The election authorities were impartial
11-2 The authorities distributed information to citizens
11-3 The authorities allowed public scrutiny of their performance
11-4 The election authorities performed well
Any missing values were imputed and these scores were then combined into standardized scales. For more details, see Norris, Martínez i Coma, and Frank (2014).

References

Balule, Badala Tachilisa. 2008. "Election Management Bodies in the SADC Region: An Appraisal of the Independence of Botswana's Independent Electoral Commission." *South African Journal on Human Rights* 24: 104–122.

Bhasin, Tavishi, and Jennifer Gandhi. 2013. "State Repression in Authoritarian Elections." *Electoral Studies* 32(4): 620–631.

Birch, Sarah. 2011. *Electoral Malpractice*. Oxford: Oxford University Press.

Bowyer, Anthony. 2013. *Armenian Presidential Election: One Step Forward or Two Steps Back*. IFES. Available at: www.ifes.org/Content/Publications/Articles/2013/Armenian-Presidential-Election-One-Step-Forward-or-Two-Steps-Back.aspx (accessed December 14, 2013).

Brancati, Dawn, and Jack L. Snyder. 2013. "Time to Kill: The Impact of Election Timing on Post-Conflict Stability." *Journal of Conflict Resolution* 57(5): 822–853.

Collier, Paul. 2009. *Wars, Guns and Votes: Democracy in Dangerous Places*. New York: HarperCollins.

Collier, Paul, and Anke Hoeffler. 1998. "On Economic Causes of Civil War." *Oxford Economic Papers—New Series* 50(4): 563–573.

Collier, Paul, and Anke Hoeffler. 2002. "On the Incidence of Civil War in Africa." *Journal of Conflict Resolution* 46(1): 13–28.

Collier, Paul, and Anke Hoeffler. 2004. "Greed and Grievance in Civil War." *Oxford Economic Papers—New Series* 56(4): 563–595.

Collier, Paul, Anke Hoeffler, and Nicholas Sambanis. 2005. "The Collier-Hoeffler Model of Civil War Onset and the Case Study Project Research Design." In *Understanding Civil War*. Edited by Paul Collier and Nicolas Sambanis. Washington, DC: The World Bank, pp. 1–33.

Collier, Paul, Anke Hoeffler, and Dominic Rohner. 2009. "Beyond Greed and Grievance: Feasibility and Civil War." *Oxford Economic Papers—New Series* 61(1): 1–27.

Daxecker, Ursula E. 2012. "The Cost of Exposing Cheating: International Election Monitoring, Fraud, and Post-Election Violence in Africa." *Journal of Peace Research* 49(4): 503–516.

Diamond, Larry. 2002. "Thinking About Hybrid Regimes." *Journal of Democracy* 13(2): 21–35.

Electoral Integrity Project. 2014. *The Expert Survey of Perceptions of Electoral Integrity, Release 2 (PE2); Quality of Government Cross-National Dataset.* Available at: www.qog.pol.se/data (accessed December 1, 2013).

Gazibo, Mamoudou. 2006. "The Forging of Institutional Autonomy: A Comparative Study of Electoral Management Commissions in Africa." *Canadian Journal of Political Science* 39(3): 611–633.

Grömping, Max. 2013. "The Retreat of Electoral Authoritarianism?" *Socdem Asia Quarterly* 1(2): 13–15.

Hegre, Håvard, Tanja Ellingsen, Scott Gates, and Nils Petter Gleditsch. 2001. "Towards a Democratic Civil Peace?" *American Political Science Review* 95(1): 33–48.

Kumar, Krishna. 1998. *Post-Conflict Elections, Democratization, and International Assistance.* Boulder, CO: Lynne Rienner.

Levitsky, Steven, and Lucan A. Way. 2010a. *Competitive Authoritarianism: Hybrid Regimes after the Cold War,* New York: Cambridge University Press.

Levitsky, Steven, and Lucan A. Way. 2010b. "Why Democracy Needs a Level Playing Field." *Journal of Democracy* 21(1): 57–68.

López-Pintor, Rafael. 2000. *Electoral Management Bodies as Institutions of Governance,* New York: United Nations Development Programme.

Mansfield, Edward D., and Jack Snyder. 2007. *Electing to Fight: Why Emerging Democracies go to War.* Cambridge, MA: MIT Press.

McAdam, Doug, Sidney Tarrow, and Charles Tilly. 2001. *Dynamics of Contention.* New York: Cambridge University Press.

Mulikita, Njunga. 1999. "Democratization and Conflict Resolution in Africa: The Role of International/Regional Electoral Observers." *Peacekeeping and International Relations* 28(3): 1–4.

Norris, Pippa. 2004. *Electoral Engineering.* New York: Cambridge University Press.

Norris, Pippa. 2008. *Driving Democracy.* New York: Cambridge University Press.

Norris, Pippa. 2014. *Why Electoral Integrity Matters.* New York: Cambridge University Press.

Norris, Pippa, Ferran Martínez i Coma, and Richard W. Frank. 2014. "Assessing the Quality of Elections." *Journal of Democracy* 24(4): 124–135.

Opitz, Christian, Hanne Fjelde, and Kristine Höglund. 2013. 'Including Peace: The Influence of Electoral Management Bodies on Electoral Violence.' *Journal of Eastern African Studies.* 7(4): 713–731.

Quality of Government Dataset. 2013. Version 20Dec13. University of Gothenburg: The Quality of Government Institute. Available at: www.qog.pol.gu.se (accessed December 1, 2013).

Reilly, Benjamin. 2002. "Elections in Post-Conflict Scenarios: Constraints and Dangers." *International Peacekeeping* 9(2): 118–139.

Sisk, Timothy, and Andrew Reynolds, Eds. 1998. *Elections and Conflict Management in Africa.* Washington, DC: US Institute of Peace Press.

Snyder, Jack. 2000. *From Voting to Violence: Democratization and Nationalist Conflict.* New York: Norton.

Struwig, Jare, Benjamin J. Roberts, and Elme Vivier. 2011. "A Vote of Confidence: Election Management and Public Perceptions." *Journal of Public Administration* 46(3): 1122–1138.

Svolik, Milan W. 2012. *The Politics of Authoritarian Rule.* New York: Cambridge University Press.

Tilly, Charles. 1979. *From Mobilization to Revolution.* Reading: Addison-Wesley.

Tilly, Charles, and Sidney Tarrow. 2006. *Contentious Politics.* New York: Oxford University Press.

Ugues, Jr. Antonio. 2014. "Electoral Management in Central America." In *Advancing Electoral Integrity.* Edited by Pippa Norris, Richard W. Frank, and Ferran Martínez i Coma. New York: Oxford University Press.

Wall, Alan, Andrew Ellis, Ayman Ayoub, Carl W. Dundas, Joram Rukambe, and Sara Staino. 2006. *Electoral Management Design: The International IDEA Handbook.* Sweden: International IDEA.

SELECTED BIBLIOGRAPHY

Abbink, Jon. 2000. "Introduction: Rethinking Democratization and Election Observation." In Jon Abbink, and G. Hesseling (Eds.) 2000. *Election Observation and Democratization in Africa*. New York: St. Martin's Press, pp. 1–17.

Acemoglu, Daron, and James A. Robinson. 2005. *Economic Origins of Dictatorship or Democracy*. New York: Cambridge University Press.

Ākhatāra, Muhāmmada Iyāhaiyā. 2001. *Electoral Corruption in Bangladesh*. Burlington, VT: Ashgate.

Albaugh, E.A. "An autocrat's toolkit: Adaptation and manipulation in 'democratic' Cameroon." *Democratization* 18(2): 388–414.

Alesina, Alberto, and Enrico Spolaore. 2003. *The Size of Nations*. Cambridge, MA: MIT Press.

Allen, H.W., and K.W. Allen. 1981. "Voting fraud and data validity." In J.M. Clubb, W.H. Flanigan, and H. Zingale (Eds.) *Analyzing Electoral History*. Beverley Hills, CA: Sage, pp. 153–193.

Alston, L.J., and A.A. Gallo. "Electoral fraud, the rise of Peron and demise of checks and balances in Argentina." *Explorations in Economic History* 47(2): 179–197.

Alvarez, R. Michael, and Thad E. Hall. 2006. "Controlling democracy: The principal agent problems in election administration." *Policy Studies Journal* 34(4): 491–510.

Alvarez, R. Michael, and Thad E. Hall. 2008. "Building secure and transparent elections through standard operating procedures." *Public Administration Review* 68(5): 828–838.

Alvarez, R. Michael, Hall, Thad E., and Llewellyn Morgan. 2008. "Who should run elections in the United States?" *Policy Studies Journal* 36(3): 325–346.

Alvarez, R. Michael, Hall, Thad E., and Llewellyn, Morgan H. 2008. "Are Americans confident their ballots are counted?" *Journal of Politics* 70(3): 754–766.

Alvarez, R. Michael, José Antonio Cheibub, Fernando Limongi, and Adam Przeworski. 1996. "Classifying political regimes." *Studies in International Comparative Development* 31: 3–36.

Alvarez, R. Michael, Lonna Atkeson, and Thad E. Hall (Eds.) 2012. *Confirming Elections: Creating Confidence and Integrity through Election Auditing*. New York: Palgrave Macmillan.

Alvarez, R. Michael, Lonna Rae Atkeson, and Thad Hall and Andrew J. Lotempio. 2002. "Winning, losing and political trust in America." *British Journal of Political Science* 32(2): 335–351.

Alvarez, R. Michael, Lonna Rae Atkeson, and Thad Hall. 2012. *Evaluating Elections: A Handbook of Methods and Standards.* New York: Cambridge University Press.

Alvarez, R. Michael, Thad Hall, and Susan Hyde. 2008 (Eds.) *Election Fraud.* Washington, DC: Brookings Institution Press.

Anderson, Christopher J. 1995. *Blaming the Government: Citizens and the Economy in Five European Democracies.* New York: M.E. Sharpe.

Anderson, Christopher J., and Y.V. Tverdova. 2001. "Winners, losers, and attitudes about government in contemporary democracies." *International Political Science Review* 22: 321–338.

Anderson, Christopher J., and Yuliya V. Tverdova. 2003. "Corruption, political allegiances, and attitudes toward government in contemporary democracies." *American Journal of Political Science* 47(1): 91–109.

Anderson, Christopher J., and Christine A. Guillory. 1997. "Political institutions and satisfaction with democracy." *American Political Science Review* 91(1):66–81.

Anderson, Christopher J., Andre Blais, Shaun Bowler, Todd Donovan, and Ola Listhaug. 2005. *Losers' Consent: Elections and Democratic Legitimacy.* New York: Oxford University Press.

Anderson, Christopher, and Silvia Mendes. 2006. "Learning to lose: Election outcomes, democratic experience and political protest potential." *British Journal of Political Science* 36(1): 91–111.

Anglin, Douglas G. 1995. "International monitoring of the transition to democracy in South Africa, 1992–1994". *African Affairs*, 9(377): 519–543.

Anglin, Douglas G. 1998. "International election monitoring: The African experience." *African Affairs* 97: 471–495.

Ansolabehere, Stephen 2009. "Effects of identification requirements on voting: Evidence from the experiences of voters on election day." *PS: Political Science and Politics* 42: 127–130.

Ansolabehere, Stephen, Eitan Hersh, and Kenneth Shepsle. 2012. "Movers, stayers, and registration: Why age is correlated with registration in the U.S." *Quarterly Journal of Political Science* 7(4): 333–363.

Atkeson, Lonna Rae, and K.L. Saunders. 2007. "The effect of election administration on voter confidence: A local matter?" *PS: Political Science and Politics* 40: 655–660.

Atkeson, Lonna Rae, Bryant, Lisa Ann, and Hall, Thad E. 2010. "A new barrier to participation: Heterogeneous application of voter identification policies." *Electoral Studies* 29(1): 66–73.

Atwood, Richard. 2012. "How the EU can support peaceful post-election transitions of power: Lessons from Africa." Directorate-General for External Policies of the Union, Directorate B Policy Department, European Parliament, Brussels.

Baker, B. 2002. "When to call black white: Zimbabwe's electoral reports." *Third World Quarterly* 23 (6): 1145–1158.

Balule, Badala Tachilisa. 2008. "Election management bodies in the SADC region: An appraisal of the independence of Botswana's independent electoral commission." *South African Journal on Human Rights* 24: 104–122.

Banducci, Susan A., and Jeffrey A. Karp. 1999. "Perceptions of fairness and support for Proportional Representation." *Political Behavior* 21(3): 217–238.

Bardall, Gabrielle. 2010. "Election violence monitoring and the use of new communication technologies." *Democracy and Society* 7(2): 1–8.

Bardal, Gabrielle. 2011. *Breaking the Mold: Understanding Gender and Electoral Violence*. Washington, DC: IFES.

Barkan, Joel D. 1993. "Kenya: Lessons from a flawed election." *Journal of Democracy* 4(3): 85–99.

Basedau, Matthais, Gero Erdman, and Andreas Mehler. 2007. *Votes, Money and Violence: Political Parties in Sub-Saharan Africa*. Sweden: Nordiska Afrikainstitutet. Available at www.urn.kb.se/resolve?urn=urn:nbn:se:nai:diva-492 (accessed December 15, 2013).

Beaulieu, Emily, and Susan D. Hyde. 2009. "In the shadow of democracy promotion: Strategic manipulation, international observers, and election boycotts." *Comparative Political Studies* 42 (3): 392–415.

Beaulieu, Emily. 2013. "Political parties and perceptions of election fraud in the U.S." Paper presented at the Workshop on Challenges of Electoral Integrity, Harvard University, June 2–3.

Beber, Bernd and Alexandra Scacco. 2012. "What the numbers say: A digit-based test for election fraud." *Political Analysis* 20(2): 211–234.

Bekoe, Dorina. Ed. 2012. *Voting in Fear: Electoral Violence in Sub-Saharan Africa*. United States Institute of Peace, Washington, DC.

Benson, J.F. 2009. "Voter fraud or voter defrauded? Highlighting an inconsistent consideration of election fraud." *Harvard Civil Rights – Civil Liberties Law Review* 44 (1): 1–42.

Berinsky, Adam J. 2004. "The perverse consequences of electoral reform in the United States." *American Politics Research* 33(4): 471–491.

Bermeo, Nancy. "Interests, inequality, and illusion in the choice for fair elections." *Comparative Political Studies* 43(8–9): 1119–1147.

Bhasin, Tavishi and Jennifer Gandhi. 2013. "State repression in authoritarian elections." *Electoral Studies* (forthcoming).

Birch, Sarah. 2007. "Electoral systems and electoral misconduct." *Comparative Political Studies* 40(12): 1533–1556.

Birch, Sarah. 2008. "Electoral institutions and popular confidence in electoral processes: A cross-national analysis." *Electoral Studies* 27(2): 305–320.

Birch, Sarah. 2010. "Perceptions of electoral fairness and voter turnout." *Comparative Political Studies* 43(12): 1601–1622.

Birch, Sarah. 2011. *Electoral Malpractice*. Oxford: Oxford University Press.

Bjornlund, Eric C. 2004. *Beyond Free and Fair: Monitoring Elections and Building Democracy*. Washington, DC: Woodrow Wilson Center Press.

Bjornskov, Christian. 2010. "How does social trust lead to better governance? An attempt to separate electoral and bureaucratic mechanisms." *Public Choice* 144(1–2): 323–346.

Bland, Gary, Andrew Green, and Toby Moore. 2012. "Measuring the quality of election administration." *Democratization* 20(2): 1–20.

Blaydes, Lisa. 2011. *Elections and Distributive Politics in Mubarak's Egypt*. New York: Cambridge University Press.

Boatright, Robert G. (Ed.) 2011. *Campaign Finance: The Problems and Consequences of Reform*. New York: IDebate Press.

Boda, M.D. 2005. "Reconsidering the 'free and fair' question." *Representation* 41(3): 155–160.

Bogaards, Matthijs, Basedau, Matthias, and Hartmann, Christof. 2010. "Ethnic party bans in Africa: An introduction." *Democratization* 17(4): 599–617.

Bogaards, Matthijs. 2013. "Reexamining African elections." *Journal of Democracy* 24(4): 151–160.

Boix, Carles, Michael K. Miller, and Sebastian Rosato. "A complete dataset of political regimes, 1800–2007." *Comparative Political Studies* (forthcoming).

Bormann, Nils-Christian, and Matt Golder. 2013. "Democratic electoral systems around the world, 1946–2011." *Electoral Studies* 32: 360–369.

Boniface, Makulilo Alexander. 2011. "'Watching the watcher': An evaluation of local election observers in Tanzania." *Journal of Modern African Studies* 49(2): 241–262.

Boone, Catherine. 2011. "Politically allocated land rights and the geography of electoral violence: The case of Kenya in the 1990s." *Comparative Political Studies* 44(10): 1311–1342.

Bowler, Shaun, and Donovan, Todd. 2011. "The limited effects of election reforms on efficacy and engagement." *Australian Journal of Political Science* 47(1): 55–70.

Brancati, Dawn, and Snyder, Jack L. 2011. "Rushing to the polls: The causes of premature postconflict elections." *Journal of Conflict Resolution* 55(3): 469–492.

Brancati, Dawn. and Jack Snyder. 2013. "Time to kill: The impact of election timing on post-conflict stability." *Journal of Conflict Resolution* (forthcoming).

Bratton, Michael, and Nicholas van de Walle. 1997. *Democratic Experiments in Africa: Regime Transitions in Comparative Perspective.* New York: Cambridge University Press.

Bratton, Michael, Robert Mattes, and E. Gyimah-Boadi. 2005. *Public Opinion, Democracy and Market Reform in Africa.* Cambridge: Cambridge University Press.

Bratton, Michael. 2008. "Vote buying and violence in Nigerian election campaigns." *Electoral Studies* 27(4): 621–632.

Bratton, Michael (Ed.) 2013. *Voting and Democratic citizenship in Africa.* Boulder, CO: Lynne Rienner Publishers.

Breunig, Christian, and Goerres, Achim. 2011. "Searching for electoral irregularities in an established democracy: Applying Benford's Law tests to Bundestag elections in Unified Germany." *Electoral Studies* 30(3): 534–545.

Brusco, V., Nazareno, M., and Stokes, S.C. 2004. "Vote buying in Argentina." *Latin American Research Review*, 39(2): 66–88.

Brown, Nathan J. (Ed.) 2011. *The Dynamics of Democratization: Dictatorship, Development and Diffusion.* Baltimore, MD: The Johns Hopkins University Press.

Brownlee, Jason, 2011. "Executive elections in the Arab world: When and how do they matter?" *Comparative Political Studies* 44(7): 807–828.

Brownlee, Jason. 2007. *Authoritarianism in an Age of Democratization.* New York: Cambridge University Press.

Brownlee, Jason. 2008. "Bound to rule: Party institutions and regime trajectories in Malaysia and the Philippines." *Journal of East Asian Studies* 8(1): 89–118.

Brownlee, Jason. 2009. "Portents of pluralism: How hybrid regimes affect democratic transitions." *American Journal of Political Science* 53(3): 515–532.

Buckley, Sam. 2011. *Banana Republic UK? Vote Rigging, Fraud andEerror in British Elections since 2001.* Open Rights Group.

Bunce, Valerie J., and Sharon L. Wolchik. 2006. "Favorable conditions and electoral revolutions." *Journal of Democracy* 17: 5–18.

Bunce, Valerie J., and Sharon L. Wolchik. 2011. *Defeating Authoritarian Leaders in Post-Communist Countries.* New York: Cambridge University Press.

Bunce, Valerie J., and Sharon L. Wolchik. 2010. "Defeating dictators: Electoral change and stability in competitive authoritarian regimes." *World Politics* 62(1): 43–86.

Butler, David and Bruce E. Cain. 1992. *Congressional Redistricting: Comparative and Theoretical Perspectives.* New York: Macmillan.

Calimbahin, Cleo. 2011. "Exceeding (low) expectations: Autonomy, bureaucratic integrity, and capacity in the 2010 elections." *Philippine Political Science Journal* 32(55): 103–126.

Callahan, W.A. 2000. *Poll Watching, Elections and Civil Society in South-East Asia.* Burlington, VT: Ashgate.

Callahan, W.A. 2005. "The discourse of vote buying and political reform in Thailand." *Pacific Affairs* 78(1): 95–113.

Calingaert, D. 2006. "Election rigging and how to fight it." *Journal of Democracy* 17(3): 138–151.

Campbell, Tracy. 2006. *Deliver the Vote: A History of Election Fraud, an American Political Tradition 1742–2004.* New York: Basic Books.

Carey, Sabine. 2007. "Violent dissent and rebellion in Africa." *Journal of Peace Research* 44(1): 1–39.

Carman, Christopher, Mitchell, James, and Johns, Robert. 2008. "The unfortunate natural experiment in ballot design: The Scottish Parliamentary elections of 2007." *Electoral Studies* 27(3): 442–459.

Carothers, Thomas. 1997. "The observers observed." *Journal of Democracy* 8(3): 17–31.

Carothers, Thomas. 2002. "The end of the transition paradigm." *Journal of Democracy* 13: 5–21.

Carreras, Miguel, and Yasmin Irepoglu. 2013. "Electoral malpractices, political efficacy, and turnout in Latin America." *Electoral Studies* (forthcoming)

Carroll, David J., and Avery Davis-Roberts. "The Carter Center and election observation: An obligations-based approach for assessing elections." *Election Law Journal* 12(1): 87–93.

Casas-Zamora, Kevin. 2004. *Paying for Democracy.* Essex: ECPR Press.

Case, William. 2011. "Electoral authoritarianism and backlash: Hardening Malaysia, oscillating Thailand." *International Political Science Review* 32(4): 438–457.

Castaneda, Gonzalo, and I. Ibarra. "Detection of fraud with agent-based models: The 2006 Mexican election." *Perfiles Latinoamericanos* 18(36): 43–69.

Castaneda, Gonzalo. 2011. "Benford's law and its applicability in the forensic analysis of electoral results." *Politica Y Gobierno* 18(2): 297–329.

Cederman, Lars-Erik, Kristian S. Gleditsch, and Simon Hug. 2013. "Elections and civil war." *Comparative Political Studies* 46(3): 387–417.

Celestino, Mauricio Rivera, and Gleditsch, Kristian Skrede. 2013. "Fresh carnations or all thorn, no rose? Nonviolent campaigns and transitions in autocracies." *Journal of Peace Research* 50 (3): 385–400.

Chaisty, Paul, and Steven Whitefield. 2013. "Forward to democracy or back to authoritarianism? The attitudinal bases of mass support for the Russian election protests of 2011–2012." *Post-Soviet Affairs* 29(5): 387–403.

Chand, Vikram. 1997. "Democratisation from the outside in: NGO and international efforts to promote open elections." *Third World Quarterly* 18(3): 543–561.

Chaturvedi, Ashish. 2005. "Rigged elections with violence." *Public Choice* 125(1/2): 189–202.

Cheibub, Jose Antonio, Jennifer Gandhi, and James Raymond Vreeland. 2010. "Democracy and dictatorship revisited." *Public Choice* 143(1–2): 67–101.

Cingranelli, David L., David L. Richards, and K. Chad Clay. 2013. *The Cingranelli-Richards (CIRI) Human Rights Dataset*. Available at www.humanrightsdata.org (accessed November 28, 2013).

Collier Paul, Anke Hoeffler, and Mans Soderbom. 2008. "Post-conflict risks." *Journal of Peace Research* 45(4): 461–478.

Collier, Paul, and Anke Hoeffler. 1998. "On economic causes of civil war." Oxford Economic Papers – New Series 50(4): 563–573.

Collier, Paul, and Anke Hoeffler. 2002. "On the incidence of civil war in Africa." *Journal of Conflict Resolution* 46(1): 13–28.

Collier, Paul, and Anke Hoeffler. 2004. "Greed and grievance in civil war." *Oxford Economic Papers – New Series* 56(4): 563–595.

Collier, Paul, and Pedro Vicente. 2011. "Violence, bribery and fraud: The political economy of elections in Sub-Saharan Africa." *Public Choice*. 153(1): 1–31.

Collier, Paul, Anke Hoeffler, and Dominic Rohner. 2009. "Beyond greed and grievance: Feasibility and civil war." *Oxford Economic Papers – New Series* 61(1): 1–27.

Collier, Paul, Anke Hoeffler, and Mans Soderbom. 2008. "Post-conflict risks." *Journal of Peace Research* 45(4): 461–478.

Collier, Paul, Anke Hoeffler, and Nicholas Sambanis. 2005. "The Collier–Hoeffler model of civil war onset and the case study project research design." In Paul Collier and Nicolas Sambanis (Eds.) *Understanding Civil War*. Washington, DC: The World Bank, pp. 1–33.

Collier, Paul. 2009. *Wars, Guns and Votes: Democracy in Dangerous Places*. New York: HarperCollins.

Coppedge, Michael. 2012. *Democratization and Research Methods*. New York: Cambridge University Press.

Craig, Stephen C., Michael D. Martinez, and Jason Gainous 2006. "Winners, losers, and election context: Voter responses to the 2000 presidential election." *Political Research Quarterly* 59(4): 579–592.

Cruz, R.C. 2001. "Voting for the unexpected: Electoral fraud and political struggle in Costa Rica (1901–1948)." *Journal of Latin American Studies* 33: 893–894.

Curtice, John. 2013. "Politicians, voters and democracy: The 2011 UK referendum on the Alternative Vote." *Electoral Studies* 32(2): 215–223.

Dahl, Robert A. 1971. *Polyarchy: Participation and Opposition*. New Haven: Yale University Press.

D'Anieri, Paul. Ed. 2010. *Orange Revolution and Aftermath:Mobilization, Apathy, and the State in Ukraine*. Baltimore, MD: Johns Hopkins University Press.

Davenport, Christian and Molly Inman. 2012. "The state of state repression research since the 1990s." *Terrorism and Political Violence* 24(4): 619–634.

Davenport, Christian. 1997. "From ballots to bullets: An empirical assessment of how national elections influence state uses of political repression." *Electoral Studies* 6(4): 517–540.

Davenport, Christian. 2007. "State repression and political order." *Annual Review of Political Science* 10: 1–23.

Davenport, Christian. 2007. *State Repression and the Domestic Democratic Peace*. New York: Cambridge University Press.

Davis-Roberts, Avery and David J. Carroll. 2010. "Using international law to assess elections." *Democratization*. 17(3): 416–441.

Darnolf, Staffan. 2011. *Assessing Electoral Fraud in New Democracies: A New Strategic Approach*. Washington, DC. International Foundation for Electoral Systems: White Paper Series Electoral Fraud.

Daxecker, Ursula E. 2012. "The cost of exposing cheating: International election monitoring, fraud, and post-election violence in Africa." *Journal of Peace Research* 49(4): 503–516.

Daxecker, Ursula E. 2013. "All quiet on election day? International election observers and incentives for violent manipulation in African elections." Working Paper. University of Amsterdam.

Daxecker, Ursula E., and Gerald Schneider. 2014. "Electoral monitoring." In Pippa Norris, Richard W. Frank and Ferran Martínez i Coma (Eds.) *Advancing Electoral Integrity*. New York: Oxford University Press, pp. 73–93.

De Gaay Fortman, B. 1999. "Elections and civil strife: Some implications for international election observation." In Jon Abbink and Gerti Hesseling (Eds.) *Election Observation and Democratization in Africa*. Basingstoke: Macmillan, pp. 76–99.

Debrah, Emmanuel. 2011. "Measuring governance institutions' success in Ghana: The case of the Electoral Commission, 1993–2008." *African Studies* 70(1): 25–45.

Deckert, Joseph, Mikhail Myagkov, and Peter C. Ordeshook. 2011. "Benford's law and the detection of election fraud." *Political Analysis* 19: 245–268.

Denver, David, R. Johns, and C. Carman. 2009. "Rejected ballot papers in the 2007 Scottish Parliament Election: The voters' perspective." *British Politics* 4(1): 3–21.

Dercon, Stefan, and Gutierrez-Romero, Roxana. 2012. "Triggers and characteristics of the 2007 Kenyan electoral violence." *World Development* 40(4): 731–744.

Diamond, Larry, and Leonardo Morlino. 2004. "Quality of democracy: An overview." *Journal of Democracy* 15(4): 20–31.

Diamond, Larry. 2002. "Thinking about hybrid regimes." *Journal of Democracy* 13(2): 21–35.

Doherty, David, and Jennifer Wolak. 2012. "When do the ends justify the means? Evaluating procedural fairness." *Political Behavior* 34(2): 301–323.

Donno, Daniella. 2010. "Who is punished? Regional intergovernmental organizations and the enforcement of democratic norms." *International Organization* 64(4): 593–625.

Donno, Daniela. 2013. "Elections and democratization in authoritarian regimes." *American Journal of Political Science* 57(3): 703–716.

Donno, Daniella. 2013. *Defending Democratic Norms*. New York: Oxford University Press.

Donno, Daniella, and Alberto Simpser. 2012. "Can international election monitoring harm governance?" *Journal of Politics* 74(2): 501–513.

Donno, Daniella, and Nasos Roussias. 2012. "Does cheating pay? The effect of electoral misconduct on party systems." *Comparative Political Studies*. 45 (5):575–605.

Donsanto, C.C. 2008. "Corruption in the electoral process under U.S. federal law." In R. Michael Alvarez, Thad E. Hall, and Susan Hyde (Eds.) *Election Fraud: Detecting and Deterring Electoral Manipulation*. Washington, DC: Brookings Institute, pp. 21–36.

Downs, Anthony. 1957. *An Economic Theory of Democracy*. New York: Harper & Row.

Doyle, Michael W., and Sambanis, Nicolas. 2000. "International peace-building: A theoretical and quantitative analysis." *American Political Science Review* 94(4): 779–801.

Drometer, Marcus, and Rincke Johannes. 2009. "The impact of ballot access restrictions on electoral competition: Evidence from a natural experiment." *Public Choice* 138(3–4): 461–474.

Dunning, Thad. 2011. "Fighting and voting: Violent conflict and electoral politics." *Journal of Conflict Resolution* 55(3): 327–339.

Dunning, Thad. *2012. Natural Experiments in the Social Sciences*. New York: Cambridge University Press.

Eisenstadt, T.A. 2004. "Catching the state off guard: Electoral courts, campaign finance, and Mexico's separation of state and ruling party." *Party Politics* 10(6): 723–745.

Eisenstadt, T.A. 2004. *Courting Democracy in Mexico: Party Strategies and Electoral Institutions.* New York: Cambridge University Press.

Ekman, Joakim. 2009. "Political participation and regime stability: A framework for analyzing hybrid regimes." *International Political Science Review* 30(1): 7–31.

Elklit, Jørgen, and Palle Svensson. 1997. "What makes elections free and fair?" *Journal of Democracy* 8(3): 32–46.

Elklit, Jørgen, and Andrew Reynolds. 2002. "The impact of election administration on the legitimacy of emerging democracies: A new comparative politics research agenda." *Commonwealth and Comparative Politics* 40(2): 86–119.

Elklit, Jørgen, and Andrew Reynolds. 2005 "A framework for the systematic study of election quality." *Democratization* 12(2): 147–162.

Elklit, Jørgen, and Svend-Erik Skaaning. 2011. *Coding Manual: Assessing Election and Election Management Quality.* Available at www.democracy-assessment.dk/start/page.asp?page=22 (accessed February 5, 2014).

Elklit, Jørgen. 1999. "Electoral institutional change and democratization: You can lead a horse to water, but you can't make it drink." *Democratization* 6(4): 28–51.

Estevez, Federico, Eric Magar, and Guillermo Rosas. 2008. "Partisanship in non-partisan electoral agencies and democratic compliance: Evidence from Mexico's Federal Electoral Institute." *Electoral Studies* 27(2): 257–271.

Evrensel, Astrid. (Ed.) 2010. *Voter registration in Africa: A comparative analysis.* Johannesburg: EISA.

European Commission. 2007. *Compendium of International Standards for Elections.* 2nd ed. Brussels: European Commission, Brussels: EC/NEEDS.

Ewing, Keith. 2009. *The Funding of Political Parties in Britain.* Cambridge: Cambridge University Press.

Fawn, Rick. 2006. "Battle over the box: International election observation missions, political competition and retrenchment in the post-Soviet space." *International Affairs* 82(6): 1133–1153.

Fell, Dafydd. 2005. *Party Politics in Taiwan: Party Change and the Democratic Evolution of Taiwan, 1991–2004.* London: Routledge.

Fife, Brian L. 2010. *Reforming the Electoral Process in America.* Santa Barbara, CA: Praeger.

Finnemore, Martha, and Kathryn Sikkink. 1998. "International norm dynamics and political change." *International Organization* 52(3): 887–917.

Fisher, Jeff. 2002. *Electoral Conflict and Violence.* Washington, DC: IFES

Fishkin, Joseph. 2011. "Equal citizenship and the individual right to vote." *Indiana Law Journal* 86(4): 1289–1360.

Flores, Thomas Edward and Irfan Nooruddin. 2012. "The effect of elections on post-conflict peace and reconstruction." *Journal of Politics* 74(2): 558–570.

Forest, Benjamin. 2012. "Electoral redistricting and minority political representation in Canada and the United States." *Canadian Geographer* 56(3): 318–338.

Foweraker, Joseph and R. Krznaric. 2002. "The uneven performance of third wave democracies: Electoral politics and the imperfect rule of law in Latin America." *Latin American Politics and Society* 44(3): 29–60.

Franklin, Mark. 2004. *Voter Turnout and the Dynamics of Electoral Competition in Established Democracies since 1945.* New York: Cambridge University Press.

Franzese, R.J. 2002. "Electoral and partisan cycles in economic policies and outcomes." *Annual Review of Political Science* 5: 369–421.

Frazer, Jendayi E. and E. Gyimah-Boadi. (Eds.) 2011. *Preventing Electoral Violence in Africa.* Carnegie Mellon University.

Freedman, Eric. 2009. "When a democratic revolution isn't democratic or revolutionary?" *Journalism* 10(6): 843–861.

Fukumoto, Kentaro, and Yusaku Horiuchi. 2011. "Making outsiders' votes count: Detecting electoral fraud through a natural experiment." *American Political Science Review* 105(3): 586–603.

Fund, John H. 2004. *Stealing Elections: How Voter Fraud Threatens Our Democracy.* San Francisco, CA: Encounter Books.

Fung, Archon. 2011. "Popular election monitoring." In Heather Gerken, Guy-Uriel E. Charles, and Michael S. Kang (Eds.) *Race, Reform and Regulation of the Electoral Process: Recurring Puzzles in American Democracy.* New York: Cambridge University Press.

Gandhi, Jennifer, and Ellen Lust-Okar. 2009. "Elections under authoritarianism." *Annual Review of Political Science* 12: 403–22.

Gandhi, Jennifer. 2008. *Political Institutions under Dictatorship.* New York: Cambridge University Press.

Geddes, Barbara. 1999. "What do we know about democratization after twenty years?" *Annual Review of Political Science* 2: 115–144.

Geisler, G. 1993. "Fair—what has fairness got to do with it? Vagaries of election observations and democratic standards." *Journal of Modern African Studies* 31(4): 613–637.

Gelman, Andrew, and Gary King. 1994. "Enhancing democracy through legislative redistricting." *American Political Science Review* 88(3): 541–559.

Geys, Benny. 2006. "Explaining voter turnout: A review of aggregate-level research." *Electoral Studies* 25(4): 637–663.

Gilbert, Leah, and Mohseni Payam. 2011. "Beyond authoritarianism: The conceptualization of hybrid regimes." *Studies in Comparative International Development* 46(3): 270–297.

Gingerich, D.W. 2009. "Ballot structure, political corruption, and the performance of proportional representation." *Journal of Theoretical Politics* 21(4): 509–441.

Global Commission on Elections, Democracy and Security. 2012. *Deepening Democracy: A Strategy for improving the Integrity of Elections Worldwide.* Sweden: IDEA.

Goodwin-Gill, Guy S. 2006. *Free and Fair Elections.* 2nd ed. Geneva: Inter-parliamentary Union.

Gosnell, Herbert F. 1968. *Machine Politics: Chicago Model,* 2nd ed. Chicago and London: University of Chicago Press.

Greenberg, Ari and Robert Mattes. 2013. "Does the quality of elections affect the consolidation of democracy?" In *Voting and Democratic Citizenship in Africa,* Michael Bratton (Ed.) Boulder, CO: Lynne Rienner Publishers.

Greene, Kenneth F. 2007. *Why Dominant Parties Lose: Mexico's Democratization in Comparative Perspective.* New York: Cambridge University Press.

Grömping, Max. 2012. "Many eyes of any kind? Comparing traditional and crowd-sourced monitoring and their contribution to democracy." Paper presented at the Second International Conference on International Relations and Development, July 2012 in Thailand.

Gronke, Paul, and Daniel Krantz Toffey. 2008. "The psychological and institutional determinants of early voting." *Journal of Social Issues* 64(3): 503–524.

Gronke, Paul, Eva Galanes-Rosenbaum, and Peter Miller. 2007. "Early voting and turnout." *PS: Political Science and Politics* 40(4): 639–645.

Gronke, Paul, Eva Galanes-Rosenbaum, Peter A. Miller, and Daniel Toffey. 2008. "Convenience voting." *Annual Review of Political Science* 11:437–55.

Gronke, Paul. 2013. "Are we confident in voter confidence? Conceptual and methodological challenges in survey measures of electoral integrity." Paper presented at the Workshop on Challenges of Electoral Integrity, Harvard University, June 2–3.

Gunlicks, Arthur B. (Ed.) 1993. *Campaign and Party Finance in North America and Western Europe.* Boulder: Westview Press.

Gustafson, Marc. 2010. "Elections and the probability of violence in Sudan." *Harvard International Law Journal Online* 51: 47–62.

Hadenius, Axel, and Jan Teorell. 2007. "Pathways from authoritarianism." *Journal of Democracy* 18(1): 143–156.

Hafner Burton, Emilie M., Susan D. Hyde, and Ryan S. Jablonski. 2013. "When do governments resort to election violence?" *British Journal of Political Science* 44(1): 149–179.

Hale, Henry E. 2011. "Formal constitutions in informal politics: Institutions and democratization in post-Soviet Eurasia." *World Politics* 63(4): 581–617.

Hall, Thad E., J. Quin Monson, and Kelly D. Patterson. 2009. "The human dimension of elections: How poll workers shape public confidence in elections." *Political Research Quarterly* 62(3):507–522.

Hall, Thad. 2011. "Voter opinions about election reform: Do they support making voting more convenient?" *Election Law Journal* 10(2): 73–87.

van Ham, Carolien. 2012. *Beyond Electoralism? Electoral fraud in third wave regimes 1974–2009.* PhD Thesis. Florence: European University Institute.

van Ham, Carolien. 2014. "Getting elections right? Measuring electoral integrity." *Democratization* (forthcoming).

Hamm, Keith E., and Hogan Robert E. 2008. "Campaign finance laws and decisions in state legislative candidacy elections." *Political Research Quarterly* 61(3): 458–467.

Handley, Lisa, and Bernie Grofman. 2008. *Redistricting in Comparative Perspective.* New York: Oxford University Press.

Hanham, H.J. 1959. *Elections and Party Management: Politics in the Time of Disraeli and Gladstone.* London: Longmans.

Hanmer, Michael J. 2009. *Discount Voting: Voter Registration Reforms and Their Effects.* New York: Cambridge University Press.

Hanmer, Michael J., and Michael W. Traugott. 2004. "The impact of Vote-By-Mail on voter behavior." *American Politics Research,* 32: 375–405.

Hasen, Richard L. 2012. *The Voting Wars: From Florida 2000 to the Next Election Meltdown.* New Haven, CT: Yale University Press.

Hasseling, Gerti, and Jon Abbink. Eds. 2000. *Election Observation and Democratization in Africa.* New York: Palgrave Macmillan

Hausmann, Ricardo, and Rigobon Roberto. 2011. "In search of the black swan: Analysis of the statistical evidence of electoral fraud in Venezuela." *Statistical Science* 26(4): 543–563.

Heidenheimer, Arnold J., Michael Johnston, and V.T. Levine. (Eds.) 1990. *Political Corruption: A Handbook,* New Brunswick, NJ: Transaction Publishers.

Heinzelman, Jessica, and Patrick Meier. 2012. "Crowdsourcing for human rights monitoring: Challenges and opportunities for verification." In *Human Rights and Information Communication Technologies: Trends and Consequences of Use,* John Lannon (Ed.). IGI Global, pp. 123–138.

Hermet, Guy, Richard Rose, and Alain Rouquié. Eds. 1978. *Elections without Choice.* London: Macmillan.

Herrnson, Paul S., Richard G. Niemi, Michael J. Hanmer, Benjamin B. Bederson, Frederick G. Conrad, and Michael W. Traugott. 2008. *Voting Technology: The Not-So-Simple Act of Casting a Ballot.* Washington: Brookings.

Herrnson, Paul, Richard G. Niemi, and Michael J. Hanmer, 2012. "The impact of ballot type on voter errors." *American Journal of Political Science* 56: 716–730.

Herron, Erik S. 2009. *Elections and Democracy after Communism?* New York: Palgrave Macmillan.

Herron, Erik S. 2010. "The effect of passive observation methods on Azerbaijan's 2008 presidential election and 2009 referendum." *Electoral Studies* 29(3): 417–424.

Hershey, Marjorie Randon. 2009. "What we know about voter ID Laws, registration, and turnout." *PS: Political Science and Politics*, 42: 87–91.

Hillman, Ben. 2013. "Public administration reform in post-conflict societies: Lessons from Aceh, Indonesia." *Public Administration and Development* 33(1): 1–14

Hoglund, Kristine, and Jarstad, Anna K. 2011. "Toward electoral security: Experiences from KwaZulu-Natal." *Africa Spectrum* 46(1): 33–59.

Hoglünd, Kristine. 2009. "Electoral violence in conflict-ridden societies: Concepts, causes, and consequences." *Terrorism and Political Violence* 21(3): 412–427.

Howard, Marc Morjé, and Philip G. Roessler, 2006. "Liberalizing electoral outcomes in competitive authoritarian regimes." *American Journal of Political Science* 50(2): 365–81.

Howell, Patrick, and Florian Justwan. 2013. "Nail-biters and no-contests: The effect of electoral margins on satisfaction with democracy in winners and losers." *Electoral Studies* 32(2): 334–343.

Hubbard, Glenn, and Tim Kane. 2013. "In defense of Citizens United: Why campaign finance reform threatens American democracy." *Foreign Affairs* 92(4): 126–133.

Hyde, Susan. D. 2007. "Experimenting in democracy promotion: International observers and the 2004 presidential elections in Indonesia." *Perspectives on Politics* 8(2): 511–527.

Hyde, Susan. D. 2007. "The observer effect in international politics: Evidence from a natural experiment." *World Politics* 60(1): 37–63.

Hyde, Susan. D. 2011. *The Pseudo-Democrat's Dilemma.* Ithaca, NY: Cornell University Press.

Hyde, Susan. D., and Nikolay Marinov. 2012. "Which elections can be lost?" *Political Analysis* 20(2): 191–210.

Ichino, Nahomi, and Schuendeln, Matthias. 2012. "Deterring or displacing electoral irregularities? Spillover effects of observers in a randomized field experiment in Ghana." *Journal of Politics* 74(1): 292–307.

International IDEA. 2002. *International Electoral Standards: Guidelines for Reviewing the Legal Framework for Elections.* Stockholm: International IDEA.

International IDEA. 2004. *Handbook on the Funding of Political Parties and Election Campaigns.* Stockholm: International IDEA.

International IDEA. 2006. *Electoral Management Design: The International IDEA Handbook.* Stockholm: International IDEA.

International IDEA. 2010. *Towards a Global Framework for Managing and Mitigating Election-Related Conflict and Violence.* Stockholm: International IDEA.

Jacobs, Kristof, and Leyenaar, Monique. 2011. "A conceptual framework for major, minor, and technical electoral reform." *West European Politics* 34(3): 495–513.

James, Toby S. 2010. "Electoral administration and voter turnout: Towards an international public policy continuum." *Representation*, 45(4): 369–389.

James, Toby S. 2010. "Electoral modernisation or elite statecraft? Electoral administration in the U.K. 1997–2007." *British Politics* 5(2): 179–201.

James, Toby S. 2012. *Elite Statecraft and Election Administration: Bending the Rules of the Game.* Basingstoke: Palgrave.

Jockers, Heinz, Kohnert, Dirk, and Nugent, Paul. 2010. "The successful Ghana election of 2008: a convenient myth?" *Journal of Modern African Studies* 48(1): 95–115.

Jones, Douglas W., and Barbara Simons. 2012. *Broken Ballots: Will your Vote Count?* Chicago: University of Chicago Press.

Kairys, David. 2013. "The contradictory messages of Rehnquist-Roberts era speech law: Liberty and justice for some." *University of Illinois Law Review* 1: 195–220.

Kalandadze, Katya, and Orenstein, Mitchell A. 2009. "Electoral protests and democratization beyond the color revolutions." *Comparative Political Studies* 42(11): 1403–1425.

Kang, M.S. 2005. "The hydraulics and politics of party regulation." *Iowa Law Review* 91(1): 131–187.

Katz, Richard S., 2005. "Democratic principles and judging 'free and fair.'" *Representation* 41(3):161–179.

Keefer, Philip, and R. Vlaicu. 2008. "Democracy, credibility, and clientelism." *Journal of Law Economics and Organization* 24(2): 371–406.

Kelley, Judith. 2008. "Assessing the complex evolution of norms: The rise of international election monitoring." *International Organization* 62(2): 221–255.

Kelley, Judith. 2009. "D-Minus Elections: The politics and norms of international election observation." *International Organization* 63(4): 765–787.

Kelley, Judith. 2009. "The more the merrier? The effects of having multiple international election monitoring organizations." *Perspectives on Politics* 7: 59–64.

Kelley, Judith. 2010. "Election observers and their biases." *Journal of Democracy* 21: 158–172.

Kelley, Judith. 2010. *Quality of Elections Data Codebook.* Available at www.sites.duke.edu/kelley/data/ (accessed December 1, 2013).

Kelley, Judith. 2011. "Do international election monitors increase or decrease opposition boycotts?" *Comparative Political Studies* 44(11): 1527–1556.

Kelley, Judith. 2012. "The international influences on elections in transition states." *Annual Review of Political Science* 15: 203–220.

Kelley, Judith. 2012. *Monitoring Democracy: When International Election Observation Works and Why it Often Fails.* Princeton, NJ: Princeton University Press.

Kerr, Nicholas N. 2014. "EMB performance and African perceptions of electoral integrity." In *Advancing Electoral Integrity.* Pippa Norris, Richard W. Frank, and Ferran Martínez i Coma (Eds.) New York: Oxford University Press, pp. 189–210.

Keyssar, Alexander. 2009. *The Right to Vote: The Contested History of Democracy in the United States.* New York: Basic Books. Revised edition.

Kitschelt, Herbert and Steven L. Wilkinson (Eds.) 2007. *Patrons, Clients and Policies.* NY: Cambridge University Press.

Klein, A. "The puzzle of ineffective election campaigning in Japan." *Japanese Journal of Political Science* 12: 57–74.

Koehler, Kevin. 2008. "Authoritarian elections in Egypt: Formal institutions and informal mechanisms of rule." *Democratization* 15(5): 974–990.

Kumar, Krishna. 1998. *Post-conflict Elections, Democratization, and International Assistance.* Boulder, CO: Lynne Reinner.

Kuntz, Philipp and Thompson, Mark R. 2009. "More than just the final straw stolen elections as revolutionary triggers." *Comparative Politics* 41(3): 253–272.

Landman, Todd, and Edzia Carvalho. 2010. *Measuring Human Rights.* London: Routledge.

Lanning, K. 2008. "Democracy, voting, and disenfranchisement in the United States: A social psychological perspective." *Journal of Social Issues* 64(3): 431–446.

Lasthuizen, Karin, Huberts, Leo, and Heres, Leonie. 2011. "How to measure integrity violations." *Public Management Review* 13(3): 383–408.

Laycock, Samantha, Alan Renwick, Daniel Stevens, and Jack Vowles. 2013. "The UK's electoral reform referendum of May 2011." *Electoral Studies* 32(2): 211–214.

Lean, S.F. 2007. "Democracy assistance to domestic election monitoring organizations: Conditions for success." *Democratization* 14(2): 289–312.

Leduc, Lawrence, Richard Niemi, and Pippa Norris. (Eds.) 2010. *Comparing Democracies 3: Elections and Voting in the 21st Century.* London: Sage.

Lehoucq, Fabrice Edouard, and Iván Molina Jiménez. 2002. *Stuffing the Ballot Box: Fraud, Electoral Reform, and Democratization in Costa Rica.* New York: Cambridge University Press.

Lehoucq, Fabrice Edouard. 2002. "Can parties police themselves? Electoral governance and democratization." *International Political Science Review* 23(1): 29–46.

Lehoucq, Fabrice Edouard. 2003. "Electoral fraud: Causes, types, and consequences." *Annual Review of Political Science* 6: 233–256.

Lessig, Lawrence. 2011. *Republic, Lost.* New York: Twelve.

Levitsky, Steven, and Way, Lucan A. 2010. "Why democracy needs a level playing field." *Journal of Democracy* 21(1): 57–68.

Levitsky, Steven, and Lucan Way. 2010. *Competitive Authoritarianism: Hybrid Regimes after the Cold War,* New York: Cambridge University Press.

Leyenaar, Monique, and Hazan, Reuven Y. 2011. "Reconceptualising electoral reform." *West European Politics* 34(3): 437–455.

Lijphart, Arend. 1994. *Electoral Systems and Party Systems: A Study of Twenty-Seven Democracies, 1945–1990.* New York: Oxford University Press.

Lindberg, Stafan. (Ed.) 2009. *Democratization by Elections: A New Mode of Transition.* Baltimore, MD: The Johns Hopkins University Press.

Lindberg, Stafan. I. 2005. "Consequences of electoral systems in Africa: A preliminary inquiry." *Electoral Studies* 24(1): 41–64.

Lindberg, Staffan I. 2006. "The surprising significance of African elections." *Journal of Democracy* 17(1): 139–151.

Lindberg, Staffan I. 2013. "Confusing categories, shifting targets." *Journal of Democracy* 24(4): 161–167.

Lindberg, Staffan.2006. *Democracy and Elections in Africa.* Baltimore, MD: The Johns Hopkins University Press.

Little, Andrew T. 2012. "Elections, fraud, and election monitoring in the shadow of revolution." *Quarterly Journal of Political Science* 7(3): 249–283.

Lo, B.B. 2003. "Russian elections: Uncivil state." *World Today* 59 (11): 22–24.

López-Pintor, Rafael, and Fischer, Jeff. 2005. *Getting to the CORE: On the Cost of Registration and Elections.* New York: UNDP

López-Pintor, Rafael, 2000. *Electoral Management Bodies as Institutions of Governance,* New York: United Nations Development Programme.

López-Pintor, Rafael. 2010. *Assessing Electoral Fraud in New Democracies: A Basic Conceptual Framework.* Washington, DC: The International Foundation for Electoral Systems, IFES.

Lukinova, Evgeniya, Myagkov, Mikhail, and Peter C. Ordeshook. 2011. "Ukraine 2010: Were Tymoshenko's cries of fraud anything more than smoke?" *Post-Soviet Affairs* 27(1): 37–63.

Lust-Okar, Ellen, and Amaney Jamal. 2002. "Rulers and rules: Reassessing the influence of regime type on electoral law formation." *Comparative Political Studies* 35(3): 337–366.

Lust-Okar, Ellen. 2000. "Legislative politics in the Arab world: The resurgence of democratic institutions." *International Journal of Middle East Studies* 32(3): 420–422.

Lust-Okar, Ellen. 2004. "Divided they rule: The management and manipulation of political opposition." *Comparative Politics* 36(2): 159–179.

Lynch, G., and G. Crawford. "Democratization in Africa 1990–2010: An assessment." *Democratization* 18(2): 275–310.

Lynch, Gabrielle, and Gordon Crawford. 2011. "Democratization in Africa 1990–2010: An assessment." *Democratization* 18(2): 275–310.

Magaloni, Beatriz. 2006. *Voting for Autocracy: Hegemonic Party Survival and Its Demise in Mexico.* Cambridge: Cambridge University Press.

Magaloni, Beatriz. 2008. "Credible power-sharing and the longevity of authoritarian rule." *Comparative Political Studies* 41(4–5): 715–741.

Magaloni, Beatriz. 2010. "The game of electoral fraud and the ousting of authoritarian rule." *American Journal of Political Science* 54(3): 751–765.

Makulilo, Alexander Boniface. 2011. "'Watching the watcher': An evaluation of local election observers in Tanzania." *Journal of Modern African Studies* 49(2): 241–262.

Martínez i Coma, Ferran and Richard W. Frank. 2014. "Expert judgments." In *Advancing Electoral Integrity.* Eds. Pippa Norris, Richard W. Frank and Ferran Martínez i Coma. New York: Oxford University Press, pp. 51–70.

Massicotte, Louis, Andre Blais, and Antoine Yoshinaka. 2004. *Establishing the Rules of the Game.* Toronto: University of Toronto Press.

McAllister, Ian, and White, Stephen. 2011. "Public perceptions of electoral fairness in Russia." *Europe-Asia Studies* 63(4): 663–683.

McCann, J.A., and Jorge I. Dominguez. 1998. "Mexicans react to electoral fraud and political corruption: An assessment of public opinion and voting behavior." *Electoral Studies* 17(4): 483–503.

McDonald, Michael P. 2004. "A comparative analysis of redistricting institutions in the United States, 2001–02." *State Politics and Policy Quarterly* 4: 371–395.

McDonald, Michael P., and Samuel Popkin. 2001. "The myth of the vanishing voter." *American Political Science Review* 95(4): 963–974.

McFaul, Michael, and N. Petrov. 2004. "What the elections tell us." *Journal of Democracy* 15(3): 20–31.

McGrath, Amy. 1997. *Corrupt Elections: Ballot Rigging in Australia.* Sydney, NSW: H.S.Chapman Society.

Mebane, Walter R. Jr. 2012. "Comment on Benford's Law and the detection of election fraud." *Political Analysis* 19(3): 269–272.

Meyer, M., and J. Booker. 1991. *Eliciting and Analyzing Expert Judgment: A Practical Guide.* London: Academic Press.

Mickiewicz, Ellen. 1997. *Changing Channels: Television and the Struggle for Power in Russia.* New York: Oxford University Press.

Mickiewicz, Ellen. 2008. *Television, Power, and the Public in Russia.* New York: Cambridge University Press.

Minnite, Lorraine Carol. 2010. *The Myth of Voter Fraud.* Ithaca: Cornell University Press.

Moehler, D.C. 2009. "Critical citizens and submissive subjects: Elections losers and winners in Africa." *British Journal of Political Science* 39(2): 345–366.

Moehler, Devra C., and Staffan I. Lindberg. 2009. "Narrowing the legitimacy gap: Turnovers as a cause of democratic consolidation." *Journal of Politics* 71(4): 1448–1466.

Molina, I., and Fabrice Edouard Lehoucq. 1999. "Political competition and electoral fraud: A Latin American case study." *Journal of Interdisciplinary History* 30(2): 199–234.

Moller, Jorgen, and Skaaning, Svend-Erik. 2010. "Post-communist regime types: Hierarchies across attributes and space." *Communist and Post-Communist Studies* 43(1): 51–71.

Moller, Jorgen, and Svend-Erik Skaaning. "Beyond the radial delusion: Conceptualizing and measuring democracy and non-democracy." *International Political Science Review* 31(3): 261–283.

Montjoy, Robert S. 2008. "The public administration of elections." *Public Administration Review* 68(5): 788–799.

Montjoy, Robert S. 2010. "The changing nature . . . and costs . . . of election administration." *Public Administration Review* 70(6): 867–875.

Morse, Yonatan L. 2012. "The era of electoral authoritarianism." *World Politics* 64(1): 161–198.

Mozaffar, Shaheen, and Andreas Schedler. 2002. "The comparative study of electoral governance: Introduction." *International Political Science Review* 23(1): 5–27.

Munck, Geraldo L. 2009. *Measuring Democracy: A Bridge between Scholarship and Politics.* Baltimore, MD: The Johns Hopkins Press.

Munck, Geraldo L. and Jay Verkuilen. 2002. "Conceptualizing and measuring democracy: Evaluating alternative indices." *Comparative Political Studies* 35 (1): 5–34.

Myagkov, Mikhail and Ordeshook, Peter C. 2008. "Ukraine's 2007 parliamentary elections free and fair, or fraud once again?" *Problems of Post-Communism* 55(6): 33–41.

Myagkov, Mikhail, and Peter C. Ordeshook. 2005. "The trail of votes in Ukraine's 1998, 1999, and 2002 elections." *Post-Soviet Affairs* 21(1): 56–71.

Myagkov, Mikhail, Peter C. Ordeshook, and Dimitri Shakin. 2005. "Fraud or fairytales: Russia and Ukraine's electoral experience." *Post-Soviet Affairs* 21(2): 91–131.

Myagkov, Mikhail, Peter C. Ordeshook, and Dimitri Shakin. 2009. *The Forensics of Election Fraud: Russia and Ukraine.* New York: Cambridge University Press.

Nagle, J.C. 2004. "How not to count votes." *Columbia Law Review* 104(6): 1732–1763.

Nassmacher, Karl-Heinz. 2001. Ed. *Foundations for Democracy: Approaches to Comparative Political Finance.* Baden-Baden: Nomos.

Nassmacher, Karl-Heinz. 2009. *The Funding of Party Competition: Political Finance in 25 Democracies.* Berlin: Nomos.

National Democratic Institute. 2005. *Money in Politics: A Study of Party Financing Practices in 22 countries.* Washington, DC: National Democratic Institute.

Nazzarine, S.R. 2003. "A faceless name in the crowd: Freedom of association, equal protection, and discriminatory ballot access laws." *University of Cincinnati Law Review* 72(1): 309–361.

Neiheisel, Jacob R. and Burden, Barry C. 2012. "The impact of election day registration on voter turnout and election outcomes." *American Politics Research* 40(4): 636–664.

Newell, James. *The Politics of Italy: Governance in a Normal Country.* New York: Cambridge University Press.

Norris, Pippa, Ferran Martínez i Coma, and Richard W. Frank. 2014. "Assessing the quality of elections." *Journal of Democracy* 24(4): 124–135.

Norris, Pippa, Ferran Martínez i Coma, and Richard W. Frank. 2014. "Measuring the quality of elections." *PS: Political Science and Politics.* 47(4): 789–798.

Norris, Pippa, Ferran Martínez i Coma, and Richard W. Frank. 2014. *The Expert Survey of Perceptions of Electoral Integrity.* Available at www.electoralintegrityproject.com (accessed March 1, 2014).

Norris, Pippa, Richard W. Frank, and Ferran Martínez I Coma. (Eds.) 2014. *Advancing Electoral Integrity.* New York: Oxford University Press.

Norris, Pippa. 2003. *Democratic Phoenix.* New York: Cambridge University Press.

Norris, Pippa. 2004 *Electoral Engineering: Voting Rules and Political Behavior.* New York: Cambridge University Press.

Norris, Pippa. 2008. *Driving Democracy: Do Power-Sharing Institutions Work?* New York: Cambridge University Press.

Norris, Pippa. 2011. "Cultural explanations of electoral reform: A policy cycle model." *West European Politics.* 34(1): 531–550.

Norris, Pippa. 2011. *Democratic Deficit: Critical Citizens Revisited* New York: Cambridge University Press.

Norris, Pippa. 2012. *Making Democratic Governance Work: How Regimes Shape Prosperity, Welfare and Peace.* New York: Cambridge University Press.

Norris, Pippa. 2013. "Does the world agree about standards of electoral integrity? Evidence for the diffusion of global norms." Special issue of *Electoral Studies* 34(4): 563–575.

Norris, Pippa. 2013. "The new research agenda studying electoral integrity." Special issue of *Electoral Studies* 34(4): 576–588.

Norris, Pippa. 2014. "Electoral integrity and political legitimacy." In Lawrence LeDuc, Richard Niemi, and Pippa Norris (Eds.) *Comparing Democracies 4.* London: Sage, pp. 150–172.

Norris, Pippa. 2014. *Why Electoral Integrity Matters.* New York: Cambridge University Press.

Norris, Pippa. (Ed.) 1999. *Critical Citizens.* Oxford: Oxford University Press.

Norris, Pippa. (Ed.) 2010. *Public Sentinel: News Media and the Governance Agenda.* Washington, DC: The World Bank.

Nou, J. 2009. "Privatizing democracy: Promoting election integrity through procurement contracts." *Yale Law Journal* 118(4): 744–793.

Nunnally, Shayla C. 2011. "(Dis)counting on democracy to work: Perceptions of electoral fairness in the 2008 presidential election." *Journal of Black Studies* 42(6): 923–942.

Nyblade, B., and S.R. Reed. "Who cheats? Who loots? Political competition and corruption in Japan, 1947–1993." *American Journal of Political Science* 52(4): 926–941.

O'Leary, Cornelius. 1962. *The Elimination of Corrupt Practices in British Elections, 1968–1911.* Oxford: Oxford University Press.

Obi, Cyril. 2011. "Taking back our democracy? The trials and travails of Nigerian elections since 1999." *Democratization* 18(2): 366–387.

Öhman, Magnus and Hani Zainulbhai. 2011. *Political Finance Regulation: The Global Experience.* Washington, DC: IFES. Available at www.ifes.org/files/Political_Finance_Regulation_The_Global_Experience.pdf (accessed October 11, 2013).

Omotola, J.S. "Elections and democratic transition in Nigeria under the Fourth Republic." *African Affairs* 109(437): 535–553.

Organisation of American States/International IDEA. 2005. *Funding of Political Parties and Election Campaigns in the Americas.* OAS/International IDEA.

Organization for Security and Cooperation in Europe (OSCE). 2010. *Election Observation Handbook.* 6th ed. Warsaw: OSCE/ODIHR.

Organization for Security and Cooperation in Europe. 2007. *Handbook for Long-Term Election Observers: Beyond Election Day Observation.* Warsaw: OSCE/ODIHR.

Ottaway, Marina. 2003. *Democracy Challenged: The Rise of Semi-Authoritarianism* Washington, DC: Carnegie Endowment for International Peace.

Overton, Spencer. 2006. *Stealing Democracy: The New Politics of Voter Suppression.* New York: Norton.

Paris, Roland.2004. *At War's End: Building Peace after Civil Conflict.* Cambridge: Cambridge University Press.

Pastor, Robert A. 1999. "The role of electoral administration in democratic transitions." *Democratization* 6(4):1–27.

Pastor, Robert A., Robert Santos, and Alison Prevost. 2011. "Voting and ID requirements: A survey of registered voters in three states." *American Review of Public Administration* 40(4): 461–481.

Paxton, Pamela, Kenneth A. Bollen, Deborah M. Lee, and HyoJuong Kim. 2003. "A half-century of suffrage: New data and a comparative analysis." *Studies in Comparative International Development* 38:93–122.

Persily, N. 2001. "Candidates *v.* parties: The constitutional constraints on primary ballot access laws." *Georgetown Law Journal* 89(7): 2181–2225.

Pinto-Duschinsky, Michael. 2005. "Financing politics: A global view." *Journal of Democracy* 13(4): 69–86.

Popova, Marina. 2006. "Watchdogs or attack dogs? The role of the Russian Courts and the Central Election Commission in the resolution of electoral disputes." *Europe-Asia Studies* 58(3): 391–414.

Powell, G. Bingham. 2000. *Elections as Instruments of Democracy.* New Haven, CT: Yale University Press.

Powell, G. Bingham. 2004. "The chain of responsiveness." *Journal of Democracy* 15(4): 91–105.

Powell, G. Bingham. 2014. "Why elections matter." In Lawrence LeDuc, Richard Niemi, and Pippa Norris (Eds.) *Comparing Democracies 4.* London: Sage, pp. 187–204.

Power, Timothy J., and Matthew MacLeod Taylor. *Corruption and Democracy in Brazil: The Struggle for Accountability*, Notre Dame, Ind.: University of Notre Dame Press.

Przeworski, Adam, Michael E. Alvarez, Jose Antonio Cheibub, and Fernando Limongi. 2000. *Democracy and Development: Political Institutions and Well-Being in the World, 1950–1990.* New York: Cambridge University Press.

Quimpo, N.G. 2009. "The Philippines: Predatory regime, growing authoritarian features." *Pacific Review* 22(3): 335–353.

Qvortup, M. 2005. "First past the postman: Voting by mail in comparative perspective." *Political Quarterly* 76(3):414–419.

Rahat, Gideon and Hazan, Reuven Y. 2011. "The barriers to electoral system reform: A synthesis of alternative approaches." *West European Politics* 34(3): 478–494.

Rallings, Colin, Michael Thrasher, and G. Borisyuk. "Much ado about not very much: The electoral consequences of postal voting at the 2005 British General Election." *British Journal of Politics and International Relations* 12(2): 223–238.

Rapoport, David C., and Leonard Weinberg. 2001. "Elections and violence." In David C. Rapoport, and Leonard Weinberg (Eds.) *The Democratic Experience and Political Violence.* London: Frank Cass Publishers, pp. 15–50.

Regan, Patrick M., Frank, Richard W., and Clark, David H. 2009. "Political institutions and elections: New datasets." *Conflict Management and Peace Science* 26(3): 320–337.

Reilly, Benjamin. 2002. "Post-conflict elections: Constraints and dangers." *International Peacekeeping* 9(2): 118–139.

Reilly, Benjamin. 2004. "Elections in post-conflict societies." In Edward Newman, and Roland Rich (Eds.) *The UN Role in Promoting Democracy: Between Ideals and Reality.* Tokyo: United Nations University Press, pp. 113–134.

Reilly Benjamin. 2006. "Political engineering and party politics in conflict prone societies", *Democratization* 13(5): 811–827.

Renwick, Alan. 2011. *The Politics of Electoral Reform: Changing the Rules of Democracy.* New York: Cambridge University Press.

Reynolds, Andrew, and M. Steenbergen. 2006. "How the world votes: The political consequences of ballot design, innovation and manipulation." *Electoral Studies* 25(3): 570–598.

Reynolds, Andrew. 2011. *Designing Democracy in a Dangerous World.* New York: Oxford University Press.

Romanelli, Raffaele. (Ed.) 1998. *How did they become voters? The History of Franchise in Modern European Representation.* The Hague: Kluwer Law.

Rosas, Guillermo. 2010. "Trust in elections and the institutional design of electoral authorities: Evidence from Latin America." *Electoral Studies* 29(1): 74–90.

Rose, Richard, and William Mishler. 2009. "How do electors respond to an 'unfair' election? The experience of Russians." *Post-Soviet Affairs* 25(2): 118–136.

Rose, Richard, William Mishler, and Neil Monroe. 2011. *Popular Support for an Undemocratic Regime: The Changing Views of Russians.* New York: Cambridge University Press.

Rothstein, Bo. 2009. "Creating political legitimacy: Electoral democracy versus quality of government." *American Behavioral Scientist* 53(3): 311–330.

Samples, John Curtis. 2006. *The Fallacy of Campaign Reform.* Chicago: University of Chicago Press.

Santa-Cruz, Arturo. 2005. "Constitutional structures, sovereignty, and the emergence of norms: The case of international election monitoring." *International Organization* 59(3): 663–693.

Santiso, C., and A. Loada. 2003. "Explaining the unexpected: Electoral reform and democratic governance in Burkina Faso." *Journal of Modern African Studies* 41(3): 395–419.

Scarrow, Susan. 2004."Explaining political finance reforms: Competition and context." *Party Politics* 10: 653–675.

Scarrow, Susan. 2007. "Political finance in comparative perspective." *Annual Review of Political Science* 10: 193–210.

Schaffer, Frederic Charles, and Tova Andrea Wang. 2009. "Is everyone else doing it? Indiana's voter identification law in international perspective." *Harvard Law and Policy Review* 3: 397–413.

Schaffer, Fredric Charles. (Ed.) 2007. *Elections for Sale: The Causes and Consequences of Vote Buying.* Boulder and London: Lynne Rienner.

Schaffer, Fredric Charles. 2002. "Might cleaning up elections keep people away from the polls? Historical and comparative perspectives." *International Political Science Review* 23(1): 69–84.

Schaffer, Fredric Charles. 2008. *The Hidden Costs of Clean Election Reform.* Ithaca, NY: Cornell University Press.

Schedler, Andreas. (Ed.). 2006. *Electoral Authoritarianism: The Dynamics of Unfree Competition* Boulder, CO and London: Lynne Rienner.

Schedler, Andreas. 1999. "Civil society and political elections: A culture of distrust?" *Annals of the American Academy of Political and Social Science* 565: 126–141.

Schedler, Andreas. 2002. "The menu of manipulation." *Journal of Democracy* 13(2): 36–50.

Schedler, Andreas. 2010. "Authoritarianism's last line of defense." *Journal of Democracy* 21(1): 69–80.

Schedler, Andreas. 2012. "Judgment and measurement in political science." *Perspectives on Politics* 10(1): 21–36

Schedler, Andreas. 2012. *The Politics of Uncertainty Sustaining and Subverting Electoral Authoritarianism.* CIDE: Mexico City.

Scher, Richard K. 2010. *The Politics of Disenfranchisement: Why Is It So Hard to Vote in America?* New York: M.E. Sharpe.

Schmeets, Hans. (Ed.) 2010. *International Election Observation and Assessment of Elections.* The Hague: Statistics Netherlands.

Schuler, Ian. 2008. "SMS as a Tool in Election Observation." *Innovations* 3(2): 143–157.

Schumpeter, Joseph. 1942. *Capitalism, Socialism and Democracy.* London: George Allen & Unwin.

Sekhon, Jasjeet S., and Titiunik, Rocio. 2012. "When natural experiments are neither natural nor experiments." *American Political Science Review* 106(1): 35–57.

Seymour, Charles. 1970. *Electoral Reform in England and Wales: The Development and Operation of the Parliamentary Franchise 1832–1885.* Hamden, CT: Archon Books.

Sharafutdinova, Gulnaz. *Political Consequences of Crony Capitalism inside Russia.* Notre Dame, IN: University of Notre Dame Press.

Shock, David R. 2008. "Securing a line on the ballot: Measuring and explaining the restrictiveness of ballot access laws for non-major party candidates in the United States." *Social Science Journal* 45(1): 48–60.

Simmons, Beth A. 2009. *Mobilizing for Human Rights: International Law in Domestic Politics.* New York: Cambridge University Press.

Simpser, Alberto. 2012. "Does electoral manipulation discourage voter turnout? Evidence from Mexico." *Journal of Politics* 74(3): 782–795.

Simpser, Alberto. 2013. *Why Parties and Governments Manipulate Elections: Theory, Practice and Implications.* New York: Cambridge University Press.

Sisk, Timothy and Andrew Reynolds. (Eds.) 1998. *Elections and Conflict Management in Africa.* Washington, DC: US Institute of Peace Press.

Sjoberg, Fredrik. 2012. "Making voters count: Evidence from field experiments about the efficacy of domestic election observation." Harriman Institute Working Paper 1.

Slater, Dan. 2010. *Ordering Power: Contentious Politics and Authoritarian Leviathans in Southeast Asia.* New York: Cambridge University Press.

Smets, Kaat, and Carolien van Ham. 2013. "The embarrassment of riches? A meta-analysis of individual-level research on voter turnout." *Electoral Studies* 32(2): 344–359.

Smith, Lahra. 2009. "Explaining violence after recent elections in Ethiopia and Kenya." *Democratization* 16(5): 867–897.

Snyder, Jack. 2000. *From Voting to Violence: Democratization and Nationalist Conflict.* New York: Norton.

Steenbergen, Marco R., and Gary Marks. 2007. "Evaluating expert judgments." *European Journal of Political Research* 46: 347–366.

Stewart, J. 2006. "A banana republic? The investigation into electoral fraud by the Birmingham Election Court." *Parliamentary Affairs* 59(4): 654–667.

Stockemer, Daniel, Bernadette LaMontagne, and Lyle Scruggs. 2013. "Bribes and ballots: The impact of corruption on voter turnout in democracies." *International Political Science Review* 34(1): 74–90.

Stokes, Susan, Thad Dunning, Marcelo Nazareno, and Valeria Brusco. 2013. *Brokers, Voters, and Clientelism: The Puzzle of Distributive Politics.* New York: Cambridge University Press.

Straus, Scott and Charles Taylor. 2012. "Democratization and electoral violence in Sub-Saharan Africa, 1990–2008." In Dorina Bekoe (Ed.) *Voting in Fear: Electoral Violence in Sub-Saharan Africa.* United States Institute of Peace: Washington, DC.

Straus, Scott, 2012. "Wars do end! Changing patterns of political violence in Sub-Saharan Africa." *African Affairs* 111(443): 179–201.

Straus, Scott, and Charlie Taylor. 2012. "Democratization and electoral violence in Sub-Saharan Africa, 1990–2008." In *Voting in Fear,* Dorina A. Bekoe (Ed.). Washington, DC: United States Institute of Peace, pp. 15–38.

Straus, Scott. 2011. "It's sheer horror here": Patterns of violence during the first four months of Cote d'Ivoire's post-electoral crisis." *African Affairs* 110(440): 481–489.

Stroh, Alexander. 2010. "Electoral rules of the authoritarian game: Undemocratic effects of proportional representation in Rwanda." *Journal of Eastern African Studies* 4(1): 1–19.

Struwig, Jare, Benjamin J. Roberts, and Elme Vivier. 2011. "A vote of confidence: Election management and public perceptions." *Journal of Public Administration* 46(3): 1122–1138.

Svolik, Milan W. 2012. *The Politics of Authoritarian Rule.* New York: Cambridge University Press.

Tan, Nettina. 2013. "Electoral engineering and hegemonic party resilience in Singapore." *Electoral Studies* (forthcoming).

Tancangco, Luzviminda G. 1992. *The Anatomy of Electoral Fraud: Concrete Bases for Electoral Reforms.* Manila: MJAGM: Distributor Matrix.

Taylor, Charles, Jon Pevehouse, and Scott Straus. 2013. "Perils of pluralism: Electoral violence and competitive authoritarianism in Sub-Saharan Africa." Simons Papers in Security and Development 23, School for International Studies, Simon Fraser University.

Taylor, Steven L. 2009. *Voting Amid Violence: Electoral Democracy in Colombia.* Boston, MA: Northeastern University Press.

The Carter Center.2013. *Database of Obligations for Democratic Elections.* Carter Center: Atlanta. Available at www.cartercenter.org/des-search/des/Introduction.aspx (accessed November 15, 2013).

Thompson, Mark R. and Kuntz, Philipp. 2004. "Stolen elections: The case of the Serbian October." *Journal of Democracy* 15(4): 159–172.

Thompson, Mark R. and Philipp Kuntz, 2009. "More than just the final straw: Stolen elections as revolutionary triggers." *Comparative Politics* 41(3):253–272.

Trenschel, Alexander and Fernando Mendez. (Eds.) 2005. *The European Union and e-voting.* London: Routledge.

Tucker, Joshua. 2007. "Enough! Electoral fraud, collective action problems, and post-communist colored revolutions." *Perspectives on Politics* 5(3): 535–551.

Tyler, Tom R. 1984. "The role of perceived injustice in defendants' evaluations of their courtroom experience." *Law and Society Review* 18(1): 51–74.

Tyler, Tom R. 1990. *Why People Obey the Law.* New Haven: Yale University Press.

Tyler, Tom R. 1994. "Governing amid diversity: The effect of fair decision-making procedures on the legitimacy of government." *Law and Society Review* 28(4): 809–31.

Tyler, Tom R., Jonathan D. Casper, and Bonnie Fisher. 1989. "Maintaining allegiance toward political authorities: The role of prior attitudes and the use of fair procedures." *American Journal of Political Science* 33(3): 629–652.

Tyler, Tom R., Kenneth A. Rasinski, and Kathleen M. McGraw. 1985. "The influence of perceived injustice on the endorsement of political leaders." *Journal of Applied Social Psychology* 15(8): 700–725.

Ugues, Jr., Antonio. 2014. "Electoral management in Central America." In Pippa Norris, Richard W. Frank, and Ferran Martínez i Coma (Eds.) *Advancing Electoral Integrity.*New York: Oxford University Press, pp. 118–134.

Ugues, Jr., Antonio. 2010. "Citizens" views on electoral governance in Mexico." *Journal of Elections, Public Opinion and Parties* 20(4): 495–527.

UNDP. 2011. *Understanding Electoral Violence in Asia.* UNDP Asia-Pacific Regional Center.

UNDP. 2012. *Evaluation of UNDP Contribution to Strengthening Electoral Systems and Processes.* New York: UNDP.

United Nations General Assembly resolution 63/163 (April 12, 2012) "*Strengthening the role of the United Nations in enhancing periodic and genuine elections and the promotion of democratization.*"

United Nations. 2005. *Declaration of Principles for International Election Observation and Code of Conduct for International Elections Observers.* New York: United Nations. Available at www.cartercenter.com/documents/2231.pdf (accessed December 1, 2013).

Verba, Sidney, and Norman Nie. 1972. *Participation in America: Political Democracy and Social Equality.* New York: Harper and Row.

Verba, Sidney, Kay Schlozman and Henry E. Brady. 1995. *Voice and Equality: Civic Voluntarism in American Politics.* Cambridge, MA: Harvard University Press.

Verba, Sidney, Norman Nie, and Jae-on Kim. 1978. *Participation and Political Equality: A Seven-Nation Comparison.* New York: Cambridge University Press.

Vickery, Chad, and Erica Shein. 2012. "Assessing electoral fraud in new democracies." IFES: Washington, DC. Available at www.ifes.org/~/media/Files/Publications/White%20 PaperReport/2012/Assessing_Electoral_Fraud_Series_Vickery_Shein.pdf (accessed July 19, 2013).

Volkov, Denis. 2012. "The protesters and the public." *Journal of Democracy* 23(3): 55–62.

Wahmn, Michael, Jan Teorell, and Axel Hadenius. 2013. "Authoritarian regime types revisited: Updated data in comparative perspective." *Contemporary Politics* 19(1):19–34.

Wall, Alan, Andrew Ellis, Ayman Ayoub, Carl W. Dundas, Joram Rukambe, and Sara Staino. 2006. *Electoral Management Design: The International IDEA Handbook.* Stockholm: International IDEA.

Walle, Nicholas van der. 2003. "Presidentialism and clientelism in Africa's emerging party systems." The *Journal of Modern African Studies* 41(02):297–321 DOI: dx.doi.org/ 10.1017/S0022278X03004269.

Wand, J.N., K.W. Shotts, J.S. Sekhon, Walter Mebane, M.C. Herron, and Henry E. Brady. 2001. "The butterfly did it: The aberrant vote for Buchanan in Palm Beach County, Florida." *American Political Science Review* 95(4): 793–810.

Wand, Jonathan, Gary King, and Olivia Lau. 2011. "Anchors: Software for anchoring vignettes data." *Journal of Statistical Software* 42(3): 1–25. Wang, Tova Andrea. 2012. *The Politics of Voter Suppression: Defending and Expanding Americans' Right to Vote.* Ithaca, NY: Cornell University Press.

Weghorst, Keith R., and Lindberg, Staffan I. 2011. "Effective opposition strategies: Collective goods or clientelism?" *Democratization* 18(5): 1193–1214.

Weidmann, Nils B., and Michael Callen. 2011. *Violence and Election Fraud: Evidence from Afghanistan*

White, Stephen. "Non-competitive elections and national politics: The USSR Supreme Soviet elections of 1984." *Electoral Studies* 4(3): 215–229.

White, Stephen. 2011. "Elections Russian-style." *Europe-Asia Studies* 63(4): 531–556.

Wigell, M. 2008. "Mapping 'hybrid regimes': Regime types and concepts in comparative politics." *Democratization* 15(2): 230–250.

Wilking, Jennifer R. 2011. "The portability of electoral procedural fairness: Evidence from experimental studies in China and the United States." *Political Behavior* 33(1): 139–159.

Wilkinson, Steven. 2006. *Votes and Violence: Electoral Competition and Ethnic Riots in India*: New York: Cambridge University Press.

Willis, Justin, and el Battahani, Atta. 2010. "'We changed the laws': Electoral practice and malpractice in Sudan since 1953." *African Affairs* 109(435): 191–212.

Wilson, Kenneth. 2012. "How Russians view electoral fairness: A qualitative analysis." *Europe-Asia Studies* 64(1): 145–168.

Wlezien, Christopher and Stuart Soroka. 2012. "Political institutions and the opinion–policy link." *West European Politics* 35(6): 1407–1432.

Wong, Chin-Huat, Chin James, and Othman Norani. 2010. "Malaysia: Towards a topology of an electoral one-party state." *Democratization* 17(5): 920–949.

Young, John Hardin. 2009. *International Election Principles: Democracy and the Rule of Law*. Chicago: American Bar Association.

Ziblatt, Daniel. 2009. "Shaping democratic practice and the causes of electoral fraud: The case of nineteenth-century Germany." *American Political Science Review* 103(1): 1–21.

INDEX